GOOD $ENSE

COUNSELOR TRAINING WORKSHOP

Equipping You to Help Others
Transform Their Finances and Lives

GOOD $ENSE

COUNSELOR TRAINING WORKSHOP

Equipping You to Help Others
Transform Their Finances and Lives

Leader's Guide

Dick Towner

With contributions from
the Good $ense Ministry team of
Willow Creek Community Church

RESOURCES

GRAND RAPIDS, MICHIGAN 49530

Good $ense Counselor Training Workshop Leader's Guide
Copyright © 2002 by Willow Creek Community Church

Requests for information should be addressed to:

Willow Creek Association   Zondervan Publishing House
67 E. Algonquin Road   5300 Patterson SE
Barrington, IL 60010   Grand Rapids, MI 49530

ISBN:0-744-13731-4

Cover design by Rick Devon, Adam Beasley

Interior design by Ann Gjeldum

Produced with the assistance of the Livingstone Corporation. Project staff includes: Ashley Taylor, Christopher D. Hudson, Carol Barnstable, and Paige Drygas.

Printed in the United States of America

02 03 04 05 06 07 / / 10 9 8 7 6 5 4 3 2 1

DEDICATION

To Pop and Gram Wernicke who raised me and modeled for me a simple and frugal lifestyle. While their lifestyle was shaped in part by income circumstances, it was lived with contentment, making it easy for me to later accept the biblical truth that a person's life does not consist in the abundance of their possessions.

To my incredibly gifted and incredibly loving wife, Sibyl, who helped me to understand that frugality for its own sake simply leads to sinful hoarding, but that the true end result of frugality is liberality. Thank you, dear Sibyl, for modeling this for me and for helping me to experience the joy of giving.

And finally, to the body of believers known as College Hill Presbyterian Church in Cincinnati, Ohio. Not only did you baptize me as a child, nurture me as a teenager, marry me as a young adult, mature my faith, ordain me as an elder, and allow me to serve as part of the ministerial team for fourteen years, but you encouraged and provided the platform for the development of the vast majority of what is contained within these pages. My gratitude is beyond expression.

CONTENTS

FOREWORD

In school they tell us we're being equipped to earn it. Then for the rest of our lives—for about fifty or sixty hours a week—we're busy making it. We invest countless hours in thought and discussion deciding how to deal with it. We walk around shopping malls for hours on end determining how we're going to spend it. We're caught up more often than we'd like to admit worrying we won't have enough of it. We dream and scheme to figure out ways to acquire more of it.

Arguments over it are a leading cause for marital disintegration. Despair over losing it has even led to suicide. Passion for it causes much of society's crime. The absence of it causes many of society's nightmares. Some view it the root of all evil, while others think of it as the means for great good.

One thing is clear: We cannot afford to ignore the reality of the importance of *money.*

Over the years at Willow Creek Community Church we've been committed to tackling every important issue that faces the people who attend—from nutrition to sexuality, from building character to deepening relationships, from discovering and adoring the identity of God to preparing for death and eternity. One topic, however, that we've learned we must address regularly and directly is the subject that Christians wrestle with almost every day—the issue of how we handle personal finances.

Thankfully, there's no shortage of information on this crucial matter in the Bible, and it provides the basis for the materials you're about to dive into. More than two thousand Scripture passages touch on the theme of money. Jesus spoke about it frequently. About two-thirds of Jesus' parables make reference to our use of financial resources. He once warned that "where your treasure is, there your heart will be also." He talked often about these matters because he understood what was at stake. He knew that, left to our own devices, this area would quickly become a source of pain and frustration—and some-times bondage. Worse, he saw how easily our hearts would be led astray from pure devotion to God into areas of worry and even obsession over possessions. He wanted to protect us from these pitfalls and to show us the liberty that comes from following him fully in every area of life, including this one.

So get ready to join the ranks of thousands of people from our church and other churches who have received tangible help in this area through *Good $ense.* This vital ministry has been refined and proven over many years by my friend and trusted co-laborer, Dick Towner, along with his Good $ense Ministry team. I'm confident you'll find fresh avenues to increased financial freedom and, along the way, grow a more grateful spirit and generous heart.

As you and others from your congregation experience this, your church will be liberated so it can reflect more and more of that giving spirit and heart to the community around you, making it a magnet to people who are desperately looking for the kind of freedom, life, and love they see in you.

Bill Hybels
Founding and Senior Pastor
Willow Creek Community Church

ACKNOWLEDGMENTS

There are literally hundreds of people at Willow Creek Community Church and the Willow Creek Association whose expertise, support, wide array of contributions and encouragement were crucial throughout the development and completion of this project. Though space limitations prohibit naming all of them, their ranks include the following:

- The early group of volunteers and staff member George Lindholm who responded to God's vision in 1985 and began the Good $ense Ministry. Their leadership ranks included Warren Beach, Bill and Loretta Gaunt, John Frederick, Chuck Keenon, Jim Kinney, and Carl Tielsch. Stalwarts of the early counseling team included Bill and Joann Allen, Bob Baker, Candy Borst, Barry Gardner, Don and Zona Hackman, Dan Hollerick, Charlie Maxwell, Elizabeth Maring, Tom Stevens, Cyndy Sutherland, and Carol White. Staff assistance in the early years also came from Bruce Bugbee and Ken Fillipini.

- Current Good $ense volunteers, especially the following who have played an active role in the development of the materials: Russ Haan, Jerry Wiseman, Steve Sherbondy, Jenifer Nordeen-Lugar, Dan Rotter and Sue Drake. Thank you for your creativity and passion and the many contributions you made. Thanks, too, to the volunteer Good $ense Ministry Board, not only for your wise counsel and direction over the years, but even more for the deep bonds of friendship and mutual call to ministry we have shared.

- John Tofilon, whom God touched in a special way to become deeply involved in the *Good $ense Budget Course* and whose commitment to this project can only be characterized as "above and beyond." Your contribution has been huge and your life has touched mine.

- Norm Vander Wel and Jon Kopke, two friends of the heart who, though not connected with Willow Creek, provided insight and creativity and encouragement that was exceedingly helpful.

- Jim Riley, who followed me as director of the Good $ense Ministry at Willow Creek Community Church, and has been a true companion of the heart in seeking to help folks understand and implement biblical principles of stewardship in their lives. Thank you, Jim, for your commitment to this project and for your deep friendship.

- Wendy Seidman and her team—Bridget Purdome, Sue Drake, and Rebecca Adler. Their expertise in instructional design makes these materials effective in training and equipping people. Thanks to each of you not only for sharing your expertise but for taking the core values of this project into your own hearts.

- Christine M. Anderson, who managed the project, interjected her insights and wisdom at all the right times, provided encouragement when it was most needed, and exhibited amazing patience as we worked and reworked and reworked the material.

- Bob Gustafson, Steve Pederson, and Sharon Sherbondy for their expertise and enthusiasm in creating video segments that not only teach and train but also touch the heart.

- Bill Hybels, senior pastor. Early in his ministry Bill recognized and affirmed the vital connection between a biblical understanding of material possessions and ones spiritual well being. Over the years, his commitment to regular, passionate teaching on this topic has been an invaluable support and encouragement to the Good $ense Ministry . . . and a significant contribution to its effectiveness.

- Jim Mellado, Sharon Swing, and the entire Willow Creek Association Leadership Team for catching the vision for this project and for their support and encouragement as we worked to realize that vision.

- Joe Sherman and the publishing and marketing team at the Willow Creek Association for providing the resources to produce this curriculum and for believing it can make a difference is so many lives.

- Several donors whose faith in this project and generous financial contributions not only provided initial funding but were also a great encouragement to me personally.

Special Acknowledgments for the *Good $ense Counselor Training Workshop*

The *Good $ense Counselor Training Workshop* materials have been developed by the Good $ense Ministry at Willow Creek Community Church to train volunteers in the art of budget counseling. The workshop is the fruit of nearly two decades of ministry as well as research and review of other resources—both Christian and secular—that offer helpful information and wisdom.

Special acknowledgment goes to:

- Larry Burkett and Christian Financial Concepts. We have gleaned great insights from some of their concepts. The *Christian Financial Concepts Manual of Financial Counseling* was a resource in designing this guide, particularly in the area of counseling guidelines and dealing with creditor issues.

- Ron Blue, especially for his book, *Master Your Money,* and for his monthly newsletter by the same name.

- Jerrold Mundis, for wisdom from his book, *How to Get Out of Debt, Stay out of Debt, and Live Prosperously.* His insights into the ministry of Debtors Anonymous provided inspiration for our teaching on "The Creditor," including "When Negotiations with Creditors Fail."

In addition, numerous Willow Creek Community Church members gave of their professional expertise and insights, including:

- Richard Watson, an agent with the U.S. Internal Revenue Service, who provided expertise on tax matters.

- Steve Sherbondy, a family therapist whose insights on counseling principles are integrated throughout the fabric of the workshop.

- Russ Robinson, Judson Strain, and Elizabeth Maring, all of whom provided guidance and direction on a host of legal topics.

- Charles Keenon, a consumer credit professional who supplied insights on credit matters and how best to deal with creditors.

- Warren Beach, whose name has become almost synonymous with Good $ense due to his excellent leadership, modeling, and teaching in the first days of the Good $ense Ministry.

PREFACE

I applaud you for teaching the *Good $ense Counselor Training Workshop.* There is a tremendous need for churches today to educate and assist people with managing their resources in God-honoring ways. Your willingness to teach this course so that counselors can be equipped to help others is a vital part of making this happen.

Everything you need to effectively teach the course is provided. However, these materials alone cannot train a roomful of new counselors. There is no substitute for study and preparation. Read the Leader's Guide carefully and thoroughly. Make notes on the facing pages and personalize the material. Consult the Recommended Resources list in the Appendix and do additional reading. If you can consult only one additional resource, I strongly recommend Randy Alcorn's *Money, Possessions and Eternity.* If you have questions you can't find answers to, consult the Good $ense website at www.GoodSenseMinistry.com.

In addition to thoroughly studying the content and practicing your presentation, I urge you to also prepare yourself spiritually. Reflect on the biblical texts and let them speak to you personally. Go beyond the material you will teach and delve more deeply into the scriptures that form the basis for the Good $ense Ministry. Spend time in prayer and ask others to pray that God will speak through you. Pray diligently about your role as a teacher. You are preparing counselors to confront materialism—the chief rival god in the lives of many clients. This puts counselors on the forefront of a spiritual battle. Pray that you will prepare them well.

Your teaching will train counselors to help others in powerful ways. When money is no longer a rival god, people are freed up to relate to God and to serve God in profoundly new and deeper ways. And you get to be a part of God's liberating work!

Thank you for stepping forward to undertake this very important task. My prayer is that God will use you in a special and powerful way.

Dick Towner

HOW TO USE THE LEADER'S GUIDE

This Leader's Guide has been prepared to help you present this course in the most effective manner possible. These introductory pages provide ideas for presenting the sessions and list the materials and equipment required.

Group Size

The *Good $ense Counselor Training Workshop* works with any size group. However, due to the nature of the activities, a minimum of two participants is required in order to perform role-playing activities.

Format Options

The *Good $ense Counselor Training Workshop* can be presented successfully in a number of delivery formats:

- **One-day workshop**
  The recommended presentation format for this course is a one-day workshop. There are five sessions, totaling approximately six hours and thirty minutes of content. Approximate teaching times for each session are:

  Session 1   80 minutes (1 hour and 20 minutes)
  Session 2   70 minutes (1 hour and 10 minutes)
  Session 3   35 minutes
  Session 4   120 minutes (2 hours)
  Session 5   70 minutes (1 hour and 10 minutes)

  In a one-day format, you need to allow time for lunch (45 to 60 minutes) and also for breaks. A ten-minute break is recommended following Session 1, and fifteen- to twenty-minute breaks following Sessions 2 and 4. You may wish to use the following as a suggested schedule:

8:30 - 9:50 A.M.	Session 1: *Foundations of the Good $ense Ministry*
9:50 - 10:00 A.M.	*Break*
10:00 - 11:10 A.M.	Session 2: *Prepare for the First Meeting*
11:10 - 11:25 A.M.	*Break*
11:25 - 12:00 A.M.	Session 3: *Listening Skills*
12:00 - 1:00 P.M.	*Lunch*
1:00 - 3:00 P.M.	Session 4: *First Meeting*
3:00 - 3:15 P.M.	*Break*
3:15 - 4:30 P.M.	Session 5: *Ongoing Counseling*

Rather than leaving for lunch, consider providing a simple meal so participants can relax and spend time with each other. In addition to promoting camaraderie and interaction, this is also a great way to make sure you stick to the schedule.

- **Two sessions delivered over two days**
  The workshop may be broken down into two shorter sessions taught over two days. A logical breaking point is to teach Sessions 1, 2, and 3 the first day; and Sessions 4 and 5 the second day. Day one would include approximately three hours of material; day two approximately three-and-a-half hours of material.

  To present the workshop in a Friday night and Saturday format, you also have the option of teaching Sessions 1 and 2 on Friday evening, and Sessions 3, 4, and 5 on Saturday. Friday evening would include approximately two-and-a-half hours of material; Saturday would include approximately four hours of material.

Participant Pre-Reading

Prior to attending the *Good $ense Counselor Training Workshop,* participants are strongly encouraged to complete the pre-reading section—pages P-1 to P-16—of the Participant's Guide and Manual. Completing the reading in advance makes the workshop more valuable and productive.

Participant Activity

In this course, the deepest learning occurs when participants are working—in individual or group activities—not when the instructor is working (lecturing or presenting the content). The participant clearly gains new insights and knowledge from the lecture/content and it is an invaluable part of the course; however, for participants to be transformed by that new information, they need time to process it.

The *Good $ense Counselor Training Workshop* provides several ways for participants to process what they learn. These include individual, partner, and small group activities. For example:

- Individual activity—analyzing a Client Profile just as they would prior to an actual first meeting with a client

- Partner activity—role-playing in a safe environment to practice skills needed to conduct an effective client meeting

- Group activity—discussing new insights, ideas, and reflections

How this Leader's Guide Is Organized

Each of the five sessions is divided into the following parts:

Session Snapshot

Provides a brief summary of the content to be discussed in the session and the overall context into which the session fits.

Objectives

Describes what participants are to accomplish and learn in that session.

Outline

Provides an overview of the content and sequence to be covered in the session.

Session Introduction, Discovery, and Summary

Describes the actual "teaching" part of the session containing the content to be presented, which is keyed to the visual aids to be used in the session. This material is presented in two columns as shown in the following example:

TIME & MEDIA	CONTENTS
2 minutes 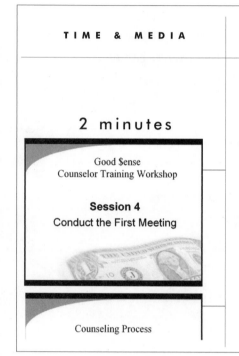	**INTRODUCTION** Participant's Guide, page 53. Remember where we left off in the counseling process? We've analyzed the Client Profile and called the client. Now, that we are equipped with some counseling skills, we are ready to conduct the first meeting.

The Time and Media Column

The TIME notations indicate suggested times for each content block. Note: These times include just the CONTENTS portion of each session. They do not allow for any question-and-answer time, nor extra time participants may need to complete activities.

The MEDIA graphics indicate when video and PowerPoint slides (or overhead transparencies, if you're using that option) should be presented.

Included on the *Good $ense Counselor Training Workshop* CD-ROM are two folders. If your facility is equipped with the computer equipment required to use PowerPoint software, the folder named "Sessions for Viewing" contains files for a four-color, electronic presentation.

If you will be using a standard overhead projector and transparencies, the folder "Sessions for Printing" contains files for black-and-white transparencies. To make overhead transparencies, you may use one of two methods.

1. Print out the files on your computer printer, using the appropriate type of transparency for your particular printer.

2. First print the files on white paper. Place a sufficient number of overhead transparency sheets (the kind specifically made for copiers) in the paper tray of a photocopier, and then run the printout through the copier. Your local full-service copy center should be equipped to make transparencies if you do not have access to the necessary equipment.

The Contents Column

The CONTENTS column is a detailed guide to the course material. If you had to, you could read this column start to finish, word-for-word, and the material would be presented completely and in the correct order. However, the more effective way is for you to use this information as a resource as you prepare to present the five sessions.

We recommend that you personalize this material by using your own words and illustrations. You might want to highlight key words and phrases so you'll be able to teach without having to read it word-for-word. If you prefer to write down your own material, there is space provided under the NOTES area (see "Notes" on page 31). Practice each session—including PowerPoint and video—at least once before presenting it to make sure you are comfortable with the material and are able to keep to the time you have allotted for the session. Also, be sure to have all visual aids organized and ready to use.

The CONTENTS column includes the following key elements:
1. The instructor narrative is shown in this standard typeface.

> In this regard, be aware that as a Good $ense counselor you are engaged in a matter of deepest spiritual significance and impact. There has been a historic feud between God and money as they both compete for our allegiance.

2. Statements the instructor should read verbatim are set off with an arrow ——➤. It is important to read these texts word-for-word because they appear in the Participant's Guide. Sometimes more than one paragraph is indented following an arrow. *Every indented paragraph following an arrow should be read verbatim.*

The objectives of the workshop are:

——➤ To help you understand the foundations of the Good $ense Ministry;

To equip you with the skills to successfully complete a case using the Good $ense counseling process;

---

3. Words shown in ALL CAPITAL LETTERS are words participants need to fill in the blanks found on the corresponding pages in their Participant's Guides.

——➤ "Red" cases are those with NEGATIVE cash flow.

"Green" cases have positive cash flow.

---

4. If you are using PowerPoint slides (rather than transparencies) the slides corresponding to content appear in the TIME & MEDIA column as show in the example below. When a slide has multiple points and "builds," the following symbol ▶ appears as a prompt to advance to the next point.

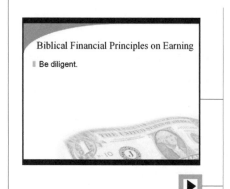

Biblical Financial Principles on Earning

Participant's Guide, page 25.

——➤ Colossians 3:23 commands us to be diligent. "Work hard and cheerfully at whatever you do" (NLT).

This same verse also calls us to be PURPOSEFUL. We are to work "as though you were working for the Lord rather than people." When we work, we

5. Scripture verses, other quotes, and words and phrases to be emphasized are italicized.

> One or more resources, skills, or talents you possess with that are relevant to budget counseling. For example:
>
> *"I used to do peer counseling at a weight loss center. The manager there told me I'm great at motivating people."*

6. Directions to the instructor are enclosed in a shaded box. These directions are *not to be spoken* by the instructor.

> You may wish to provide everyone in the class with copies of the "My Team" worksheets generated by the groups. Call the group back together after 15 minutes.

7. A variety of activities are included throughout the course to help participants learn by talking to each other or reflecting on their own experiences. These include individual, partner, and small group activities.

Notes
Provides space to write your own words and illustrations to customize your presentation and replace portions of the instructor narrative.

Participant's Guide Pages
Allows you to view the page(s) participants are seeing as you talk without having to hold two books at the same time. It also helps you immediately know where the participants are in their books when someone asks.

Master Materials List

To present the *Good $ense Counselor Training Workshop,* the following materials and supplies are needed:

- Leader's Guide

- Participant's Guides

- Name tags and markers

- Computer and projection equipment with CD-ROM disk if using PowerPoint slides. Be sure to test all components together before each class. Or, overhead projector, screen, transparencies, and pens if using overheads. Before each class, check to be sure transparencies are in the correct order, the projector works, and there are spare bulbs and pens.

- *Good $ense Counselor Training Workshop* video cassette

- Video player and monitor—set up and ready to play—as well as all necessary cords and cables

- Extra calculators

- Extra pencils with erasers

- Optional: tape or CD player for music. Use this before and after sessions, as well as during breaks, to create a welcoming and relaxed atmosphere.

Facility Setup

To create a comfortable and relaxed atmosphere, we recommend using round tables. As shown in the diagram on the next page, seat four to six people at each table, leaving an open space at the front so no one has their back to the instructor.

FOUNDATIONS OF
THE GOOD $ENSE
MINISTRY

SESSION SNAPSHOT

OVERVIEW

Session 1 begins with a vision video that conveys the mission of the Good $ense Ministry and underscores the importance of the counselor's role in both the financial and spiritual development of their clients. Participants share their reflections on this vision in a group introduction activity. The Biblical Financial Principles, which are the foundation of the Good $ense Ministry, are introduced in this session, and participants have a chance to begin to apply them to "real life" situations.

OBJECTIVES

In this session, participants will:

1. Share why God brought them into the Good $ense Ministry

2. Apply Biblical Financial Principles to "real life" situations

OUTLINE

I. Introduction

II. The Good $ense Ministry Vision
    A. Video: *The Good $ense Ministry Vision*
    B. Group Activity: *The Good $ense Ministry Vision*

III. Workshop Objectives and Overview

IV. Whom We Serve

V. The Pull of the Culture vs. the Mind and Heart of God

VI. The Foundation of a Good $ense Ministry: Biblical Financial Principles
    A. The Steward's Mindset
    B. Video: *The Pearl of Great Price*
    C. Individual Reflection Activity: *The Steward's Mindset*
    D. The Five Financial Areas
    E. Group Activity: *Applying the Biblical Financial Principles*

VII. Session Summary

FOUNDATIONS OF THE GOOD $ENSE MINISTRY

TIME & MEDIA	CONTENTS

3 minutes

INTRODUCTION

Participant's Guide, page 16.

1. Call the group together.
2. Introduce yourself.

Welcome to the Good $ense
Counselor Training Workshop

Session 1
Foundations of the
Good $ense Ministry

Welcome. I'm so glad you are here. There is a tremendous need for folks like you to come alongside people who are struggling with their finances. As you help your clients, you will be relieving tremendous stress and anxiety caused by consumer debt, aiding marriages torn by the conflict over money, and restoring self-esteem and confidence. There are few things that are more life changing to the individual or more satisfying to yourself than helping someone learn to control their money rather than have it control them.

But even more significantly, you will be removing a key roadblock to your client's spiritual growth and development.

A Key Roadblock:

Money is often the chief rival god in people's lives.

➡ For money is often the chief rival god in people's lives.

NOTES

INTRODUCTION

**Welcome to the Good $ense Counselor
Training Workshop!**

Money is often the chief rival god in people's lives.

We cannot serve two masters; we cannot serve both money and
God.

It is important that your efforts are grounded in prayer and a
deep understanding of what scripture says about money and
our relationship to it.

The Good $ense Ministry Vision

Video: *The Good $ense Ministry Vision*

Notes

In this regard, be aware that as a Good $ense counselor you are engaged in a matter of deepest spiritual significance and impact. There has been a historic feud between God and money as they both compete for our allegiance.

But the Bible is very clear:

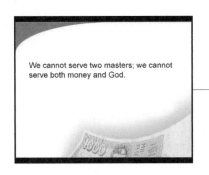

We cannot serve two masters; we cannot serve both money and God.

Because you will be engaged in what is first and foremost a spiritual battle, it is important that your efforts are grounded in prayer and a deep understanding about what Scripture says about money and our relationship to it.

Before we go any further, let's take a moment to pray.

> You may wish to substitute your own prayer for the prayer below.

Father, thank you for bringing together today these committed individuals who want to use their abilities to help others. We thank you for your presence here today as we learn how to listen to the hearts—not just the words—of the clients who will be in our care. Thank you for the strength to provide hope to clients in the midst of their struggles. Help us to gain the wisdom and knowledge we need from your Word. We gratefully acknowledge that all material things are yours, that we are stewards of your abundant gifts, and that we can teach others this important message by example and through the power of the Holy Spirit. In Christ's name, amen.

NOTES

INTRODUCTION

Welcome to the Good $ense Counselor Training Workshop!

Money is often the chief rival god in people's lives.

We cannot serve two masters; we cannot serve both money and God.

It is important that your efforts are grounded in prayer and a deep understanding of what scripture says about money and our relationship to it.

The Good $ense Ministry Vision

Video: *The Good $ense Ministry Vision*

Notes

THE GOOD $ENSE MINISTRY VISION

We're going to start with a video that reveals the lure of our materialistic culture and why ministries like Good $ense are so necessary today. You're also going to see some real people whose lives have been changed as a result of Good $ense budget counseling. The impact of your work as a budget counselor can be enormous, as I think you'll soon learn.

13 minutes

Video: *The Good $ense Ministry Vision*

> View video: *The Good $ense Ministry Vision.*

Now, let's spend some time discussing your reactions to the video.

16 minutes

Group Activity: *The Good $ense Ministry Vision*

> Participant's Guide, page 17.

Group Activity:

The Good $ense
Ministry Vision

Objectives:

For participants to:

- Get to know one another

- Share their reactions to the video

- Share why God brought them into the Good $ense Ministry

- Identify each other's skills

For classes of *seven or fewer* participants, do this and all other group activities as one group.

NOTES

INTRODUCTION

Welcome to the Good $ense Counselor Training Workshop!

Money is often the chief rival god in people's lives.

We cannot serve two masters; we cannot serve both money and God.

It is important that your efforts are grounded in prayer and a deep understanding of what scripture says about money and our relationship to it.

The Good $ense Ministry Vision

Video: *The Good $ense Ministry Vision*

Notes

Group Activity: *The Good $ense Ministry Vision*

Directions

1. Form a small group with three or four other people.

2. Share with your group:

   - Your name

   - Your reaction to the video

   - Why you believe God brought you into the Good $ense Ministry

   - One or more resources, skills, or talents you possess that are relevant to budget counseling. For example:

   "I used to do peer counseling at a weight loss center. The manager there told me I'm great at motivating people."

   "I'm just out of college and spent a lot of time researching on the Internet. I can find just about anything on the web."

   "I'm a stay-at-home parent. I'm an expert at balancing our budget."

   "I work in an accounting department. I'm good at using a spreadsheet to do loan amortization tables."

3. As each person introduces themselves, write down their name, phone number, and skills on the "My Team" worksheet on the following page.

Directions (1 minute)

1. Form a group with three or four other people.

2. Share with your group:

   • Your name

   • Your reaction to the video

   • Why you believe God brought you into the Good $ense Ministry

   • One or more resources, skills, or talents you possess that are relevant to budget counseling. For example:

     "I used to do peer counseling at a weight loss center. The manager there told me I'm great at motivating people."

     "I'm just out of college and spent a lot of time researching on the Internet. I can find just about anything on the web."

     "I'm a stay-at-home parent. I'm an expert at balancing our budget."

     "I work in an accounting department. I'm good at using a spread sheet to do loan amortization tables."

3. As each person introduces themselves, write down their name, phone number, and skills on the "My Team" worksheet on the following page.

We will take 15 minutes to do this.

> You may wish to provide everyone in the class with copies of the "My Team" worksheets generated by the groups. Call the group back together after 15 minutes.

NOTES

_____

_____

_____

_____

_____

_____

_____

_____

_____

_____

_____

_____

_____

_____

_____

_____

_____

_____

_____

_____

_____

_____

Group Activity: *The Good $ense Ministry Vision*

Directions

1. Form a small group with three or four other people.

2. Share with your group:
   - Your name
   - Your reaction to the video
   - Why you believe God brought you into the Good $ense Ministry
   - One or more resources, skills, or talents you possess that are relevant to budget counseling. For example:

   "I used to do peer counseling at a weight loss center. The manager there told me I'm great at motivating people."

   "I'm just out of college and spent a lot of time researching on the Internet. I can find just about anything on the web."

   "I'm a stay-at-home parent. I'm an expert at balancing our budget."

   "I work in an accounting department. I'm good at using a spreadsheet to do loan amortization tables."

3. As each person introduces themselves, write down their name, phone number, and skills on the "My Team" worksheet on the following page.

My Team

Name/Phone	Skills, Resources, Talents
1. _____	_____
2. _____	_____
3. _____	_____
4. _____	_____
5. _____	_____
6. _____	_____
7. _____	_____

2 minutes

WORKSHOP OBJECTIVES AND OVERVIEW

Participant's Guide, page 19.

Now that you've seen the Good $ense vision and shared your own thoughts and insights with each other, let's consider what we're here to accomplish today.

The objectives of the workshop are:

Workshop Objectives
- To help you understand the foundations of the Good $ense Ministry
- To equip you with the skills to successfully complete a case using the Good $ense counseling process
- To build your confidence while you experience fellowship and fun!

To help you understand the foundations of the Good $ense Ministry;

To equip you with the skills to successfully complete a case using the Good $ense counseling process;

To build your confidence while you experience fellowship and fun!

Now let's look at an overview of this workshop:

Workshop Overview
- Session 1: The Foundations of the Good $ense Ministry
- Session 2: Prepare for the First Meeting
- Session 3: Listening Skills
- Session 4: Conduct the First Meeting
- Session 5: Ongoing Counseling

We will begin by covering the foundations of the Good $ense Ministry—whom we serve, what motivates them, and how we can take a biblical approach to providing counsel.

In Session 2, we will discuss how to prepare for the first client meeting.

In Session 3, we will practice listening skills for building a strong relationship with our client.

Then, in Session 4, we will cover how to conduct the first meeting in detail, and you will have an opportunity to practice these steps while applying the listening skills you just learned.

NOTES

Workshop Objectives

- To help you understand the foundations of the Good $ense Ministry

- To equip you with the skills to successfully complete a case using the Good $ense counseling process

- To build your confidence while you experience fellowship and fun!

Workshop Overview

- Session 1: The Foundations of the Good $ense Ministry

- Session 2: Prepare for the First Meeting

- Session 3: Listening Skills

- Session 4: Conduct the First Meeting

- Session 5: Ongoing Counseling

In the final session, we will discuss ongoing counseling by applying Good $ense strategies, forms, and the Biblical Financial Principles to provide ongoing counseling to our clients.

Let's start by discussing whom we serve.

Turn to page 20.

2 minutes

WHOM WE SERVE

Participant's Guide, page 20.

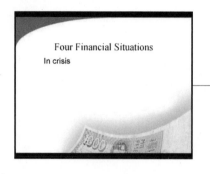

Our clients usually fall into one of four financial situations:

Clients in the first situation are in crisis.

These folks are experiencing serious financial problems, requiring immediate help and ongoing encouragement and assistance.

 Next are those who are living one paycheck from disaster.

These people aren't experiencing any immediate crisis, but they are living from paycheck to paycheck. They sense that their debt is too high and their savings too low. However, they are often lulled into a false sense of security by the cultural message that everything is okay as long as they are making minimum payments on their debts.

Some clients are in good "financial" shape.

They're not in consumer debt, they save on a regular basis, and they invest wisely. From a purely financial standpoint, they are good money managers. But they haven't yet grasped the vision of leading a financial lifestyle from a Christian perspective.

NOTES

_____
_____
_____
_____
_____
_____
_____
_____
_____
_____
_____
_____
_____
_____
_____
_____
_____
_____
_____
_____
_____
_____
_____

Workshop Objectives

- To help you understand the foundations of the Good $ense Ministry

- To equip you with the skills to successfully complete a case using the Good $ense counseling process

- To build your confidence while you experience fellowship and fun!

Workshop Overview

- Session 1: The Foundations of the Good $ense Ministry

- Session 2: Prepare for the First Meeting

- Session 3: Listening Skills

- Session 4: Conduct the First Meeting

- Session 5: Ongoing Counseling

Whom We Serve

- In Crisis

- One Paycheck from Disaster

- Good "Financial" Shape

- God-Honoring Lifestyle

- "Red" cases are those with _____ cash flow.

- "Green" cases have positive cash flow.

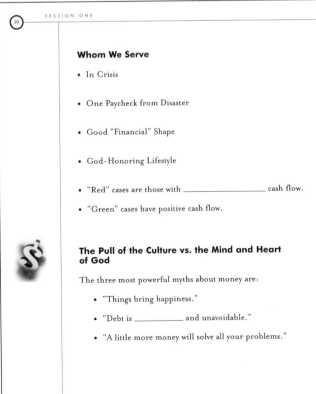

The Pull of the Culture vs. the Mind and Heart of God

The three most powerful myths about money are:

- "Things bring happiness."

- "Debt is _____ and unavoidable."

- "A little more money will solve all your problems."

▶ Finally, there are those who have a God-honoring lifestyle.

This group has applied the Biblical Financial Principles to their lives. They understand that they have been entrusted with what belongs to God, and they are handling their finances in a God-honoring way. Our ministry's leaders and counselors are drawn from this group. Those of you sitting in this room are part of this group. Our ultimate goal is that everyone in our church would be in this category.

You're here today to learn how to counsel the "in crisis" and "one-paycheck-from-disaster" cases that we define as "red" cases; that is, cases in which clients have a negative cash flow and are experiencing some financial difficulties.

A key point to remember is that people in difficulty are often those most open to hearing about God's love and forgiveness. It is possible that not all your clients will be Christians, even if they regularly attend church. Therefore, it's important to be ready to share your own faith story and to be prepared to lead them to a faith commitment.

Case Types

"Red" Cases: NEGATIVE cash flow

"Green" Cases: positive cash flow

"Red" cases are those with NEGATIVE cash flow.

"Green" cases have positive cash flow.

Although our workshop today is focused on red cases, there is also green case counseling for people who have positive cash flow

A new Good $ense Ministry may choose to begin by focusing only on red case counseling and then eventually move to also providing green case counseling. If your ministry will only be providing red case counseling, explain this to the participants.

NOTES

(lined note-taking space)

Whom We Serve

- In Crisis

- One Paycheck from Disaster

- Good "Financial" Shape

- God-Honoring Lifestyle

- "Red" cases are those with _____ cash flow.

- "Green" cases have positive cash flow.

The Pull of the Culture vs. the Mind and Heart of God

The three most powerful myths about money are:

- "Things bring happiness."

- "Debt is _____ and unavoidable."

- "A little more money will solve all your problems."

A green case might involve someone who receives an inheritance and wants to invest it wisely, or someone who has been living within their means but has recently earned a large pay increase. Or perhaps it is simply a person who is in good shape financially but wants to understand more deeply what Scripture has to say about finances and how to apply those principles.

Since we're learning about red cases today, let's spend a few moments trying to understand what's going on with those who find themselves in financial crisis.

4 minutes

THE PULL OF THE CULTURE VS. THE MIND AND HEART OF GOD

It's very important that we give our clients good tools and techniques for managing their financial lives. But it's even more important that we help them understand at a deep level what the Bible says about our relationship to money and how the cultural messages about money are often in direct contradiction to it.

Let's look at what we will refer to as the Pull of the Culture. The video we watched a few minutes ago showed the tremendous pull our materialistic culture has on our clients and, also, on us.

The culture shouts that we will find financial freedom, fulfillment, contentment, and peace by acquiring more things. Its power derives in large measure through the perpetuation of myths about money.

As we saw, the three most powerful myths about money are:

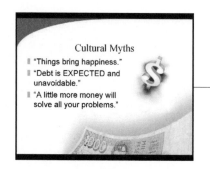

➤ "Things bring happiness."

"Debt is EXPECTED and unavoidable."

"A little more money will solve all your problems."

NOTES

Whom We Serve

- In Crisis

- One Paycheck from Disaster

- Good "Financial" Shape

- God-Honoring Lifestyle

- "Red" cases are those with _____ cash flow.

- "Green" cases have positive cash flow.

The Pull of the Culture vs. the Mind and Heart of God

The three most powerful myths about money are:

- "Things bring happiness."

- "Debt is _____ and unavoidable."

- "A little more money will solve all your problems."

Many of our clients have succumbed to these myths. It is helpful to understand their thoughts and feelings.

Participant's Guide, page 21.

Two basic human motivators are pleasure and pain. Much of our behavior results from trying to avoid pain or experience pleasure. Many people will procrastinate, bend the truth, and do almost anything to avoid painful situations or to experience pleasurable ones.

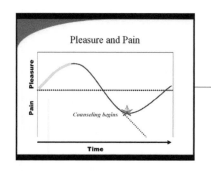

This pleasure and pain diagram depicts the cycle for many of our clients. One of the realities of debt is that getting into it can be fun at the outset. You get to purchase and experience all kinds of things that are pleasurable in the short run. This is illustrated by the initial upward slope of the diagram.

Unfortunately, as we accumulate more and more debt to pay for these possessions, the initial feelings of pleasure turn to pain. Creditors are calling, we can't meet minimum payments, and life becomes increasingly stressful. You can see on the diagram that the pleasure decreases, turns to pain, and the pain is intensifying.

Most of our clients arrive at Good $ense in the midst of this painful downslide. What they discover through their counseling is that in order to reduce their expenses, they will typically need to sacrifice some comforts or habits they don't want to let go of, and that can increase their feelings of pain and frustration. However, the hope and encouragement you offer them can offset the additional pain of sacrifice. As illustrated by the dotted line on the diagram, were it not for your presence, the pain would likely intensify and perhaps discourage the client from following through. Thus, your offering of hope and encouragement throughout the counseling process is very important.

NOTES

Pleasure and Pain Diagram

Notes

With your assistance, as shown by the final upward slope of the diagram, your client can begin to reduce the pain and move back toward the freedom and pleasure of being out of debt, reducing the pain as each debt is retired. Your client will experience not only the pleasure of reduced anxiety but also the pleasure of accomplishment and ultimately of financial freedom.

It's important that we understand this principle. We can offer the hope and encouragement to counter the increased pain of sacrifice that the client initially faces and thereby greatly increase the chances that they will successfully continue to take the necessary steps toward financial freedom.

How can we begin to do this?

Turn to page 22.

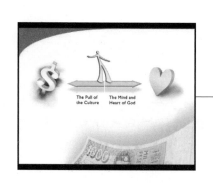

We can do this by helping them to understand the Mind and Heart of God. While the Pull of the Culture is hard at work trying to influence and control our financial behavior, the Mind and Heart of God is quietly encouraging us. God doesn't shout or plead. In his ever-quiet voice, he asks us to be faithful to him. Financial freedom is the byproduct of that faithfulness.

Matthew 6:33 says, "Seek first his kingdom and his righteousness, and all these things will be given to you as well."

This includes the promise of financial freedom.

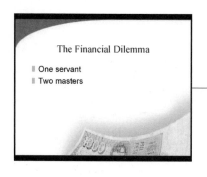

The financial dilemma in biblical terms is that of one servant and two masters.

The Bible makes it clear that we can't serve two masters.

Matthew 6:24 says, "No one can serve two masters. For you will hate one and love the other, or be devoted to one and despise the other. You cannot serve both God and money" (NLT).

NOTES

_____

_____

_____

_____

_____

_____

_____

_____

_____

_____

_____

_____

_____

_____

_____

_____

_____

_____

_____

_____

_____

_____

_____

_____

_____

_____

_____

The Bible also makes clear where following each of these masters leads. Luke 12:20 points out that the Pull of the Culture leads to foolishness. Following the Mind and Heart of God leads to faithfulness as illustrated by the parable of the talents in Matthew 25:21.

We can offer our clients the practical tools and encouragement to turn toward the Mind and Heart of God and to resist the Pull of the Culture.

A solid understanding of the Biblical Financial Principles will provide a framework in which we can do this.

THE FOUNDATION OF A GOOD $ENSE MINISTRY: BIBLICAL FINANCIAL PRINCIPLES

Participant's Guide, page 23.

The following Biblical Financial Principles form the foundation of a Good $ense Ministry.

The Steward's Mindset

3 minutes

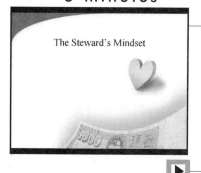

The overarching and most important of the principles is the cultivation of a steward's mindset. Let me explain this principle by sharing the fundamental truths embodied in all that the Bible says about money.

These truths are:

➡ God created everything.

Genesis 1:1 says that in the beginning there was nothing, and God created.

He created every grain of sand on the earth and every star in the galaxies. Sometimes it's easy to lose sight of that fact because we live and work in environments humans have created. But the truth is that first there was nothing, and then there was everything. God created everything.

NOTES

_____

_____

_____

_____

_____

_____

_____

_____

_____

_____

_____

_____

_____

_____

_____

_____

_____

_____

_____

_____

_____

_____

The Pull of the Culture vs. the Mind and Heart of God

Matthew 6:33—_"Seek first his kingdom and his righteousness, and all these things will be given to you as well."_

The Financial Dilemma

- One servant
- Two masters

Matthew 6:24 (NLT)—_"No one can serve two masters. For you will hate one and love the other, or be devoted to one and despise the other. You cannot serve both God and money."_

The Foundation of a Good $ense Ministry: Biblical Financial Principles

The Steward's Mindset

- God created everything.

  Genesis 1:1 says that in the beginning there was nothing, and God created.

- God _____ everything.

  Psalm 50:10, 12b—_"Every animal of the forest is mine, and the cattle on a thousand hills . . . for the world is mine, and all that is in it."_

  Psalm 24:1—_"The earth is the Lord's, and everything in it, the world, and all who live in it."_

- We are trustees.

  A trustee has no rights, only responsibilities.

  1 Corinthians 4:2— _"Now it is required that those who have been given a trust must prove faithful."_

—→ God OWNS everything.

God did not create everything and then go off somewhere else in infinity and turn his back on his creation. Scripture makes it clear that God continues to be involved in creation and has retained ownership of all he created.

—→ In Psalm 50 God declares, "Every animal of the forest is mine, and the cattle on a thousand hills . . . for the world is mine, and all that is in it."

And Psalm 24:1 says, "The earth is the Lord's, and everything in it, the world, and all who live in it."

God owns everything.

 —→ We are trustees.

God created and retained ownership. He then entrusted to each of us—who are created in his image—a portion of his creation to manage on his behalf. Our titles and deeds convey ownership only in earthly terms. In the eternal perspective, we own nothing; everything belongs to God. Thus, we are trustees, trustees for God of whatever we have been given.

In order to prove faithful it is important to understand the role of a trustee.

—→ A trustee has no rights, only responsibilities—the responsibility to care for what belongs to someone else.

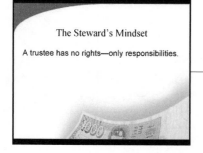

The Steward's Mindset

A trustee has no rights—only responsibilities.

NOTES

**The Foundation of a Good $ense Ministry:
Biblical Financial Principles**

The Steward's Mindset

- God created everything.

  Genesis 1:1 says that in the beginning there was nothing, and God created.

- God _____ everything.

  > Psalm 50:10, 12b—"*Every animal of the forest is mine, and the cattle on a thousand hills . . . for the world is mine, and all that is in it.*"
  >
  > Psalm 24:1—"*The earth is the Lord's, and everything in it, the world, and all who live in it.*"

- We are trustees.

  A trustee has no rights, only responsibilities.

  > 1 Corinthians 4:2— "*Now it is required that those who have been given a trust must prove faithful.*"

For example, if you were incapacitated and I were made trustee of your estate, I would have no rights to your assets, only the responsibility of handling them wisely on your behalf. If I were to violate that trust and manage your affairs in my best interests instead of yours, I could be hauled into court to stand before a judge and explain why I had violated that trust. Each of us will someday be called to give an account of our trusteeship of God's resources.

 First Corinthians 4:2 says, "Now it is required that those who have been given a trust must prove faithful."

This concept of trustee versus owner is the key Biblical Financial Principle from which all others flow.

To drive home this point, we're going to watch a video based on the parable of the pearl of great price in Matthew 13:45–46. It has been created with illustrations rather than live actors and is set in the 1940s.

Turn to page 24.

5 minutes

Video: *The Pearl of Great Price*

Participant's Guide, page 24.

View video: *The Pearl of Great Price*

4 minutes

Individual Reflection Activity: *The Steward's Mindset*

Directions:
How does this truth impact you? Take a couple minutes to reflect on this principle. In your Participant's Guide use the space provided to write down any thoughts you may have.

Individual Reflection Activity:

The Steward's Mindset

Call the group back together after 2 minutes.

NOTES

_____
_____
_____
_____
_____
_____
_____
_____
_____
_____
_____
_____
_____
_____
_____
_____
_____
_____
_____
_____
_____
_____

The Foundation of a Good $ense Ministry: Biblical Financial Principles

The Steward's Mindset

- God created everything.

  Genesis 1:1 says that in the beginning there was nothing, and God created.

- God _____ everything.

  > Psalm 50:10, 12b—"*Every animal of the forest is mine, and the cattle on a thousand hills . . . for the world is mine, and all that is in it.*"
  >
  > Psalm 24:1—"*The earth is the Lord's, and everything in it, the world, and all who live in it.*"

- We are trustees.

  A trustee has no rights, only responsibilities.

  > 1 Corinthians 4:2— "*Now it is required that those who have been given a trust must prove faithful.*"

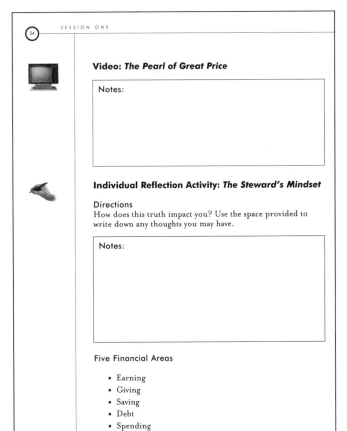

Video: *The Pearl of Great Price*

Notes:

Individual Reflection Activity: *The Steward's Mindset*

Directions
How does this truth impact you? Use the space provided to write down any thoughts you may have.

Notes:

Five Financial Areas

- Earning
- Giving
- Saving
- Debt
- Spending

Wrap-up

What were some thoughts you had as you reflected on this video?

> Solicit two or three comments from the group. Be sure to repeat their answers so everyone hears the response.
>
> Possible responses:
>
> • It's a great reminder of who really owns "our stuff."
>
> • I don't think I ever realized that before.

This profound and fundamental concept means we are trustees, not owners, of *everything* we have, even our children. Our children are not really *ours* but are the beloved sons and daughters of God who are entrusted to us.

10 minutes

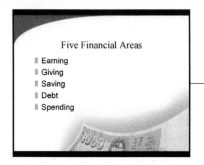

The Five Financial Areas

The remaining foundational Biblical Financial Principles have to do with the five financial areas in our lives. The five areas are:

 Earning

    Giving

    Saving

    Debt

    Spending

These areas represent the usual way in which we get money, which is earning, and the four things we can do with it once we have it: we can give it away, save it, pay debt with it, or spend it.

Let's look at the Biblical Financial Principles that surround these areas.

Let's start with the Biblical Financial Principles for earning.

NOTES

Video: *The Pearl of Great Price*

Notes:

Individual Reflection Activity: *The Steward's Mindset*

Directions
How does this truth impact you? Use the space provided to write down any thoughts you may have.

Notes:

Five Financial Areas

- Earning
- Giving
- Saving
- Debt
- Spending

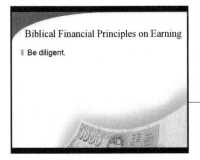

Biblical Financial Principles on Earning

Participant's Guide, page 25.

 Colossians 3:23 commands us to be diligent. "Work hard and cheerfully at whatever you do" (NLT).

This same verse also calls us to be PURPOSEFUL. We are to work "as though you were working for the Lord rather than people." When we work, we serve God. First Timothy 5:8 further clarifies a key purpose of our work by calling us to provide for ourselves and for those dependent on us. This verse says that "those who won't care for their own relatives . . . have denied what we believe" (NLT).

As we earn, we are also to be GRATEFUL. Deuteronomy 8:17-18 reminds us that even our ability to earn is a gift from God.

"You may say to yourself, 'My power and the strength of my hands have produced this wealth for me, but remember the Lord your God, for it is he who gives you the ability to produce wealth."

Now, let's look at giving.

Turn to page 26.

Biblical Financial Principles on Giving

Participant's Guide, page 26.

The main Biblical Financial Principle on giving is that we are made to give, to be generous.

NOTES

_____
_____
_____
_____
_____
_____
_____
_____
_____
_____
_____
_____
_____
_____
_____
_____
_____
_____
_____
_____

Biblical Financial Principles on Earning

• Be diligent.

> Colossians 3:23 (NLT)—_"Work hard and cheerfully at whatever you do."_

• Be _____.

> Colossians 3:23 (NLT)—Work _"as though you were working for the Lord rather than people."_

  ◦ Serve God.

  ◦ Provide for ourselves and for those dependent on us.

> I Timothy 5:8 (NLT)— _"Those who don't care for their own relatives . . . have denied what we believe."_

• Be _____.

> Deuteronomy 8:17-18— _"You may say to yourself, 'My power and the strength of my hands have produced this wealth for me.' But remember the Lord your God, for it is he who gives you the ability to produce wealth."_

Biblical Financial Principles on Giving

• We are made to give.

• Why God wants us to give:

  ◦ As a response to God's _____

> James 1:17— _"Whatever is good and perfect comes to us from God above."_

  ◦ To focus on him as our source and security

> Matthew 6:19-20a (NLT)— _"Don't store up treasures here on earth, where they can be eaten by moths and get rusty, and where thieves break in and steal. Store your treasures in heaven."_

> Matthew 6:32b-33 (NLT)— _"Your heavenly Father already knows all your needs, and he will give you all you need from day to day if you live for him and make the Kingdom of God your primary concern."_

  ◦ To help achieve economic justice

  ◦ To bless others (Genesis 12:2-3)

  ◦ To break the _____ of money

We're made to be channels, not reservoirs. A body of water without an outlet becomes stagnant. A life without an outlet for some of its resources becomes stagnant. Giving is the channel for God's heart to flow through us—a heart of love, generosity, and compassion. When we give, we become more of who God wants us to be. Created in his image, we are not complete or fully satisfied unless we share a portion of what we have with others. Simply put, giving changes lives.

Let's take a look at what the Bible says about why God wants us to give.

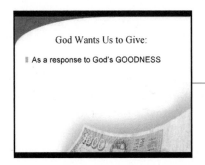

→ First of all, giving is a response to God's GOODNESS. James 1:17 says, "Whatever is good and perfect comes to us from God above" (NLT).

Our giving is simply a way to say, "Thank you, I'm grateful."

→ Second, God wants us to focus on him as our source and security. Our earthly resources are not dependable. In Matthew 6:19-20 Jesus issues this warning to his followers: "Don't store up treasures here on earth, where they can be eaten by moths and get rusty, and where thieves break in and steal. Store your treasures in heaven" (NLT).

In other words, don't base your security on riches that one economic downturn could quickly destroy, but base your security on things of God that will last forever.

We are to trust God, who is totally dependable, for our ultimate provision.

→ In this same chapter of Matthew, Jesus goes on to say, "Your heavenly Father already knows all your needs, and he will give you all you need from day to day if you live for him and make the Kingdom of God your primary concern" (Matthew 6:32b–33).

NOTES

Biblical Financial Principles on Giving

- We are made to give.

- Why God wants us to give:

  ○ As a response to God's _____

  > James 1:17— *"Whatever is good and perfect comes to us from God above."*

  ○ To focus on him as our source and security

  > Matthew 6:19-20a (NLT)— *"Don't store up treasures here on earth, where they can be eaten by moths and get rusty, and where thieves break in and steal. Store your treasures in heaven."*

  > Matthew 6:32b-33 (NLT)— *"Your heavenly Father already knows all your needs, and he will give you all you need from day to day if you live for him and make the Kingdom of God your primary concern."*

  ○ To help achieve economic justice

  ○ To bless others (Genesis 12:2-3)

  ○ To break the _____ of money

When we give generously we are acting out our belief that God will continue to provide for our needs.

▶ → Third, God wants to use us to help achieve economic justice in the world.

Throughout Scripture, material blessing has been linked to obedience, particularly in reference to justice and compassion for the poor. If God has blessed us beyond our needs, chances are it is not for the purpose of raising our standard of living but for the purpose of raising our standard of giving. We are called to love. We can give without loving, but we cannot love without giving.

▶ → Fourth, God wants us to give to bless others.

The relationship between giving and blessing goes all the way back to God's original covenant with Abraham. In Genesis 12:2-3, God tells Abraham that he is being blessed in part so that he can be a blessing to others. It is more blessed to give than to receive. We do reap what we sow. We miss that joy and blessing in our own lives when we hold on to what we have rather than sharing freely with others.

▶ → A final and very important reason for giving is that it breaks the HOLD that money can otherwise have on us.

Money is a very powerful thing. It wants to have our allegiance, to capture our hearts, to control us! But the unnatural act of giving it away rather than using it for other purposes breaks the hold money might otherwise have over us.

Now, let's move to saving—the second thing we can do with money.

NOTES

Biblical Financial Principles on Giving

- We are made to give.

- Why God wants us to give:

  ○ As a response to God's _____

    > James 1:17— *"Whatever is good and perfect comes to us from God above."*

  ○ To focus on him as our source and security

    > Matthew 6:19-20a (NLT)— *"Don't store up treasures here on earth, where they can be eaten by moths and get rusty, and where thieves break in and steal. Store your treasures in heaven."*

    > Matthew 6:32b-33 (NLT)— *"Your heavenly Father already knows all your needs, and he will give you all you need from day to day if you live for him and make the Kingdom of God your primary concern."*

  ○ To help achieve economic justice

  ○ To bless others (Genesis 12:2-3)

  ○ To break the _____ of money

Biblical Financial Principles on Saving

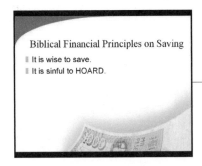

Participant's Guide, page 27.

Scripture says two things about saving:

First, it is wise to save. Proverbs 21:20 says, "In the house of the wise are stores of choice food and oil but [the] foolish . . . devour all [they have]."

Second, it is sinful to HOARD. This is demonstrated in the parable of the rich fool with the overflowing barn in Luke 12:16-21.

In this parable, the rich fool decides to build bigger barns to store even more crops so he can then relax and live in luxury. However, that very night his life was demanded of him.

It is wise to save and foolish to hoard; therefore, we need to be able to assess when we've crossed the line from saving to hoarding. We need to be able to answer the key question,

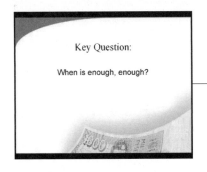

"When is enough, enough?"

I hope that each of you has wrestled with your answer to that question. There are some guidelines on addressing this question in the Appendix on page 121.

Now, let's move to debt.

Turn to page 28.

Biblical Financial Principles on Debt

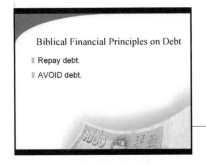

Participants Guide, page 28.

Scripture has two guidelines for us about debt.

First, if we owe debt, we must repay it. Psalm 37:21 says, "The wicked borrow and do not repay. . . ."

NOTES

_____

_____

_____

_____

_____

_____

_____

_____

_____

_____

_____

_____

_____

_____

_____

_____

_____

_____

_____

_____

_____

_____

_____

_____

Biblical Financial Principles on Saving

- It is wise to save.

> Proverbs 21:20— _"In the house of the wise are stores of choice food and oil . . . but [the] foolish . . . devour all [they have]."_

- It is sinful to _____ (Luke 12:16-21).

Key Question: "When is enough, enough?"

Biblical Financial Principles on Debt

- Repay debt.

> Psalm 37:21— _"The wicked borrow and do not repay . . ."_

- _____ debt.

> Proverbs 22:7— _"The borrower is servant to the lender."_

Spiritual Dangers of Debt:

- Presumes on the future

> James 4:14— _"You do not even know what will happen tomorrow."_

- Denies God the opportunity to _____

> Ecclesiastes 7:14— _"When times are good, be happy; but when times are bad, consider: God has made the one as well as the other."_

- Fosters _____ and greed

> Luke 12:15, (NLT)— _"Beware! Don't be greedy for what you don't have. Real life is not measured by how much we own."_

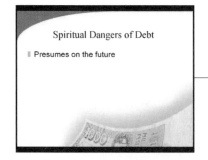

Second, and better yet, AVOID debt altogether, because it produces bondage. When you owe someone money, they own a piece of you. Proverbs 22:7 says, "The borrower is servant to the lender."

We can also surmise from Scripture that there are spiritual dangers of debt.

The first danger is that debt presumes on the future.

Every time we take on debt, we are presuming that we will be able to pay it back. The ad says, "You can afford a $120 monthly payment," and we believe it. While it may be true at the moment, we may not be able to pay it for the life of the loan.

James 4:14 says, "You do not even know what will happen tomorrow."

The second spiritual danger is that we deny God the opportunity to TEACH US.

He may wish to teach us about his love and provision, but we can deny him that opportunity. For example, I desire something I don't have the money for, but I buy it anyway and put it on my credit card. I can just imagine God saying, "I'm so sorry you did that. I was going to have a friend give you that very thing. Not only have you denied me the opportunity to bless you and show you my love, but you've also placed yourself in bondage to debt."

There's another way God sometimes tries to teach us. It's through withholding. For those of you who are parents, can you recall a time when your children wanted something that you didn't give them? Of course. Why do we sometimes withhold from our children? Because we know there are many things they want that are not in their best interests. That may be the way it is with God. He desires to teach us through withholding, but we can circumvent his intentions by incurring debt to get what we want.

NOTES

Biblical Financial Principles on Debt

- Repay debt.

> Psalm 37:21— *"The wicked borrow and do not repay . . ."*

- _____ debt.

> Proverbs 22:7— *"The borrower is servant to the lender."*

Spiritual Dangers of Debt:

- Presumes on the future

> James 4:14— *"You do not even know what will happen tomorrow."*

- Denies God the opportunity to _____

> Ecclesiastes 7:14— *"When times are good, be happy; but when times are bad, consider: God has made the one as well as the other."*

- Fosters _____ and greed

> Luke 12:15, (NLT)— *"Beware! Don't be greedy for what you don't have. Real life is not measured by how much we own."*

Ecclesiastes 7:14 says, "When times are good, be happy; but when times are bad, consider: God has made the one as well as the other."

The third spiritual danger is that debt often fosters ENVY and greed.

We all have a natural inclination to want more, and debt and credit can be used to satisfy that envious, greedy part of us.

In Luke 12:15 Jesus says, "Beware! Don't be greedy for what you don't have. Real life is not measured by how much we own" (NLT).

Biblical Financial Principles on Spending

Participant's Guide, page 29.

The last thing we can do with money is spend it. Let's examine three Biblical Financial Principles about spending and our behavior as consumers. These principles deal with focusing on God and living a lifestyle of moderation and contentment.

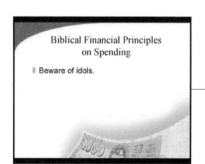

Beware of idols.

In Deuteronomy 5:7-8, God declares himself to be a jealous God and commands that we have no other gods before him.

Yet, since the beginning of time, we have wrestled with the temptation to replace God with things.

In New Testament times, in Romans 1:25, the Apostle Paul described the wicked as those who "worshiped and served created things rather than the Creator."

Today that worship of created things is called materialism. It is a competing theology that makes idols of material possessions.

NOTES

_____

_____

_____

_____

_____

_____

_____

_____

_____

_____

_____

_____

_____

_____

_____

_____

_____

_____

_____

_____

_____

_____

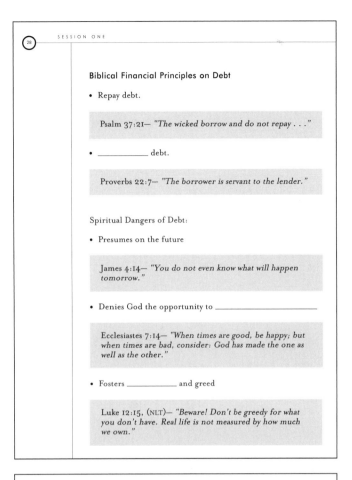

SESSION ONE

28

Biblical Financial Principles on Debt

- Repay debt.

> Psalm 37:21— _"The wicked borrow and do not repay . . ."_

- _____ debt.

> Proverbs 22:7— _"The borrower is servant to the lender."_

Spiritual Dangers of Debt:

- Presumes on the future

> James 4:14— _"You do not even know what will happen tomorrow."_

- Denies God the opportunity to _____

> Ecclesiastes 7:14— _"When times are good, be happy; but when times are bad, consider: God has made the one as well as the other."_

- Fosters _____ and greed

> Luke 12:15, (NLT)— _"Beware! Don't be greedy for what you don't have. Real life is not measured by how much we own."_

SESSION ONE

29

Biblical Financial Principles on Spending

- Beware of idols (Deuteronomy 5:7-8).

> Romans 1:25— _They "worshiped and served created things rather than the Creator."_

- Guard against _____.

> Luke 12:15 (NLT)— _"Beware! Don't be greedy for what you don't have. Real life is not measured by how much we own."_
>
> Proverbs 30:8 (NLT)— _"Give me neither poverty nor riches. Give me just enough to satisfy my needs."_

- Be _____.

> Philippians 4:12— _"I know what it is to be in need, and I know what it is to have plenty. I have learned the secret of being content in any and every situation, whether well fed or hungry, whether living in plenty or in want."_

The second principle is to guard against GREED. In Luke 12:15 Jesus says, "Beware! Don't be greedy for what you don't have. Real life is not measured by how much we own" (NLT). In contrast to greed, the Bible calls us to seek moderation. Proverbs 30:8 says, "Give me neither poverty nor riches! Give me just enough to satisfy my needs" (NLT).

The third principle is to be CONTENT. In Philippians 4:12, Paul explains that he has learned to be content in all circumstances. He writes, "I know what it is to be in need, and I know what it is to have plenty. I have learned the secret of being content in any and every situation, whether well fed or hungry, whether living in plenty or in want."

It is very important that, as a Good $ense counselor, you become familiar with these and other Biblical Financial Principles. Your counseling should be grounded in them. It is what distinguishes your counsel from a number of secular agencies a client could go to.

Turn to page 201 in the Appendix.

You'll notice a Biblical Financial Principles page, which contains the principles we just discussed as well as some additional ones. Please go ahead and remove that page now; it's perforated. You might want to laminate it for durability. Keep it handy, study it often, and use it as a reference in your counseling. We'll talk more about this later.

At this point, let's look at some sample situations and see how good we are at choosing which principles apply to these situations.

Turn to page 30.

NOTES

_____
_____
_____
_____
_____
_____
_____
_____
_____
_____
_____
_____
_____
_____
_____
_____
_____
_____
_____
_____
_____
_____
_____

Biblical Financial Principles on Spending

- Beware of idols (Deuteronomy 5:7-8).

> Romans 1:25— They "worshiped and served created things rather than the Creator."

- Guard against _____.

> Luke 12:15 (NLT)— "Beware! Don't be greedy for what you don't have. Real life is not measured by how much we own."

> Proverbs 30:8 (NLT)— "Give me neither poverty nor riches. Give me just enough to satisfy my needs."

- Be _____.

> Philippians 4:12— "I know what it is to be in need, and I know what it is to have plenty. I have learned the secret of being content in any and every situation, whether well fed or hungry, whether living in plenty or in want."

18 minutes

Group Activity:

Applying the
Biblical Financial
Principles

Group Activity: *Applying the Biblical Financial Principles*

Participant's Guide, pages 30–33.

Objective:
For participants to practice relating the Biblical Financial Principles to their clients' situations.

Directions

1. Get back into your groups.

2. Select one person to read Situation 1.

3. Discuss the situation and write the applicable Biblical Financial Principle(s) from pages 201 and 202 in the box. If you know of other verses or principles that might apply to the situation, go ahead and write them down also.

4. Do the same for Situations 2 and 3.

When you get to Situation 3, note that it is not a red case situation, but there's value in looking at it.

You'll have 10 minutes to work in your groups then we'll discuss this activity together.

The three situations are listed below.

Situation 1

This is a Christian couple.

"My spouse would like a new car. The one she drives is very reliable, but it has almost 100,000 miles on it and it's pretty dinged up. It has a little rust also. We don't have any money saved to get a car (fact is, we hardly have any savings, period), but we're very confident that we could afford monthly payments because next month I'm getting a raise and that will give me about $350 additional take-home pay. We don't have any other debt except our mortgage.

(Continued on next page.)

NOTES

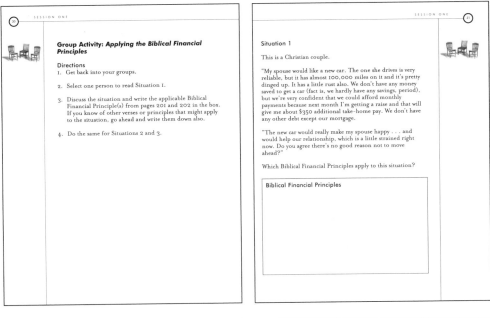

Group Activity: *Applying the Biblical Financial Principles*

Directions

1. Get back into your groups.

2. Select one person to read Situation 1.

3. Discuss the situation and write the applicable Biblical Financial Principle(s) from pages 201 and 202 in the box. If you know of other verses or principles that might apply to the situation, go ahead and write them down also.

4. Do the same for Situations 2 and 3.

Situation 1

This is a Christian couple.

"My spouse would like a new car. The one she drives is very reliable, but it has almost 100,000 miles on it and it's pretty dinged up. It has a little rust also. We don't have any money saved to get a car (fact is, we hardly have any savings, period), but we're very confident that we could afford monthly payments because next month I'm getting a raise and that will give me about $350 additional take-home pay. We don't have any other debt except our mortgage.

"The new car would really make my spouse happy . . . and would help our relationship, which is a little strained right now. Do you agree there's no good reason not to move ahead?"

Which Biblical Financial Principles apply to this situation?

Biblical Financial Principles

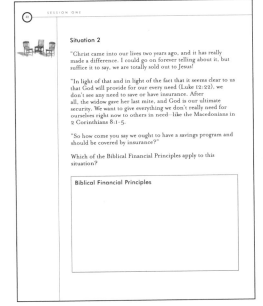

Situation 2

"Christ came into our lives two years ago, and it has really made a difference. I could go on forever telling about it, but suffice it to say, we are totally sold out to Jesus!

"In light of that and in light of the fact that it seems clear to us that God will provide for our every need (Luke 12:22), we don't see any need to save or have insurance. After all, the widow gave her last mite, and God is our ultimate security. We want to give everything we don't really need for ourselves right now to others in need—like the Macedonians in 2 Corinthians 8:1-5.

"So how come you say we ought to have a savings program and should be covered by insurance?"

Which of the Biblical Financial Principles apply to this situation?

Biblical Financial Principles

Situation 3

This person professes that Christ is his Lord and Savior.

"I make big bucks! I tithe to the church (and even give some additional money to other charities from time to time). I'm out of debt except for the mortgage on our present $400,000 house—we owe just under $160,000. Most of the people we know who make as much as we do live in much more expensive homes.

"There's an $800,000 estate for sale that we have our eye on. We're convinced we can afford it. It has a lake, and we like to fish and swim. Our kids could have their friends over. People know we're Christians, and this could be tangible evidence of how God has blessed us. And we'd have lots of room to have our church friends stay over.
Any counsel as to why we should or shouldn't buy it?"

Which Biblical Financial Principles apply to this situation?

Biblical Financial Principles

"The new car would really make my spouse happy . . . and would help our relationship, which is a little strained right now. Do you agree there's no good reason not to move ahead?"

Which Biblical Financial Principles apply to this situation?

Situation 2

"Christ came into our lives two years ago, and it has really made a difference. I could go on forever telling about it, but suffice it to say, we are totally sold out to Jesus!

"In light of that and in light of the fact that it seems clear to us that God will provide for our every need (Luke 12:22), we don't see any need to save or have insurance. After all, the widow gave her last mite, and God is our ultimate security. We want to give everything we don't really need for ourselves right now to others in need—like the Macedonians in 2 Corinthians 8:1-5.

"So how come you say we ought to have a savings program and should be covered by insurance?"

Which of the Biblical Financial Principles apply to this situation?

Situation 3

This person professes that Christ is his Lord and Savior.

"I make big bucks! I tithe to the church (and even give some additional money to other charities from time to time). I'm out of debt except for the mortgage on our present $400,000 house—we owe just under $160,000. Most of the people we know who make as much as we do live in much more expensive homes.

(Continued on next page.)

NOTES

Group Activity: *Applying the Biblical Financial Principles*

Directions

1. Get back into your groups.

2. Select one person to read Situation 1.

3. Discuss the situation and write the applicable Biblical Financial Principle(s) from pages 201 and 202 in the box. If you know of other verses or principles that might apply to the situation, go ahead and write them down also.

4. Do the same for Situations 2 and 3.

Situation 1

This is a Christian couple.

"My spouse would like a new car. The one she drives is very reliable, but it has almost 100,000 miles on it and it's pretty dinged up. It has a little rust also. We don't have any money saved to get a car (fact is, we hardly have any savings, period), but we're very confident that we could afford monthly payments because next month I'm getting a raise and that will give me about $350 additional take-home pay. We don't have any other debt except our mortgage.

"The new car would really make my spouse happy . . . and would help our relationship, which is a little strained right now. Do you agree there's no good reason not to move ahead?"

Which Biblical Financial Principles apply to this situation?

Biblical Financial Principles

Situation 2

"Christ came into our lives two years ago, and it has really made a difference. I could go on forever telling about it, but suffice it to say, we are totally sold out to Jesus!

"In light of that and in light of the fact that it seems clear to us that God will provide for our every need (Luke 12:22), we don't see any need to save or have insurance. After all, the widow gave her last mite, and God is our ultimate security. We want to give everything we don't really need for ourselves right now to others in need—like the Macedonians in 2 Corinthians 8:1–5.

"So how come you say we ought to have a savings program and should be covered by insurance?"

Which of the Biblical Financial Principles apply to this situation?

Biblical Financial Principles

Situation 3

This person professes that Christ is his Lord and Savior.

"I make big bucks! I tithe to the church (and even give some additional money to other charities from time to time). I'm out of debt except for the mortgage on our present $400,000 house—we owe just under $160,000. Most of the people we know who make as much as we do live in much more expensive homes.

"There's an $800,000 estate for sale that we have our eye on. We're convinced we can afford it. It has a lake, and we like to fish and swim. Our kids could have their friends over. People know we're Christians, and this could be tangible evidence of how God has blessed us. And we'd have lots of room to have our church friends stay over. Any counsel as to why we should or shouldn't buy it?"

Which Biblical Financial Principles apply to this situation?

Biblical Financial Principles

"There's an $800,000 estate for sale that we have our eye on. We're convinced we can afford it. It has a lake, and we like to fish and swim. Our kids could have their friends over. People know we're Christians, and this could be tangible evidence of how God has blessed us. And we'd have lots of room to have our church friends stay over. Any counsel as to why we should or shouldn't buy it?"

Which Biblical Financial Principles apply to this situation?

Wrap-up

Call the group back together after 10 minutes.

Begin with Situation 1. Ask the class which Biblical Financial Principles their group chose to apply to the situation.

Repeat the process with Situations 2 and 3.

Possible answers are listed below, as well as additional narrative you may choose to use to enrich the discussion. Participants may also have their own favorite passages to apply to the situations.

Situation 1
Which Biblical Financial Principles apply to Situation 1?

Answers:

- Avoid the bondage of debt (Proverbs 22:7).

  You may wish to add: "Although the clients could be commended for not having any consumer debt, it would be foolish to incur it now, when they have little savings and a reliable car that doesn't need replacing."

- Debt presumes on the future (James 4:13-14).

  You may wish to add: "The client is presuming they will get a raise and presuming they will be able to afford the payment for as long as it is due."

- It is wise to save (Proverbs 21:20).

(Continued on next page.)

NOTES

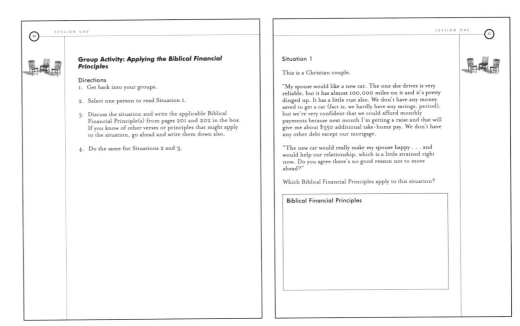

Group Activity: *Applying the Biblical Financial Principles*

Directions

1. Get back into your groups.

2. Select one person to read Situation 1.

3. Discuss the situation and write the applicable Biblical Financial Principle(s) from pages 201 and 202 in the box. If you know of other verses or principles that might apply to the situation, go ahead and write them down also.

4. Do the same for Situations 2 and 3.

Situation 1

This is a Christian couple.

"My spouse would like a new car. The one she drives is very reliable, but it has almost 100,000 miles on it and it's pretty dinged up. It has a little rust also. We don't have any money saved to get a car (fact is, we hardly have any savings, period), but we're very confident that we could afford monthly payments because next month I'm getting a raise and that will give me about $350 additional take-home pay. We don't have any other debt except our mortgage.

"The new car would really make my spouse happy . . . and would help our relationship, which is a little strained right now. Do you agree there's no good reason not to move ahead?"

Which Biblical Financial Principles apply to this situation?

Biblical Financial Principles

Situation 2

"Christ came into our lives two years ago, and it has really made a difference. I could go on forever telling about it, but suffice it to say, we are totally sold out to Jesus!

"In light of that and in light of the fact that it seems clear to us that God will provide for our every need (Luke 12:22), we don't see any need to save or have insurance. After all, the widow gave her last mite, and God is our ultimate security. We want to give everything we don't really need for ourselves right now to others in need—like the Macedonians in 2 Corinthians 8:1-5.

"So how come you say we ought to have a savings program and should be covered by insurance?"

Which of the Biblical Financial Principles apply to this situation?

Biblical Financial Principles

Situation 3

This person professes that Christ is his Lord and Savior.

"I make big bucks! I tithe to the church (and even give some additional money to other charities from time to time). I'm out of debt except for the mortgage on our present $400,000 house—we owe just under $160,000. Most of the people we know who make as much as we do live in much more expensive homes.

"There's an $800,000 estate for sale that we have our eye on. We're convinced we can afford it. It has a lake, and we like to fish and swim. Our kids could have their friends over. People know we're Christians, and this could be tangible evidence of how God has blessed us. And we'd have lots of room to have our church friends stay over.
Any counsel as to why we should or shouldn't buy it?"

Which Biblical Financial Principles apply to this situation?

Biblical Financial Principles

You may wish to add: "It's better to use the raise, if it does come through, to save toward the next car and to continue to drive the car they have."

- A person's life does not consist of the abundance of their possessions (Luke 12:15).

You may wish to add: "It is very doubtful that a new car will help this strained marital relationship."

Situation 2

Which Biblical Financial Principles apply to this situation?

Answers:

- Provide for ourselves and those dependent on us (1 Timothy 5:8).

- Saving for the unexpected is wise (Proverbs 6:8; 21:20).

You may wish to add, "It is absolutely true that our ultimate security lies with God and not our financial resources. However, we are in fact trusting God when we do as his Word counsels us, which is to make provision for the unexpected. In some rare instances, God may call upon someone to sell all they have and give it to the poor. But that is clearly not prescriptive for all us. The general norm is to provide for those dependent upon us by reasonably planning for the unexpected through such vehicles as saving and insurance."

Situation 3

Which Biblical Financial Principles apply to this situation?

Answers:

- Seek moderation (Proverbs 30:7-9).

- Be content (1 Timothy 6:6-10 and Philippians 4:12).

- Calculate cost; prioritize (Luke 14:28-30).

(Continue on next page.)

NOTES

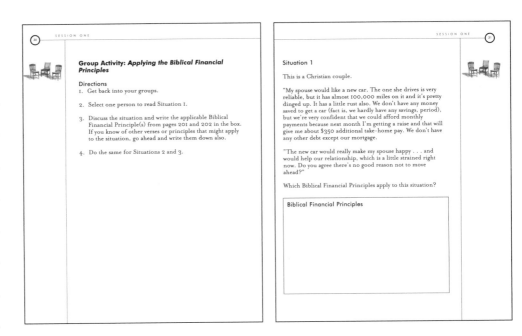

Group Activity: *Applying the Biblical Financial Principles*

Directions

1. Get back into your groups.

2. Select one person to read Situation 1.

3. Discuss the situation and write the applicable Biblical Financial Principle(s) from pages 201 and 202 in the box. If you know of other verses or principles that might apply to the situation, go ahead and write them down also.

4. Do the same for Situations 2 and 3.

Situation 1

This is a Christian couple.

"My spouse would like a new car. The one she drives is very reliable, but it has almost 100,000 miles on it and it's pretty dinged up. It has a little rust also. We don't have any money saved to get a car (fact is, we hardly have any savings, period), but we're very confident that we could afford monthly payments because next month I'm getting a raise and that will give me about $350 additional take-home pay. We don't have any other debt except our mortgage.

"The new car would really make my spouse happy . . . and would help our relationship, which is a little strained right now. Do you agree there's no good reason not to move ahead?"

Which Biblical Financial Principles apply to this situation?

Biblical Financial Principles

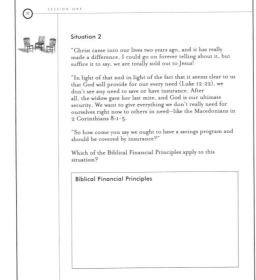

Situation 2

"Christ came into our lives two years ago, and it has really made a difference. I could go on forever telling about it, but suffice it to say, we are totally sold out to Jesus!

"In light of that and in light of the fact that it seems clear to us that God will provide for our every need (Luke 12:22), we don't see any need to save or have insurance. After all, the widow gave her last mite, and God is our ultimate security. We want to give everything we don't really need for ourselves right now to others in need—like the Macedonians in 2 Corinthians 8:1-5.

"So how come you say we ought to have a savings program and should be covered by insurance?"

Which of the Biblical Financial Principles apply to this situation?

Biblical Financial Principles

Situation 3

This person professes that Christ is his Lord and Savior.

"I make big bucks! I tithe to the church (and even give some additional money to other charities from time to time). I'm out of debt except for the mortgage on our present $400,000 house—we owe just under $160,000. Most of the people we know who make as much as we do live in much more expensive homes.

"There's an $800,000 estate for sale that we have our eye on. We're convinced we can afford it. It has a lake, and we like to fish and swim. Our kids could have their friends over. People know we're Christians, and this could be tangible evidence of how God has blessed us. And we'd have lots of room to have our church friends stay over.
Any counsel as to why we should or shouldn't buy it?"

Which Biblical Financial Principles apply to this situation?

Biblical Financial Principles

> You may wish to discuss whether material possessions are, in fact, evidence of God's blessing. If so, one would have to surmise that God has blessed criminals who have gained a great deal of wealth illegally.
>
> This situation can also be used to point out how easy it is for us to rationalize and thereby justify doing or getting what we would like. While it would certainly be appropriate to share this estate if the folks bought it, think of all the ways they could bless others with the financial resources they would have if they didn't buy it.
>
> Another issue that could be discussed is how the question, "When is enough, enough?" applies to this situation.

You are now familiar with the Biblical Financial Principles, which we learned are the foundation of a Good $ense Ministry. We will talk further about how to incorporate them into our counseling sessions later in the course.

SESSION SUMMARY

So far we've covered the types of clients you'll be working with—those in crisis and those that are one paycheck from disaster. We've discussed how the Pull of the Culture impacts them and how we can help them move toward the Mind and Heart of God by applying the Biblical Financial Principles.

In Session 2, we will cover how to prepare for the first meeting with our client.

PREPARE FOR THE FIRST MEETING

SESSION SNAPSHOT

OVERVIEW

In Session 2, the major parts of the counseling process are presented. The first two parts, analyzing the Client Profile and calling the client, are discussed in detail. Participants have a chance to practice analyzing sample profiles and are able to observe sample phone calls on video.

OBJECTIVES

In this session, participants will:

1. Analyze the Client Profile

2. Identify the key points to remember when calling the client

OUTLINE

   I.   Introduction

  II.   Analyze the Client Profile

       A.   Client Profile for the Olsens

       B.   Individual Activity: *Analyze Moore or Leonard Client Profile*

 III.   Call the Client

       A.   Video: *Phone Call to the Olsens*

 IV.   Session Summary

PREPARE FOR THE FIRST MEETING

TIME & MEDIA	CONTENTS

1 minute

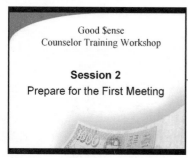

Good $ense
Counselor Training Workshop

Session 2
Prepare for the First Meeting

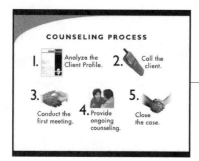

COUNSELING PROCESS

1. Analyze the Client Profile. 2. Call the client.

3. Conduct the first meeting. 4. Provide ongoing counseling. 5. Close the case.

INTRODUCTION

Participant's Guide, page 36.

In this session, we will look at the counseling process and focus on preparing for the first meeting by analyzing the Client Profile and identifying the key points to remember when calling the client.

The Good $ense counseling process consists of five parts:

1. Analyze the Client Profile.

2. Call the client.

3. Conduct the first meeting.

4. Provide ongoing counseling.

5. Close the case.

We will walk through each of these parts of the process today.

NOTES

COUNSELING PROCESS

1. Analyze the Client Profile.

2. Call the client.

3. Conduct the first meeting.

4. Provide ongoing counseling.

5. Close the case.

23 minutes

Purpose of Analyzing the Client Profile

▌ Gain an initial understanding of the client's financial picture

▌ Develop questions, points of affirmation, and encouragement for the first meeting with the client

ANALYZE THE CLIENT PROFILE

> Participant's Guide, page 37.

Let's begin with step one, Analyze the Client Profile.

Your pre-reading described the process by which a client enters the Good $ense Ministry. Once you have been assigned a case by your Good $ense administrator, you will receive a copy of your client's completed Client Profile.

If you are assigned a case in which you are well acquainted with the client, you may wish to notify your Good $ense administrator of that fact and have them check with the client as to their comfort level with having you as their counselor. There can be both pros and cons to working with someone you know, and the determining factor should be each party's comfort level.

The purpose of analyzing the profile is to:

➔ Gain an initial understanding of the client's financial picture, and to develop questions, points of affirmation, and encouragement for the first meeting with the client.

We'll start by walking through a Client Profile to see what it tells us about our clients. Be aware that as you review many of the profiles you receive, your first reaction may be, "This is ridiculous. How could anyone be so foolish and mismanage their finances so badly?" While it is true that many of our clients have made very poor choices, our attitude needs to be one of empathy rather than judgment. Your client is on their side of the table and you are on your side because you have strengths in an area in which they are weak. Your role is to share God's love from the position of your strength.

NOTES

Analyze the Client Profile

Purposes of Analyzing the Client Profile

- Gain an initial understanding of the client's financial picture

- Develop questions and points of affirmation and encouragement for the first meeting with the client

The profile is a _____ point only.

Turn to pages 221 to 224 in the Appendix and remove the Client Profile for Mark and Carol Olsen.

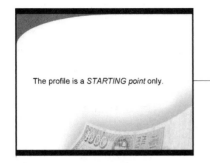

The profile is a *STARTING* point only.

As we walk through the profile, it is important to remember this key point:

 The profile is a STARTING point only.

It should be used to make observations, note questions, and begin to seek clarity. No conclusions or judgments should be made based solely on the profile data.

Think of the profile as a coloring book. The basic outline is there, but you can't fill in the colors until you meet the client and get to know the story behind the numbers. Only then will you begin to get a completed picture.

Client Profile for the Olsens

Let's take a look at a sample Client Profile.

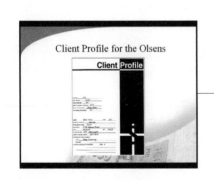

Client Profile for the Olsens

Participant's Guide, page 38.

 Turn to the Client Profile for Mark and Carol Olsen on pages 221 to 224 in the Appendix and remove them now.

We're going to go through Mark and Carol's profile page by page in a moment. But first turn to page 38.

This is a Client Profile Analysis Chart. The Client Profile Analysis Chart is a helpful tool for you to record two types of information as you review the profile.

The first column contains a checklist of things to look for as you review the Client Profile.

 The second and third columns are labeled with a plus sign and a question mark. The final column gives you room to take notes. When you write down the positive things you notice, place a check in the plus-sign column.

NOTES

Analyze the Client Profile

Purposes of Analyzing the Client Profile

- Gain an initial understanding of the client's financial picture

- Develop questions and points of affirmation and encouragement for the first meeting with the client

. The profile is a _____ point only.

Turn to pages 221 to 224 in the Appendix and remove the Client Profile for Mark and Carol Olsen.

Date:_____

Client Profile Analysis Chart

As you review the Client Profile, note positive things you can affirm and questions you want to ask. Place a check in the + or ? colums to indicate whether it is an affirmation or a question.

CHECKLIST	+	?	NOTES
FRONT COVER			
Is the client married? If so, the spouse should participate in the counseling meetings.			
How old is the client? This will give you an idea about future career income and of how adequate their savings are for college expenses and retirement, etc.			
What is the nature of the client's employment? If self-employed, there may be income stability issues and a question of whether they are current on their quarterly estimated tax payments.			
What are the names and ages of the client's children? This will help you understand the types and amount of their expenses as well as provide information that may be helpful in building rapport with your client.			
WHAT I OWN			
How much money is in the checking and savings accounts? This indicates whether your client has any buffer to work with.			
Are there any other savings listed for the client to draw on? The cash value of life insurance may be such a resource.			

When you write down any questions you have about the data, place a check in the question-mark column.

Take a few minutes and familiarize yourself with the information on this chart.

Pause for 3 minutes while participants read through the Client Profile Analysis Chart.

We are going to analyze the Client Profile for the Olsens using the Client Profile Analysis Chart. I'm going to have you actually record information on this chart so we don't miss anything important.

Although we will record most of our notes on the Client Profile Analysis Chart, feel free to mark up or highlight the Client Profile itself in any way that makes sense to you. Remember to use a different-colored pen to make your markings so that they can be distinguished from the client's writing. Avoid using red ink since it has a negative connotation for many people.

One other thing I'd like to mention is that the Client Profile Analysis Chart is for capturing your initial questions and affirmations. Once it is complete, you may want to narrow down the number of questions you actually cover during the first meeting, or rephrase or reorder them.

Now, let's begin with the first category on the Client Profile Analysis Chart, the front cover.

Front Cover
What does the first question on the Client Profile Analysis Chart ask?

Answer: Is the client married? If so, the spouse should participate in the counseling meetings.

NOTES

Date:_____

Client Profile Analysis Chart

As you review the Client Profile, note positive things you can affirm and questions you want to ask. Place a check in the + or ? colums to indicate whether it is an affirmation or a question.

CHECKLIST	+	?	NOTES
FRONT COVER			
Is the client married? If so, the spouse should participate in the counseling meetings.			
How old is the client? This will give you an idea about future career income and of how adequate their savings are for college expenses and retirement, etc.			
What is the nature of the client's employment? If self-employed, there may be income stability issues and a question of whether they are current on their quarterly estimated tax payments.			
What are the names and ages of the client's children? This will help you understand the types and amount of their expenses as well as provide information that may be helpful in building rapport with your client.			
WHAT I OWN			
How much money is in the checking and savings accounts? This indicates whether your client has any buffer to work with.			
Are there any other savings listed for the client to draw on? The cash value of life insurance may be such a resource.			

Now look at the profile. Is Mark married?

Answer: Yes.

We want to be sure to include his spouse, Carol, in the first meeting.

What is the next question on the chart?

Answer: How old is the client?

→ This will give you an idea about future career income and how adequate their savings are for college expenses and retirement, etc.

Now look at the profile. What's Mark's age?

Answer: Mark is thirty-two.

Although we don't need to note anything on the chart, we'll need this information later.

→ The next question on the chart is, "What is the nature of the client's employment?" If self-employed, there may be income stability issues and a question of whether they're current on their quarterly estimated tax payments.

Look on the profile. What is the nature of Mark's employment?

Answer: He does data processing work.

Be prepared to ask about his work. It's a good starting point for getting to know him and for establishing your relationship. Go ahead and note this question on your chart.

Client Profile Analysis Chart for Mark and Carol Olsen

NOTES

Date:_____

Client Profile Analysis Chart

As you review the Client Profile, note positive things you can affirm and questions you want to ask. Place a check in the + or ? colums to indicate whether it is an affirmation or a question.

CHECKLIST	+	?	NOTES
FRONT COVER			
Is the client married? If so, the spouse should participate in the counseling meetings.			
How old is the client? This will give you an idea about future career income and of how adequate their savings are for college expenses and retirement, etc.			
What is the nature of the client's employment? If self-employed, there may be income stability issues and a question of whether they are current on their quarterly estimated tax payments.			
What are the names and ages of the client's children? This will help you understand the types and amount of their expenses as well as provide information that may be helpful in building rapport with your client.			
WHAT I OWN			
How much money is in the checking and savings accounts? This indicates whether your client has any buffer to work with.			
Are there any other savings listed for the client to draw on? The cash value of life insurance may be such a resource.			

➔ The next question on the chart asks for the names and ages of the client's children. This will help you understand the types and amount of their expenses as well as provide information that may be helpful in building rapport with your client.

You can see from the profile that Mark and Carol have a four-year-old child named Ben. Let's make a note to ask about Ben.

What I Own
You can see that the next section on the chart is "What I Own."

➔ The first question asks, "How much money is in the checking and savings accounts?" This indicates whether your client has any buffer to work with.

How much money do the Olsens have in these accounts?

Answer: Thirty dollars in checking and $100 in savings.

They have no buffer to work with. Let's make a note about this on the chart.

➔ The next question asks whether there are any other savings listed for the client to draw on. The cash value of life insurance may be such a resource.

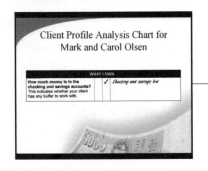

NOTES

Date:_____

Client Profile Analysis Chart

As you review the Client Profile, note positive things you can affirm and questions you want to ask. Place a check in the + or ? colums to indicate whether it is an affirmation or a question.

CHECKLIST	+	?	NOTES
FRONT COVER			
Is the client married? If so, the spouse should participate in the counseling meetings.			
How old is the client? This will give you an idea about future career income and of how adequate their savings are for college expenses and retirement, etc.			
What is the nature of the client's employment? If self-employed, there may be income stability issues and a question of whether they are current on their quarterly estimated tax payments.			
What are the names and ages of the client's children? This will help you understand the types and amount of their expenses as well as provide information that may be helpful in building rapport with your client.			
WHAT I OWN			
How much money is in the checking and savings accounts? This indicates whether your client has any buffer to work with.			
Are there any other savings listed for the client to draw on? The cash value of life insurance may be such a resource.			

Notice that there aren't any other savings listed on the Olsens' profile.

➤ The next question on page 39 is, "Has the client begun to save for retirement?"

Have they?

> Answer: Yes.

The $20,000 in 401(k) savings is a good start for a couple in their early thirties. Let's make a note to affirm them for having begun this savings and encourage them to continue.

> Pause to allow participants to fill in their charts.

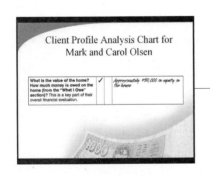

➤ The next question asks for the value of the home and how much money is owed on the home—from the "What I Owe" section. This is a key part of the overall financial situation.

Under the "What I Own" section of the profile, we see that the market value of their home is $174,000. If we look at the next section, "What I Owe," we see that the current balance of the mortgage is $125,000. Let's make a note on our chart that they have about $50,000 in equity in the house.

> Pause to allow participants to fill in their charts.

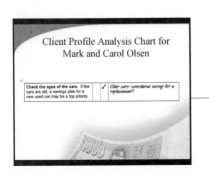

➤ Now, let's check the ages of the cars. If the cars are old, a savings plan for a new used car may be a top priority.

You can see that they own two older cars. Let's make a note to ask whether they have considered a savings plan for a replacement car.

NOTES

CHECKLIST	+	?	NOTES
WHAT I OWN (continued)			
Has the client begun to save for retirement?			
What is the value of the home? How much money is owed on the home (from the "What I Owe" section)? This is a key part of their overall financial evaluation.			
Check the ages of the cars. If the cars are old, a savings plan for a new used car may be a top priority.			
What is the value of other possessions? If high, there may be an opportunity to sell some assets to jump-start debt repayment.			
WHAT I OWE			
Total all the consumer debts. Include all debts, *except* mortgage.			
WHAT I MAKE			
Verify the total monthly income figure. Note the frequency of paychecks. "Every other week" means that there are twenty-six paychecks per year. "Weekly" means fifty-two checks per year. Since we are interested in monthly income, you'll have to do the math to calculate the monthly income. Note also that these pay arrangements can create some cash flow complexities since paydays come on different dates each month.			

Pause to allow participants to fill in their charts.

→ The last question in this section asks, "What is the value of other possessions?" If high, there may be an opportunity to sell some assets to jump-start debt repayment.

The Olsens did not list any other possessions, but notice at the bottom of the "What I Owe" section there is a note concerning a travel trailer.

Participants may ask what the note about the tax-deductible trailer means. Under certain circumstances in the United States, a travel trailer qualifies for a tax deduction if it meets second home qualification criteria.

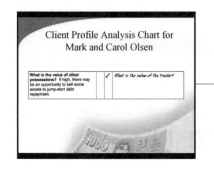

Let's make a note to ask about the value of the trailer.

Pause to allow participants to fill in their charts.

What I Owe

→ The next category on the chart is "What I Owe."

Take a moment and total all their consumer debts. Include all debts, *except* mortgage.

Pause.

How much does our client owe in consumer debt?

Answer: More than $17,000.

Let's note this on our chart.

NOTES

CHECKLIST	+	?	NOTES
WHAT I OWN (continued)			
Has the client begun to save for retirement?			
What is the value of the home? How much money is owed on the home (from the "What I Owe" section)? This is a key part of their overall financial evaluation.			
Check the ages of the cars. If the cars are old, a savings plan for a new used car may be a top priority.			
What is the value of other possessions? If high, there may be an opportunity to sell some assets to jump-start debt repayment.			
WHAT I OWE			
Total all the consumer debts. Include all debts, *except* mortgage.			
WHAT I MAKE			
Verify the total monthly income figure. Note the frequency of paychecks. "Every other week" means that there are twenty-six paychecks per year. "Weekly" means fifty-two checks per year. Since we are interested in monthly income, you'll have to do the math to calculate the monthly income. Note also that these pay arrangements can create some cash flow complexities since paydays come on different dates each month.			

Let's also note that one of the debts is for hospital bills. You might ask if the situation that caused the hospital stay is now okay.

Pause to allow participants to fill in their charts.

 Does it appear that the client understands the difference between the total amount owed and the minimum payment?

Answer: Yes.

What I Make

Let's look at the next category on the chart, "What I Make." It says, "Verify the total monthly income figure." Note the frequency of paychecks. "Every other week" means that there are twenty-six paychecks per year. "Weekly" means fifty-two checks per year. Since we are interested in monthly income, you'll have to do the math to calculate the monthly income. Note also that these pay arrangements can create some cash flow complexities since paydays come on different dates each month.

Let's verify the total monthly income figure. Is $4,494 per month correct?

Answer: Yes: Monthly income = ($2,074 X 26) / 12 = $4,494 per month.

Now look at page 40.

What I Spend
The next category on the chart is "What I Spend."

The first question in this category asks if the client is giving and saving anything.

NOTES

CHECKLIST	+	?	NOTES
WHAT I OWN (continued)			
Has the client begun to save for retirement?			
What is the value of the home? How much money is owed on the home (from the "What I Owe" section)? This is a key part of their overall financial evaluation.			
Check the ages of the cars. If the cars are old, a savings plan for a new used car may be a top priority.			
What is the value of other possessions? If high, there may be an opportunity to sell some assets to jump-start debt repayment.			
WHAT I OWE			
Total all the consumer debts. Include all debts, *except* mortgage.			
WHAT I MAKE			
Verify the total monthly income figure. Note the frequency of paychecks. "Every other week" means that there are twenty-six paychecks per year. "Weekly" means fifty-two checks per year. Since we are interested in monthly income, you'll have to do the math to calculate the monthly income. Note also that these pay arrangements can create some cash flow complexities since paydays come on different dates each month.			

QUESTIONS	+	?	NOTES
WHAT I SPEND			
Is the client giving and saving anything?			
How do the consumer debt payments in this section compare to the minimum monthly payments listed in the "What I Owe" section?			
Based on the ages of the cars in the "What I Own" section, is a realistic amount listed for auto maintenance?			
Are there any missing items? Pay attention to the household/personal section. Clothes/dry cleaning, gifts, cosmetics, and barber/beauty are typically underestimated or left blank, yet just about everyone has these expenses.			
Total the monthly expenses and subtract from the monthly income to get an idea of cash flow.			
Check for any expenses in any of the categories that appear to be unusually high. Be prepared to learn why these expenses are high.			

What does the profile show?

> Anwer: They aren't giving or saving on a regular basis, except possibly in their 401(k).

We want to explore their thoughts and feelings regarding their lack of giving and saving, but we need to do so in a nonjudgmental way. Let's make a note about this.

> Pause to allow participants to fill in their charts.

→ The next question asks how the consumer debt payments in this section compare to the minimum monthly payments listed in the "What I Owe" section.

What do you notice?

> Answer: The Olsens are making just the minimum payments on their consumer debts.

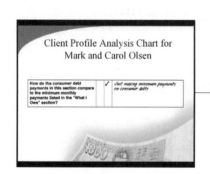

Let's note this on our chart.

→ The next question asks, "Based on the ages of the cars in the 'What I Own' section, is a realistic amount listed for auto maintenance?" We noticed earlier that the client has older cars. Is the maintenance amount realistic?

> Answer: No.

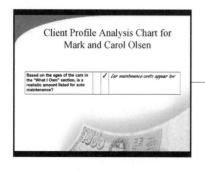

Let's make a note of that on our chart.

> Pause to allow participants to fill in their charts.

NOTES

QUESTIONS	+	?	NOTES
WHAT I SPEND			
Is the client giving and saving anything?			
How do the consumer debt payments in this section compare to the minimum monthly payments listed in the "What I Owe" section?			
Based on the ages of the cars in the "What I Own" section, is a realistic amount listed for auto maintenance?			
Are there any missing items? Pay attention to the household/personal section. Clothes/dry cleaning, gifts, cosmetics, and barber/beauty are typically underestimated or left blank, yet just about everyone has these expenses.			
Total the monthly expenses and subtract from the monthly income to get an idea of cash flow.			
Check for any expenses in any of the categories that appear to be unusually high. Be prepared to learn why these expenses are high.			

➤ The next point begins with, "Are there any missing items?" Read the rest of that and see if you can see anything missing.

> Pause for responses.
>
> Take one answer at a time until all bullet points below are covered.
>
> Answers:
>
> - Maintenance and insurance for the house (ask if insurance is part of the mortgage)
>
> - Clothes/dry cleaning
>
> - Gifts
>
> - Cosmetics
>
> - Barber/beauty expenses
>
> - Travel/vacation

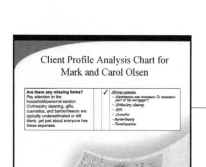

Let's add these items to the notes section of our chart and put a check in the question-mark column.

> Pause to allow participants to fill in their charts.

➤ The next item asks us to total the monthly expenses and subtract from the monthly income to get an idea of cash flow.

This has already been done at the bottom right-hand corner of the page. You can see that income is greater than expenses by $1,343.

In this case, the fact that they are heavily in debt, even though their income is much higher than their listed expenses, tells us that their estimated expenses are way off . . . or that something catastrophic happened in the immediate past. Let's make a note of this.

NOTES

QUESTIONS	+	?	NOTES
WHAT I SPEND			
Is the client giving and saving anything?			
How do the consumer debt payments in this section compare to the minimum monthly payments listed in the "What I Owe" section?			
Based on the ages of the cars in the "What I Own" section, is a realistic amount listed for auto maintenance?			
Are there any missing items? Pay attention to the household/personal section. Clothes/dry cleaning, gifts, cosmetics, and barber/beauty are typically underestimated or left blank, yet just about everyone has these expenses.			
Total the monthly expenses and subtract from the monthly income to get an idea of cash flow.			
Check for any expenses in any of the categories that appear to be unusually high. Be prepared to learn why these expenses are high.			

> Pause to allow participants to fill in their charts.

The final point in this section asks us to check for any expenses that appear to be unusually high and to be prepared to learn why these expenses are high. Does anyone notice anything?

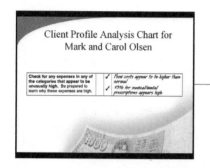

> Answers:
>
> - Food costs appear to be higher than normal.
> - $316 for medical/dental/prescriptions appears high.

Let's make a note ask about these expenses.

> Pause to allow participants to fill in their charts.

Request

On page 41, the next section of the chart is "Request." It says, "Carefully read the answers to the open-ended questions. Look for clues about the client's attitude toward his/her situation and for action steps you can affirm."

Let's go to the last page of the Client Profile. What do you discover from this couple's answer to the question, "How can the Good $ense Ministry help you?"

> Answer: It appears that their child, Ben, is deaf since they would like a babysitter who knows sign language.

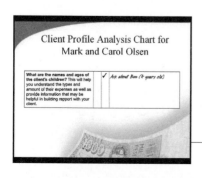

Ben's hearing situation is something to show interest in—to hear what they are feeling in their hearts. Showing interest in Ben is one of the best ways to build a relationship with them. We will talk more about the importance of establishing rapport shortly.

Let's make a note to ask about Ben's hearing situation.

NOTES

QUESTIONS	+	?	NOTES
WHAT I SPEND			
Is the client giving and saving anything?			
How do the consumer debt payments in this section compare to the minimum monthly payments listed in the "What I Owe" section?			
Based on the ages of the cars in the "What I Own" section, is a realistic amount listed for auto maintenance?			
Are there any missing items? Pay attention to the household/personal section. Clothes/dry cleaning, gifts, cosmetics, and barber/beauty are typically underestimated or left blank, yet just about everyone has these expenses.			
Total the monthly expenses and subtract from the monthly income to get an idea of cash flow.			
Check for any expenses in any of the categories that appear to be unusually high. Be prepared to learn why these expenses are high.			

QUESTIONS	+	?	NOTES
REQUEST			
Carefully read the answers to the open-ended questions. Look for clues about the client's attitude toward his/her situation and for action steps you can affirm.			
AGREEMENT			
If your clients are married, check whether they both signed the agreement. If not, ask about it at the first meeting.			

Needed for the first meeting:

> Pause to allow participants to fill in their charts.

▶ In addition, note that their answer to the next question shows that the couple has taken steps to improve their present situation. This is something to affirm and provide encouragement for. Let's list it on our chart.

> Pause to allow participants to fill in their charts.

One more thing I'd like to point out is that Mark and Carol are hoping to find work they can do from home to bring in additional income. We will discuss Good $ense strategies in Session 5 and will point out that in most circumstances more income is not the best answer. However, before we can assume this, we need to ask them what ideas they have.

▶ Let's add it to our chart.

> Pause to allow participants to fill in their charts.

Agreement

→ The next section on our chart is the "Agreement." If your clients are married, check whether they both signed the agreement. If not, ask about it at the first meeting. You can see that Mark and Carol both signed it.

At the end of the chart is one final section called "Needed for the First Meeting." There is room here to indicate anything that would be helpful for the client to bring to the first meeting. In the case of the Olsens, let's make a note to make sure Carol is included in the first meeting, as we have already discussed.

> Pause to allow participants to fill in their charts.

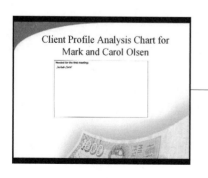

Client Profile Analysis Chart for
Mark and Carol Olsen

NOTES

QUESTIONS	+	?	NOTES
REQUEST			
Carefully read the answers to the open-ended questions. Look for clues about the client's attitude toward his/her situation and for action steps you can affirm.			
AGREEMENT			
If your clients are married, check whether they both signed the agreement. If not, ask about it at the first meeting.			

Needed for the first meeting:

Once you've completed the Client Profile Analysis Chart, go back through the affirmations and questions and reorder them as appropriate. For example, one of the last questions we wrote down on Mark and Carol's chart was to ask about their son, Ben's, hearing situation. This is one of the first questions we'd ask about. Also, it's important to check your wording to insure that your questions are nonjudgmental. For example, we wrote, "Checking and savings low" on the Olsens' chart. A better way to word this would be "Tell me about your checking and savings accounts."

Any questions?

Pause.

Let's move on. Turn to page 42.

Individual Activity: *Analyze Moore or Leonard Client Profile*

30 minutes

Participant's Guide, page 42.

Now that we've analyzed one profile together, you're going to work individually to analyze another profile.

Individual Activity:

Analyze Moore or Leonard Client Profile

Objective
For participants to apply what they just learned by individually analyzing a second profile.

Divide the class into two groups. Assign half the class to analyze the profile for Sharlene and Joe Moore, and half the class to analyze the profile for Barb Leonard. It is important to have equal numbers of participants analyzing each profile since they will use this work later during the role play activity in Session 4. If you don't have an equal number, you or someone else will need to be available for the role play.

(Continued on next page.)

NOTES

Individual Activity: *Analyze Moore or Leonard Profile*

Directions

1. If you are analyzing the Client Profile for Joe and Sharlene Moore, turn to the Appendix and remove pages 225–228. If you are analyzing the client profile for Barb Leonard, turn to the Appendix and remove pages 229–232.

2. Work individually to analyze your assigned profile using the Client Profile Analysis Chart on pages 233–236. Feel free also to take notes right on the Client Profile.

Ask those participants analyzing the profile for Sharlene and Joe Moore to remove the Client Profile on pages 225–228, and those participants analyzing the Client Profile for Barb Leonard to remove the Client Profile on pages 229–232.

Directions

1. If you are analyzing the Client Profile for Joe and Sharlene Moore, turn to the Appendix and remove pages 225–228. If you are anlayzing the Client Profile for Barb Leonard, turn to the Appendix and remove pages 229–232.

2. Work individually to analyze your assigned profile using the Client Profile Analysis Chart on pages 233 to 236. Feel free also to take notes right on the Client Profile.

You'll have 15 minutes. When you are finished, we'll discuss your findings together as a group.

Call the group back together after 15 minutes.

Wrap-up

Let's start with the profile for Sharlene and Joe Moore and walk through the findings of those of you who analyzed this profile. Those who analyzed Barb Leonard's profile can follow along by referring to the Moores' profile on pages 225–228. We'll follow the order of the Client Profile Analysis Chart.

What did you note on the first section of your chart?

Pause before showing the slides with the answers so participants have a chance to give you their answers first.

Answers:

- Sharlene is self-employed. This raises questions about income stability and whether they are current on their quarterly estimated tax payments.

- Ask about Joe's work in retail and being a student.

Client Profile Analysis Chart for Sharlene and Joe Moore

NOTES

42

Individual Activity: *Analyze Moore or Leonard Profile*

Directions

1. If you are analyzing the Client Profile for Joe and Sharlene Moore, turn to the Appendix and remove pages 225–228. If you are analyzing the client profile for Barb Leonard, turn to the Appendix and remove pages 229–232.

2. Work individually to analyze your assigned profile using the Client Profile Analysis Chart on pages 233–236. Feel free also to take notes right on the Client Profile.

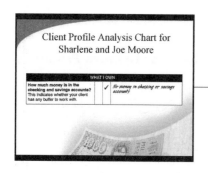

Now, we're at the "What I Own" section of the chart.

What did you note for the first question?

Answer: No money in checking or savings accounts.

What other notes did you make in this section of your Client Profile Analysis Chart?

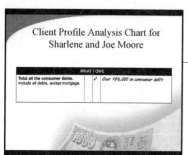

Take one answer at a time until all points below are covered.

Answers:

- No retirement savings

- How much is owed on the house? (They confused the monthly mortgage payment with how much is owed.)

- Older car—consider saving for a replacement?

Let's look at the "What I Owe" section of the chart. What did you note here?

Pause. Answer: Over $26,000 in consumer debts.

Not everything you observe will always be on the checklist. In this case, did anyone notice anything about the types of credit cards listed?

Answer: They are all premium credit cards.

▶ Since premium cards often have annual fees, you may want to ask what fees they are paying on these cards.

NOTES

_____

_____

_____

_____

_____

_____

_____

_____

_____

_____

_____

_____

_____

_____

_____

_____

_____

_____

_____

_____

_____

_____

Client: _____

Date: _____

Client Profile Analysis Chart

As you review the Client Profile, note positive things you can affirm and questions you want to ask. Place a check in the + or ? colums to indicate whether it is an affirmation or a question.

CHECKLIST	+	?	NOTES
FRONT COVER			
Is the client married? If so, the spouse should participate in the counseling meetings.			
How old is the client? This will give you an idea about future career income and of how adequate their savings are for college expenses and retirement, etc.			
What is the nature of the client's employment? If self-employed, there may be income stability issues and a question of whether they are current on their quarterly estimated tax payments.			
What are the names and ages of the client's children? This will help you understand the types and amount of their expenses as well as provide information that may be helpful in building rapport with your client.			
WHAT I OWN			
How much money is in the checking and savings accounts? This indicates whether your client has any buffer to work with.			
Are there any other savings listed for the client to draw on? The cash value of life insurance may be such a resource.			

CHECKLIST	+	?	NOTES
WHAT I OWN (continued)			
Has the client begun to save for retirement?			
What is the value of the home? How much money is owed on the home (from the "What I Owe" section)? This is a key part of their overall financial evaluation.			
Check the ages of the cars. If the cars are old, a savings plan for a new used car may be a top priority.			
What is the value of other possessions? If high, there may be an opportunity to sell some assets to jump-start debt repayment.			
WHAT I OWE			
Total all the consumer debts. Include all debts, *except* mortgage.			
WHAT I MAKE			
Verify the total monthly income figure. Note the frequency of paychecks. "Every other week" means that there are twenty-six paychecks per year. "Weekly" means fifty-two checks per year. Since we are interested in monthly income, you'll have to do the math to calculate the monthly income. Note also that these pay arrangements can create some cash flow complexities since paydays come on different dates each month.			

QUESTIONS	+	?	NOTES
WHAT I SPEND			
Is the client giving and saving anything?			
How do the consumer debt payments in this section compare to the minimum monthly payments listed in the "What I Owe" section?			
Based on the ages of the cars in the "What I Own" section, is a realistic amount listed for auto maintenance?			
Are there any missing items? Pay attention to the household/personal section. Clothes/dry cleaning, gifts, cosmetics, and barber/beauty are typically underestimated or left blank, yet just about everyone has these expenses.			
Total the monthly expenses and subtract from the monthly income to get an idea of cash flow.			
Check for any expenses in any of the categories that appear to be unusually high. Be prepared to learn why these expenses are high.			

QUESTIONS	+	?	NOTES
REQUEST			
Carefully read the answers to the open-ended questions. Look for clues about the client's attitude toward his/her situation and for action steps you can affirm.			
AGREEMENT			
If your clients are married, check whether they both signed the agreement. If not, ask about it at the first meeting.			

Needed for the first meeting:

Let's move to "What I Make." Did they calculate their monthly income correctly?

Answer: Yes: $760 + $120 = $880 × 52 weeks = $45,760 / 12 = $3813.

Now, let's talk about the "What I Spend" section.

Are they giving or saving anything?

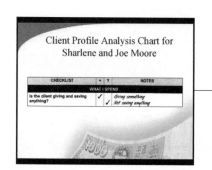

Answer: They are giving $20. They aren't saving anything.

Make sure to affirm them for giving at least something.

How do their consumer debt payments compare to the minimum monthly payments listed in the "What I Owe" section?

Answer: The client is making more than the minimum monthly payments.

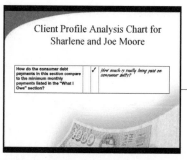

Normally you would affirm this, but when you look at their total expenses, which are $648 more than their income, you see that they can't really be making payments this high. Therefore, you should have noted this as a question.

What did you note about the maintenance expense for the car?

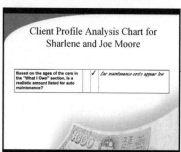

Pause. Answer: Maintenance expense is low, considering the age of the car.

Did you find any missing items?

NOTES

Client Profile Analysis Chart

Client: _____

Date: _____

As you review the Client Profile, note positive things you can affirm and questions you want to ask. Place a check in the + or ? columns to indicate whether it is an affirmation or a question.

CHECKLIST	+	?	NOTES
FRONT COVER			
Is the client married? If so, the spouse should participate in the counseling meetings.			
How old is the client? This will give you an idea about future career income and of how adequate their savings are for college expenses and retirement, etc.			
What is the nature of the client's employment? If self-employed, there may be income stability issues and a question of whether they are current on their quarterly estimated tax payments.			
What are the names and ages of the client's children? This will help you understand the types and amount of their expenses as well as provide information that may be helpful in building rapport with your client.			
WHAT I OWN			
How much money is in the checking and savings accounts? This indicates whether your client has any buffer to work with.			
Are there any other savings listed for the client to draw on? The cash value of life insurance may be such a resource.			

CHECKLIST	+	?	NOTES
WHAT I OWN (continued)			
Has the client begun to save for retirement?			
What is the value of the home? How much money is owed on the home (from the "What I Owe" section)? This is a key part of their overall financial evaluation.			
Check the ages of the cars. If the cars are old, a savings plan for a new used car may be a top priority.			
What is the value of other possessions? If high, there may be an opportunity to sell some assets to jump-start debt repayment.			
WHAT I OWE			
Total all the consumer debts. Include all debts, *except* mortgage.			
WHAT I MAKE			
Verify the total monthly income figure. Note the frequency of paychecks. "Every other week" means that there are twenty-six paychecks per year. "Weekly" means fifty-two checks per year. Since we are interested in monthly income, you'll have to do the math to calculate the monthly income. Note also that these pay arrangements can create some cash flow complexities since paydays come on different dates each month.			

QUESTIONS	+	?	NOTES
WHAT I SPEND			
Is the client giving and saving anything?			
How do the consumer debt payments in this section compare to the minimum monthly payments listed in the "What I Owe" section?			
Based on the ages of the cars in the "What I Own" section, is a realistic amount listed for auto maintenance?			
Are there any missing items? Pay attention to the household/personal section. Clothes/dry cleaning, gifts, cosmetics, and barber/beauty are typically underestimated or left blank, yet just about everyone has these expenses.			
Total the monthly expenses and subtract from the monthly income to get an idea of cash flow.			
Check for any expenses in any of the categories that appear to be unusually high. Be prepared to learn why these expenses are high.			

QUESTIONS	+	?	NOTES
REQUEST			
Carefully read the answers to the open-ended questions. Look for clues about the client's attitude toward his/her situation and for action steps you can affirm.			
AGREEMENT			
If your clients are married, check whether they both signed the agreement. If not, ask about it at the first meeting.			

Needed for the first meeting:

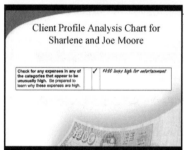

Pause. Answers:

- Home maintenance

- Life and medical insurance

- Household items

- Medical/dental prescription

We already talked about their cash flow. Expenses exceed income by $648 per month.

Did you notice any unusually high expenses?

Pause. Answer: $480 appears to be high for entertainment expenses.

Participants may ask what, if anything, a counselor should say concerning the $140/month expenditure on "liquor/tobacco." Remind participants it is not their role to judge the client. However, after rapport has been established it might be appropriate to inquire about this expense. For example, if the client indicates that he/she is attempting to cut back on smoking but finding it hard to do, encouragement from the counselor would be very much in order.

You may have also noticed that one of them is undergoing counseling. This is typically not an area where you want to recommend reducing costs; at most, you may want to ask the client if he or she feels the counseling is helping.

In the "Request" section, what did you discover when looking at the answer to the first open-ended question?

Answer: They need help in managing their budget.

NOTES

Client: _____

Date: _____

Client Profile Analysis Chart

As you review the Client Profile, note positive things you can affirm and questions you want to ask. Place a check in the + or ? colums to indicate whether it is an affirmation or a question.

CHECKLIST	+	?	NOTES
FRONT COVER			
Is the client married? If so, the spouse should participate in the counseling meetings.			
How old is the client? This will give you an idea about future career income and of how adequate their savings are for college expenses and retirement, etc.			
What is the nature of the client's employment? If self-employed, there may be income stability issues and a question of whether they are current on their quarterly estimated tax payments.			
What are the names and ages of the client's children? This will help you understand the types and amount of expenses as well as provide information that may be helpful in building rapport with your client.			
WHAT I OWN			
How much money is in the checking and savings accounts? This indicates whether your client has any buffer to work with.			
Are there any other savings listed for the client to draw on? The cash value of life insurance may be such a resource.			

CHECKLIST	+	?	NOTES
WHAT I OWN (continued)			
Has the client begun to save for retirement?			
What is the value of the home? How much money is owed on the home (from the "What I Owe" section)? This is a key part of their overall financial evaluation.			
Check the ages of the cars. If the cars are old, a savings plan for a new used car may be a top priority.			
What is the value of other possessions? If high, there may be an opportunity to sell some assets to jump-start debt repayment.			
WHAT I OWE			
Total all the consumer debts. Include all debts, *except* mortgage.			
WHAT I MAKE			
Verify the total monthly income figure. Note the frequency of paychecks. "Every other week" means that there are twenty-six paychecks per year. "Weekly" means fifty-two checks per year. Since we are interested in monthly income, you'll have to do the math to calculate the monthly income. Note also that these pay arrangements can create some cash flow complexities since paydays come on different dates each month.			

QUESTIONS	+	?	NOTES
WHAT I SPEND			
Is the client giving and saving anything?			
How do the consumer debt payments in this section compare to the minimum monthly payments listed in the "What I Owe" section?			
Based on the ages of the cars in the "What I Own" section, is a realistic amount listed for auto maintenance?			
Are there any missing items? Pay attention to the household/personal section. Clothes/dry cleaning, gifts, cosmetics, and barber/beauty are typically underestimated or left blank, yet just about everyone has these expenses.			
Total the monthly expenses and subtract from the monthly income to get an idea of cash flow.			
Check for any expenses in any of the categories that appear to be unusually high. Be prepared to learn why these expenses are high.			

QUESTIONS	+	?	NOTES
REQUEST			
Carefully read the answers to the open-ended questions. Look for clues about the client's attitude toward his/her situation and for action steps you can affirm.			
AGREEMENT			
If your clients are married, check whether they both signed the agreement. If not, ask about it at the first meeting.			

Needed for the first meeting:

How about the second question?

Pause. Answer: They've made the decision to contact Good $ense and they are giving back to God, even though it's a small amount. They are also praying about their situation.

Make sure that you made notes to affirm them on both these points.

Finally, in the last section, you should have noted to include Joe in the first meeting, and perhaps to ask them to find out before the first meeting how much they owe on their house.

Now, let's discuss the Client Profile for Barb Leonard. Those who analyzed the Moores' profile can follow along.

Let's start with the first section of the Client Profile Analysis Chart.

What did you notice about the nature of the client's employment?

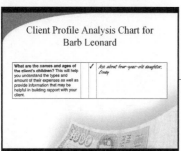

Pause. Answer: She's a sales representative. This means her income is probably commission based, which raises questions about income stability.

What else did you note on this page of the chart?

Pause. Answer: Ask about her four-year-old daughter, Cindy.

What did you note in the "What I Own" section of the chart?

NOTES

_____

_____

_____

_____

_____

_____

_____

_____

_____

_____

_____

_____

_____

_____

_____

_____

_____

_____

_____

_____

_____

_____

Client: _____

Date: _____

Client Profile Analysis Chart

As you review the Client Profile, note positive things you can affirm and questions you want to ask. Place a check in the + or ? colums to indicate whether it is an affirmation or a question.

CHECKLIST	+	?	NOTES
FRONT COVER			
Is the client married? If so, the spouse should participate in the counseling meetings.			
How old is the client? This will give you an idea about future career income and of how adequate their savings are for college expenses and retirement, etc.			
What is the nature of the client's employment? If self-employed, there may be income stability issues and a question of whether they are current on their quarterly estimated tax payments.			
What are the names and ages of the client's children? This will help you understand the types and amount of their expenses as well as provide information that may be helpful in building rapport with your client.			
WHAT I OWN			
How much money is in the checking and savings accounts? This indicates whether your client has any buffer to work with.			
Are there any other savings listed for the client to draw on? The cash value of life insurance may be such a resource.			

CHECKLIST	+	?	NOTES
WHAT I OWN (continued)			
Has the client begun to save for retirement?			
What is the value of the home? How much money is owed on the home (from the "What I Owe" section)? This is a key part of their overall financial evaluation.			
Check the ages of the cars. If the cars are old, a savings plan for a new used car may be a top priority.			
What is the value of other possessions? If high, there may be an opportunity to sell some assets to jump-start debt repayment.			
WHAT I OWE			
Total all the consumer debts. Include all debts, _except_ mortgage.			
WHAT I MAKE			
Verify the total monthly income figure. Note the frequency of paychecks. "Every other week" means that there are twenty-six paychecks per year. "Weekly" means fifty-two checks per year. Since we are interested in monthly income, you'll have to do the math to calculate the monthly income. Note also that these pay arrangements can create some cash flow complexities since paydays come on different dates each month.			

QUESTIONS	+	?	NOTES
WHAT I SPEND			
Is the client giving and saving anything?			
How do the consumer debt payments in this section compare to the minimum monthly payments listed in the "What I Owe" section?			
Based on the ages of the cars in the "What I Own" section, is a realistic amount listed for auto maintenance?			
Are there any missing items? Pay attention to the household/personal section. Clothes/dry cleaning, gifts, cosmetics, and barber/beauty are typically underestimated or left blank, yet just about everyone has these expenses.			
Total the monthly expenses and subtract from the monthly income to get an idea of cash flow.			
Check for any expenses in any of the categories that appear to be unusually high. Be prepared to learn why these expenses are high.			

QUESTIONS	+	?	NOTES
REQUEST			
Carefully read the answers to the open-ended questions. Look for clues about the client's attitude toward his/her situation and for action steps you can affirm.			
AGREEMENT			
If your clients are married, check whether they both signed the agreement. If not, ask about it at the first meeting.			

Needed for the first meeting:

Pause. Answers:

- No money in checking and savings accounts

- No retirement savings

- Older car—may need to save for a replacement

Let's talk about the "What I Owe" section.

You should have noted that Barb has no credit card debt. That should be commended.

She does have $9,300 in other debts.

Also, you may have noticed that the bank loan is listed at zero percent interest. This is not likely. You'll want to ask about it.

Barb owes money on her taxes. Make sure you ask if she's current on this year's tax payments. Also, is tax withheld from her commissions?

If you find out that taxes are not withheld, then take-home pay will actually be less than what is calculated in the next section. In such a case, it will probably be necessary for your client to seek the assistance of someone knowledgeable about taxes to help calculate her actual net pay.

Note also that the government charges interest on taxes owed. You should ask what the interest is on her debt.

Let's move to the "What I Make" section of the chart.

We had a question earlier about the stability of her income. It appears that about one-third of it, or $700, is commission. Make sure that you ask how sure she is of this commission. What has it averaged over the last year?

NOTES

Client: _____

Date: _____

Client Profile Analysis Chart

As you review the Client Profile, note positive things you can affirm and questions you want to ask. Place a check in the + or ? columns to indicate whether it is an affirmation or a question.

CHECKLIST	+	?	NOTES
FRONT COVER			
Is the client married? If so, the spouse should participate in the counseling meetings.			
How old is the client? This will give you an idea about future career income and of how adequate their savings are for college expenses and retirement, etc.			
What is the nature of the client's employment? If self-employed, there may be income stability issues and a question of whether they are current on their quarterly estimated tax payments.			
What are the names and ages of the client's children? This will help you understand the types and amount of their expenses as well as provide information that may be helpful in building rapport with your client.			
WHAT I OWN			
How much money is in the checking and savings accounts? This indicates whether your client has any buffer to work with.			
Are there any other savings listed for the client to draw on? The cash value of life insurance may be such a resource.			

CHECKLIST	+	?	NOTES
WHAT I OWN (continued)			
Has the client begun to save for retirement?			
What is the value of the home? How much money is owed on the home (from the "What I Owe" section)? This is a key part of their overall financial evaluation.			
Check the ages of the cars. If the cars are old, a savings plan for a new used car may be a top priority.			
What is the value of other possessions? If high, there may be an opportunity to sell some assets to jump-start debt repayment.			
WHAT I OWE			
Total all the consumer debts. Include all debts, *except mortgage.*			
WHAT I MAKE			
Verify the total monthly income figure. Note the frequency of paychecks. "Every other week" means that there are twenty-six paychecks per year. "Weekly" means fifty-two checks per year. Since we are interested in monthly income, you'll have to do the math to calculate the monthly income. Note also that these pay arrangements can create some cash flow complexities since paydays come on different dates each month.			

QUESTIONS	+	?	NOTES
WHAT I SPEND			
Is the client giving and saving anything?			
How do the consumer debt payments in this section compare to the minimum monthly payments listed in the "What I Owe" section?			
Based on the ages of the cars in the "What I Own" section, is a realistic amount listed for auto maintenance?			
Are there any missing items? Pay attention to the household/personal section. Clothes/dry cleaning, gifts, cosmetics, and barber/beauty are typically underestimated or left blank, yet just about everyone has these expenses.			
Total the monthly expenses and subtract from the monthly income to get an idea of cash flow.			
Check for any expenses in any of the categories that appear to be unusually high. Be prepared to learn why these expenses are high.			

QUESTIONS	+	?	NOTES
REQUEST			
Carefully read the answers to the open-ended questions. Look for clues about the client's attitude toward his/her situation and for action steps you can affirm.			
AGREEMENT			
If your clients are married, check whether they both signed the agreement. If not, ask about it at the first meeting.			

Needed for the first meeting:

One additional thing you may have caught is that this is a divorced parent, but no child support is listed. Approach this with sensitivity, but ask if child support payments are a possibility.

We are now on the "What I Spend" section of the chart.

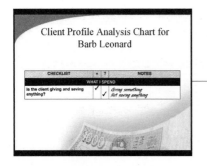

Is Barb giving and saving anything?

> Pause. Answer: She's giving $20 per month. She's not saving anything.

Make sure she's affirmed for giving something.

What did you note when comparing debt payments in this section to the total amount owed?

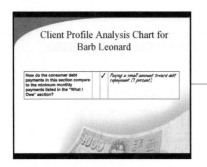

> Pause. Answer: She's paying a small amount—approximately 1 percent—toward debt repayment each month.

For the next question, it looks like she did list a realistic amount for auto maintenance. However, note that she put down the annual amount of her auto license fee rather than the monthly cost. This will need to be adjusted.

The next question asks: "Are there any missing items?" What did you find missing?

> Take one answer at a time until all points below are covered.
>
> Answers:
>
> - No utilities expenses listed. Are they covered in her rent?
>
> (Continued on next page.)

NOTES

Client: _____

Date: _____

Client Profile Analysis Chart

As you review the Client Profile, note positive things you can affirm and questions you want to ask. Place a check in the + or ? colums to indicate whether it is an affirmation or a question.

CHECKLIST	+	?	NOTES
FRONT COVER			
Is the client married? If so, the spouse should participate in the counseling meetings.			
How old is the client? This will give you an idea about future career income and of how adequate their savings are for college expenses and retirement, etc.			
What is the nature of the client's employment? If self-employed, there may be income stability issues and a question of whether they are current on their quarterly estimated tax payments.			
What are the names and ages of the client's children? This will help you understand the types and amount of their expenses as well as provide information that may be helpful in building rapport with your client.			
WHAT I OWN			
How much money is in the checking and savings accounts? This indicates whether your client has any buffer to work with.			
Are there any other savings listed for the client to draw on? The cash value of life insurance may be such a resource.			

CHECKLIST	+	?	NOTES
WHAT I OWN (continued)			
Has the client begun to save for retirement?			
What is the value of the home? How much money is owed on the home (from the "What I Owe" section)? This is a key part of their overall financial evaluation.			
Check the ages of the cars. If the cars are old, a savings plan for a new used car may be a top priority.			
What is the value of other possessions? If high, there may be an opportunity to sell some assets to jump-start debt repayment.			
WHAT I OWE			
Total all the consumer debts. Include all debts, *except* mortgage.			
WHAT I MAKE			
Verify the total monthly income figure. Note the frequency of paychecks. "Every other week" means that there are twenty-six paychecks per year. "Weekly" means fifty-two checks per year. Since we are interested in monthly income, you'll have to do the math to calculate the monthly income. Note also that these pay arrangements can create some cash flow complexities since paydays come on different dates each month.			

QUESTIONS	+	?	NOTES
WHAT I SPEND			
Is the client giving and saving anything?			
How do the consumer debt payments in this section compare to the minimum monthly payments listed in the "What I Owe" section?			
Based on the ages of the cars in the "What I Own" section, is a realistic amount listed for auto maintenance?			
Are there any missing items? Pay attention to the household/personal section. Clothes/dry cleaning, gifts, cosmetics, and barber/beauty are typically underestimated or left blank, yet just about everyone has these expenses.			
Total the monthly expenses and subtract from the monthly income to get an idea of cash flow.			
Check for any expenses in any of the categories that appear to be unusually high. Be prepared to learn why these expenses are high.			

QUESTIONS	+	?	NOTES
REQUEST			
Carefully read the answers to the open-ended questions. Look for clues about the client's attitude toward his/her situation and for action steps you can affirm.			
AGREEMENT			
If your clients are married, check whether they both signed the agreement. If not, ask about it at the first meeting.			

Needed for the first meeting:

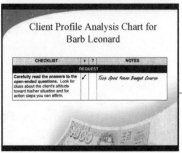

- Although auto insurance is paid for the year, what is the monthly amount?

- No life or health insurance listed. Is she covered?

- No clothes/dry cleaning listed. This seems unusual since she is in a sales position.

- No gift expense listed.

- No cosmetics expenses listed.

- Only one expense under entertainment is filled out.

How does her cash flow look?

Pause. Answer: Her monthly income is $135 more than her listed expenses.

Although this appears positive, there are so many missing expenses and no savings that we should note it as a question.

Did you notice any expenses that appear to be unusually high?

Take one answer at a time until all points are covered.

Answers:

- $40 for books/magazines

- $750 for child care. Point out that since Cindy is four, she will start school soon—one or two years from now—and this expense may go way down, which will be a huge help.

- $90 for fitness/sports

Finally, let's look at her answers to the open-ended questions in the "Request" section. Make sure you made a note to affirm her for taking the *Good $ense Budget Course*.

NOTES

_____

_____

_____

_____

_____

_____

_____

_____

_____

_____

_____

_____

_____

_____

_____

_____

_____

_____

_____

_____

Client: _____

Date: _____

Client Profile Analysis Chart

As you review the Client Profile, note positive things you can affirm and questions you want to ask. Place a check in the + or ? colums to indicate whether it is an affirmation or a question.

CHECKLIST	+	?	NOTES
FRONT COVER			
Is the client married? If so, the spouse should participate in the counseling meetings.			
How old is the client? This will give you an idea about future career income and of how adequate their savings are for college expenses and retirement, etc.			
What is the nature of the client's employment? If self-employed, there may be income stability issues and a question of whether they are current on their quarterly estimated tax payments.			
What are the names and ages of the client's children? This will help you understand the types and amount of their expenses as well as provide information that may be helpful in building rapport with your client.			
WHAT I OWN			
How much money is in the checking and savings accounts? This indicates whether your client has any buffer to work with.			
Are there any other savings listed for the client to draw on? The cash value of life insurance may be such a resource.			

CHECKLIST	+	?	NOTES
WHAT I OWN (continued)			
Has the client begun to save for retirement?			
What is the value of the home? How much money is owed on the home (from the "What I Owe" section)? This is a key part of their overall financial evaluation.			
Check the ages of the cars. If the cars are old, a savings plan for a new used car may be a top priority.			
What is the value of other possessions? If high, there may be an opportunity to sell some assets to jump-start debt repayment.			
WHAT I OWE			
Total all the consumer debts. Include all debts, *except* mortgage.			
WHAT I MAKE			
Verify the total monthly income figure. Note the frequency of paychecks. "Every other week" means that there are twenty-six paychecks per year. "Weekly" means fifty-two checks per year. Since we are interested in monthly income, you'll have to do the math to calculate the monthly income. Note also that these pay arrangements can create some cash flow complexities since paydays come on different dates each month.			

QUESTIONS	+	?	NOTES
WHAT I SPEND			
Is the client giving and saving anything?			
How do the consumer debt payments in this section compare to the minimum monthly payments listed in the "What I Owe" section?			
Based on the ages of the cars in the "What I Own" section, is a realistic amount listed for auto maintenance?			
Are there any missing items? Pay attention to the household/personal section. Clothes/dry cleaning, gifts, cosmetics, and barber/beauty are typically underestimated or left blank, yet just about everyone has these expenses.			
Total the monthly expenses and subtract from the monthly income to get an idea of cash flow.			
Check for any expenses in any of the categories that appear to be unusually high. Be prepared to learn why these expenses are high.			

QUESTIONS	+	?	NOTES
REQUEST			
Carefully read the answers to the open-ended questions. Look for clues about the client's attitude toward his/her situation and for action steps you can affirm.			
AGREEMENT			
If your clients are married, check whether they both signed the agreement. If not, ask about it at the first meeting.			

Needed for the first meeting:

Great job! We've reviewed the profile, and you know a bit about your client. You know what's missing and what they'll need to bring to the first meeting.

Does anyone have any questions?

> Pause.

Let's move to the next step, which is "Call the client."

We're on page 43.

CALL THE CLIENT

> Participant's Guide, page 43.

Some cases can look pretty hopeless at the outset. Only with God's help can we hope to move people toward a God-honoring financial lifestyle.

Therefore, before picking up the telephone, pray for your client. Pray for wisdom, discernment, compassion, and patience. You'll need all of these qualities in abundance as you help those in crisis. Also pray for the client's honesty and strength and courage to take the steps necessary to become free of their burden.

As you can see, there's a sample prayer in your Participant's Guide that you can use or modify as needed.

Psalm 50:15 should be a theme for both you and the client:

 Call upon me in the day of trouble; I will deliver you, and you will honor me.

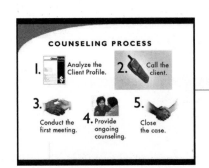

COUNSELING PROCESS

1. Analyze the Client Profile.
2. Call the client.
3. Conduct the first meeting.
4. Provide ongoing counseling.
5. Close the case.

4 minutes

NOTES

Call the Client

COUNSELING PROCESS

 1. Analyze the Client Profile.

 2. Call the client.

 3. Conduct the first meeting.

 4. Provide ongoing counseling.

 5. Close the case.

Sample Prayer:

Father, I offer myself to you and to [client(s)] for the purpose of helping them with their finances, and more importantly, aiding their spiritual growth. Help me to teach [clients] how they can grow in their faith while properly managing the material resources you've provided and by applying your biblical principles in their lives. Grant me the ability to correctly discern right from wrong and to correct the wrongs and affirm the rights. Grant me the patience to fully listen and to respond with empathy or tough love as each situation demands. In your name, amen.

Theme Verse:

Psalm 50:15— *"Call upon me in the day of trouble; I will deliver you, and you will honor me."*

Making that first phone call to a stranger can be awkward! It's important to remember that the first phone call is the beginning of the counseling relationship, so it's important to make the call in a relaxed environment and at a time you are sure you can focus solely on the call with no distractions.

Participant's Guide, pages 44 – 45.

On pages 44 – 45 you'll find a "Phone Call Reminders" list that gives you some pointers for making that first phone call.

Take a few minutes and read through them.

Pause for 3 minutes while participants read through the Phone Call Reminders. This list is included here for your reference.

Phone Call Reminders

These pointers refer specifically to the first phone call, but many of these tips also apply to any phone contact with your client.

- Review the "Needed for the First Meeting" list from the Client Profile Analysis Chart you made for the Client Profile.

- Have your calendar out as well as paper and pen ready in case the client decides to chat and provide further details on the case.

- Call from a quiet place where you will not be disturbed.

If you reach the client directly:

- Introduce yourself.

- Tell them you're calling to make an appointment.

- Arrange a date, time (allow two hours), and neutral location for the meeting. Make sure both spouses are available if your client is a couple.

(Continue on next page.)

NOTES

_____

_____

_____

_____

_____

_____

_____

_____

_____

_____

_____

_____

_____

_____

_____

_____

_____

_____

_____

_____

Phone Call Reminders

These pointers refer specifically to the first phone call, but many of these tips also apply to any phone contact with your client.

- Review the "Needed for the First Meeting" list from the Client Profile Analysis Chart you made for the Client Profile.
- Have your calendar out as well as paper and pen ready in case the client decides to chat and provide further details on the case.
- Call from a quiet place where you will not be disturbed.

If you reach the client directly:

- Introduce yourself.
- Tell them you're calling to make an appointment.
- Arrange a date, time (allow two hours), and neutral location for the meeting. Make sure both spouses are available if your client is a couple.
- Identify what items—if you listed any on your Client Profile Analysis Chart—they need to bring to the meeting.
- Explain what you plan to cover during the first meeting: get to know each other, gain a better understanding of their financial situation, and discuss steps they can begin to take to accomplish their purposes for your time together.
- Tell them you're looking forward to working with them.
- Give them your phone number in case they have a change of plans and need to reach you.
- Reiterate the date, time, and meeting place.
- End the conversation.

If you reach someone other than the client and the client is not there:

- Introduce yourself, but do not say you're from Good $ense Ministry or make any mention of budget counseling. Simply state that you are someone calling "from church." (If the person asks, "Why are you calling?" just say, "I'm returning his/her phone call.")
- Ask the person who answered if he or she can take a message or if there is a more convenient time to call back.
- If the person offers to take a message, leave your phone number and indicate whether it's a home or work number.
- Indicate the best time to reach you.
- Thank the message taker and end the phone call.

If you reach an answering device or voice mailbox:

- Keep in mind that the client may not be the only one with access to the answering device or voice mail, so be discreet!
- State your name and say you're calling "from church."
- Leave your name, number, and best time to call you back. Indicate whether the number you're leaving is a home or work number.

- Identify what items—if you listed any on your Client Profile Analysis Chart—they need to bring to the meeting.

- Explain what you plan to cover during the first meeting: get to know each other, gain a better understanding of their financial situation, and discuss steps they can begin to take to accomplish their purposes for your time together.

- Tell them you're looking forward to working with them.

- Give them your phone number in case they have a change of plans and need to reach you.

- Reiterate the date, time, and meeting place.

- End the conversation.

If you reach someone other than the client and the client is not there:

- Introduce yourself, but *do not say you are from Good $ense Ministry or make any mention of budget counseling.* Simply state that you are someone calling "from church." (If the person asks, "Why are you calling?" just say, "I'm returning his/her phone call.")

- Ask the person who answered if he or she can take a message or if there is a more convenient time to call back.

- If the person offers to take a message, leave your phone number and indicate whether it's a home or work number.

- Indicate the best time to reach you.

- Thank the message taker and end the phone call.

If you reach an answering device or voice mailbox:

- Keep in mind that the client may not be the only one with access to the answering device or voice mail, so be discreet!

- State your name and say you're calling "from church."

(Continue on next page.)

NOTES

Phone Call Reminders

These pointers refer specifically to the first phone call, but many of these tips also apply to any phone contact with your client.

- Review the "Needed for the First Meeting" list from the Client Profile Analysis Chart you made for the Client Profile.
- Have your calendar out as well as paper and pen ready in case the client decides to chat and provide further details on the case.
- Call from a quiet place where you will not be disturbed.

If you reach the client directly:

- Introduce yourself.
- Tell them you're calling to make an appointment.
- Arrange a date, time (allow two hours), and neutral location for the meeting. Make sure both spouses are available if your client is a couple.
- Identify what items—if you listed any on your Client Profile Analysis Chart—they need to bring to the meeting.
- Explain what you plan to cover during the first meeting: get to know each other, gain a better understanding of their financial situation, and discuss steps they can begin to take to accomplish their purposes for your time together.
- Tell them you're looking forward to working with them.
- Give them your phone number in case they have a change of plans and need to reach you.
- Reiterate the date, time, and meeting place.
- End the conversation.

If you reach someone other than the client and the client is not there:

- Introduce yourself, but do not say you're from Good $ense Ministry or make any mention of budget counseling. Simply state that you are someone calling "from church." (If the person asks, "Why are you calling?" just say, "I'm returning his/her phone call.")
- Ask the person who answered if he or she can take a message or if there is a more convenient time to call back.
- If the person offers to take a message, leave your phone number and indicate whether it's a home or work number.
- Indicate the best time to reach you.
- Thank the message taker and end the phone call.

If you reach an answering device or voice mailbox:

- Keep in mind that the client may not be the only one with access to the answering device or voice mail, so be discreet!
- State your name and say you're calling "from church."
- Leave your name, number, and best time to call you back. Indicate whether the number you're leaving is a home or work number.

- Leave your name, number, and best time to call you back. Indicate whether the number you're leaving is a home or work number.

Let's watch a video segment that demonstrates the first phone call. Turn to page 46.

First, Roger, the counselor, leaves a message with Mark Olsen's mother-in-law. Then, Roger receives a call back from Carol and is able to set up an appointment.

Keep an eye on that list of pointers as you watch the video.

8 minutes

Video: *Phone Call to the Olsens*

Participant's Guide, page 46.

View video: *Phone Call to the Olsens.*

Wrap-up
How did Roger do with leaving the message?

Possible response:

He left a concise and discreet message.

How did he handle the nosy mother-in-law?

Possible response:

He was tactful but firm and used generic responses.

How do you think Roger did when Carol called back?

Possible response:

He did a good job following the telephone pointers.

NOTES

46

Video: *Phone Call to the Olsens*

Notes

0 minutes

SESSION SUMMARY

Now you've seen your client on paper and have spoken briefly to him or her on the phone. Your next contact will be in person. That's when you'll begin to know the person and find out what influences are at work in his or her life. Before we walk through the first meeting, we will practice some listening skills to help you build that critically important relationship with your client.

LISTENING SKILLS

SESSION SNAPSHOT

OVERVIEW

In Session 3, listening skills are reviewed, modeled, and explored. A practice activity will give participants an opportunity to try out these techniques for themselves.

OBJECTIVES

In this session, participants will:

1. Review active listening skills

2. Practice the mirroring technique

OUTLINE

   I. Introduction

  II. Listening Skills

      A. Active Listening

      B. Mirroring

      C. Video: *Mirroring Example*

      D. Partner Activity: *Mirroring*

 III. Session Summary

LISTENING SKILLS

TIME & MEDIA	**CONTENTS**

1 minute

> Good $ense
> Counselor Training Workshop
>
> **Session 3**
> Listening Skills

INTRODUCTION

> Participant's Guide, page 47.

We've covered the first two parts of the counseling process, Analyze the Client Profile and Call the Client.

➜ Before we move on to part three, Conduct the First Meeting, we need to review active listening skills and practice using the mirroring technique, which we will use throughout these meetings.

Turn to page 48.

> **COUNSELING PROCESS**
>
> 1. Analyze the Client Profile. 2. Call the client.
>
> 3. Conduct the first meeting. 4. Provide ongoing counseling. 5. Close the case.

3 minutes

LISTENING SKILLS

> Participant's Guide, page 48.

Listening skills are just as important as your financial skills.

Your success as a counselor is more dependent upon the relationship you build than on your financial skills.

➜ In fact, your success as a counselor is more dependent upon the relationship you build than on your financial skills.

NOTES

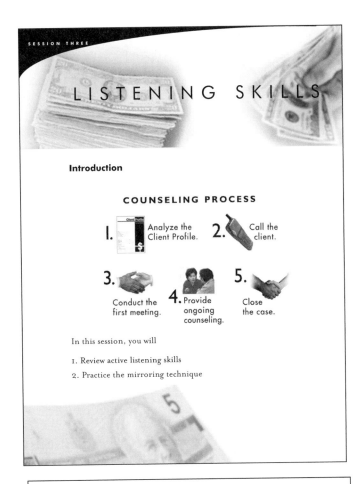

SESSION THREE

LISTENING SKILLS

Introduction

COUNSELING PROCESS

1. Analyze the Client Profile.

2. Call the client.

3. Conduct the first meeting.

4. Provide ongoing counseling.

5. Close the case.

In this session, you will

1. Review active listening skills
2. Practice the mirroring technique

Listening Skills

Your success as a counselor is more dependent upon the relationship you build than on your financial skills.

Building rapport means:

Really connecting with another person and creating a comfort zone between you.

That's why we're going to demonstrate and practice listening skills for a significant part of our time together. These skills are critical!

You won't need the expertise of a licensed therapist, but we do want to you to practice some truly useful skills to use in your counseling sessions as well as with your family, friends, and colleagues.

I'm going to begin by telling you about an emergency room doctor. A patient arrives at the emergency room with chest pains. The doctor rules out a heart attack and then gives the patient some advice: "You need to lose 100 pounds, stop smoking, exercise, and eat more fruits and vegetables."

"Can't you just give me a pill?" the patient asks.

The doctor's frustration is that, even though she knows her advice is sound and that her recommendations are proven to reduce heart problems, the patient will likely go on living like he always has, following the same bad habits.

You're like that doctor in that some clients will come to you wanting a magic pill to make their money problems go away. They're hoping for an easy answer, and you're the bearer of bad news who tells them it's going to take work, even sacrifice, to make their situation better.

However, unlike that doctor, you have an opportunity to work with the client on an ongoing basis to help change his habits.

The advantage of seeing the client on an ongoing basis is that it gives you the opportunity to build rapport.

Building rapport means really connecting with another person and creating a comfort zone between you.

Building Rapport Means:

Really connecting with another person and creating a comfort zone between you.

NOTES

Listening Skills

Your success as a counselor is more dependent upon the relationship you build than on your financial skills.

Building rapport means:

Really connecting with another person and creating a comfort zone between you.

144

It is out of this relationship—this rapport—that your counsel and advice gains credibility and motivates the client to change. You also have another huge advantage. You have God's principles and the Holy Spirit to guide you.

Keep in mind that when you are talking with a client, you are being invited into their lives. You are a guest and should act accordingly by being polite and respectful. What public rooms will they allow you to examine? What dark closets must you avoid?

10 minutes

Active Listening

Participant's Guide, page 49.

A key way to build rapport is by active listening.

➔ Active listening is focusing on the other person and what that person has to say.

Take a moment and think of a situation where you felt the other person was *not* listening to you.

Write down the situation in your Participant's Guide.

Pause a couple minutes until you see that most participants are finished writing.

Now, write down your answer to the second question:

➔ How did you know that they were not listening?

Pause a couple minutes until you see that most participants are finished writing.

What are some of the things you wrote down for the second question?

NOTES

_____

_____

_____

_____

_____

_____

_____

_____

_____

_____

_____

_____

_____

_____

_____

_____

_____

_____

_____

Listening Skills

Your success as a counselor is more dependent upon the
relationship you build than on your financial skills.

Building rapport means:

Really connecting with another person and creating a comfort
zone between you.

Active Listening

Active listening is:

Focusing on the other person and what that person has
to say.

Think of a situation where you felt that the other person was
not listening to you.

How did you know that they were not listening?

Possible responses:

- They were not looking at me.

- They were doodling while I was talking.

- They were fidgeting.

- They kept looking at their watch.

- They kept taking phone calls in the middle of our meeting.

How did this make you feel?

Possible responses:

- I felt uncomfortable.

- I wanted to walk away.

- I felt small.

Keeping these feelings in mind, put yourself in your client's shoes. They may be experiencing a number of emotions: nervousness, discomfort, embarrassment, etc. The most important thing they need is a good listener.

Turn to page 50.

There is a list of tips for good listening:

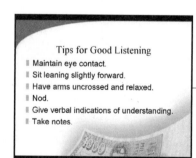

→ Maintain eye contact.

    Sit leaning slightly forward.

    Have arms uncrossed and relaxed.

    Nod.

    Give verbal indications of understanding, such as "uh-huh."

    Take notes.

NOTES

Active Listening

Active listening is:

Focusing on the other person and what that person has to say.

Think of a situation where you felt that the other person was *not* listening to you.

How did you know that they were not listening?

Tips for Good Listening

- Maintain eye contact.
- Sit leaning slightly forward.
- Have arms uncrossed and relaxed.
- Nod.
- Give verbal indications of understanding.
- Take notes.

Most often the client will interpret note taking as an indication that you are listening, but it can make some clients nervous. It is courteous to ask if it would be okay to take notes. This gives you the opportunity to explain that you want to remember what is being said.

I'm sure that these tips are not new to you, but they are critically important.

Take a moment and put a check mark by the one tip you'd like to keep in mind during your counseling sessions. Maybe it's something you've wished another person had done when listening to you, or maybe it's something you know you need to work on.

Pause.

3 minutes

Mirroring

Participant's Guide, page 51.

The tips we just talked about deal with giving our physical attention to the listener. This is only one component of building rapport. The next level of listening is mirroring. This technique is simple, but it's not always easy and it takes practice.

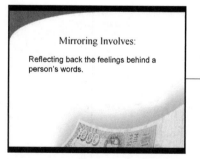

Mirroring involves reflecting back the feelings behind a person's words.

Clients may quickly verify or correct your reflected perceptions; or, they may pause and consider your perception, especially if it reflects a feeling they were not completely conscious of. In other words, your observation may be a revelation to them.

In the mirroring process, you:

Listen for the BASIC MESSAGE of the client.

NOTES

Tips for Good Listening

- Maintain eye contact.

- Sit leaning slightly forward.

- Have arms uncrossed and relaxed.

- Nod.

- Give verbal indications of understanding.

- Take notes.

Mirroring

Mirroring involves:

Reflecting back the feelings behind a person's words.

Mirroring Process

- Listen for the _____ of the client.
- Observe any cues or emotion surrounding the message.
- Relate back to them a concise summary of the message with your perception of how they feel about it.

Mirroring Example

Client: I feel really stupid for not learning more about money while I was married. My ex-husband handled all of our finances. All I cared about was my house, my kids, and having nice stuff. I never gave a thought to the cost. Now, it's different.

Counselor: You're kicking yourself for not learning this stuff before, because now you're feeling overwhelmed with all this added responsibility.

Video: *Mirroring Example*

Notes

→ Observe any cues or emotion surrounding the message.

Relate back to them a concise summary of the message with your perception of how they feel about it.

For example:

The client says:

→ "I feel really stupid for not learning more about money while I was married. My ex-husband handled all of our finances. All I cared about was my house, my kids, and having nice stuff. I never gave a thought to the cost. Now, it's different."

The counselor could mirror back by saying:

→ "You're kicking yourself for not learning this stuff before, because now you're feeling overwhelmed with all this added responsibility."

Notice that rather than asking questions, the counselor mirrored back the client's feelings.

Without learning this skill first, it may be natural for you to begin asking your client a lot of questions at the first meeting. In general, use questions sparingly. Too many questions can make a person feel interrogated. "Why" questions are especially difficult, as they tend to sound accusatory.

Let's take a look at a video demonstrating this. This video shows a counselor effectively using mirroring in a conversation.

NOTES

Mirroring

Mirroring involves:

Reflecting back the feelings behind a person's words.

Mirroring Process

- Listen for the _____ of the client.
- Observe any cues or emotion surrounding the message.
- Relate back to them a concise summary of the message with your perception of how they feel about it.

Mirroring Example

Client: I feel really stupid for not learning more about money while I was married. My ex-husband handled all of our finances. All I cared about was my house, my kids, and having nice stuff. I never gave a thought to the cost. Now, it's different.

Counselor: You're kicking yourself for not learning this stuff before, because now you're feeling overwhelmed with all this added responsibility.

Video: *Mirroring Example*

Notes

5 minutes

Video: *Mirroring Example*

> View video: *Mirroring Example.*

Wrap-up
What did you notice in this video?

> Possible responses:
>
> • The counselor didn't ask a single question. She just continued to mirror the client's response.
>
> • The counselor's mirroring seemed to help the client open up.
>
> • The counselor made great eye contact.

A portion of this script is in the Appendix on page 112. You can use it as a refresher of the process.

Turn to page 52.

12 minutes

Partner Activity:

Mirroring

Partner Activity: *Mirroring*

> Participant's Guide, page 52.

Now *you're* going to get a chance to try this technique.

> Objective:
> For participants to practice the mirroring technique.

Directions:

1. Pair up with a partner. Spouses may not partner with each other!

2. Choose who will be the first Talker and the first Listener.

3. Talkers, talk about whatever you like. There are some suggested topics you can read through in just a moment.

NOTES

_____

_____

_____

_____

_____

_____

_____

_____

_____

_____

_____

_____

_____

_____

_____

_____

_____

_____

_____

_____

Mirroring

Mirroring involves:

Reflecting back the feelings behind a person's words.

Mirroring Process

- Listen for the _____ of the client.
- Observe any cues or emotion surrounding the message.
- Relate back to them a concise summary of the message with your perception of how they feel about it.

Mirroring Example

Client: I feel really stupid for not learning more about money while I was married. My ex-husband handled all of our finances. All I cared about was my house, my kids, and having nice stuff. I never gave a thought to the cost. Now, it's different.

Counselor: You're kicking yourself for not learning this stuff before, because now you're feeling overwhelmed with all this added responsibility.

Video: *Mirroring Example*

Notes

Partner Activity: *Mirroring*

Directions

1. Pair up with a partner. Spouses may not partner with each other!

2. Choose who will be the first Talker and the first Listener.

3. Talkers, talk about whatever you like. Here are some suggested topics:

   - How did you come to be a good money manager? Were you always good at managing money, or did you learn the hard way? Explain to your listener your spiritual relationship to money.

   - We all have those days when nothing seems to go right. Somehow, the day gets off to the wrong start-we burn the toast, get a ticket for speeding, and then the computer network's down when we really need it. Recall such a day and tell your listener about it.

   - Think of a personal relationship-current or past-that has been challenging. This relationship can be with a friend, coworker, family member, or anyone. Describe the relationship to the listener.

4. Listeners, your job is to respond to the Talkers by mirroring their words and reflecting what you think they're feeling about what they're saying.

5. The only rule for Listeners is that they cannot ask any questions. This will be harder than it sounds!

4. Listeners, your job is to respond to the Talkers by mirroring their words and reflecting what you think they're feeling about what they're saying.

5. The only rule for Listeners is that they cannot ask any questions.

This will be harder than it sounds!

You will have 3 minutes for this first round. Then, we will switch.

> To view the suggested topics, see the Participant's Guide on the facing page (page 155).
>
> After 3 minutes, ask partners to switch roles. Call the group back together after 6 minutes.

Wrap-up
Let's focus on the listening part first.

What did it feel like to be unable to ask questions?

> Possible responses:
>
> - It was very difficult to do!
>
> - I asked a question and then had to take it back.
>
> - I realized that I wanted to find out some information that my partner didn't really want to share with me.

How many of you had any long silences during your exchange? Raise your hand.

> Pause.

NOTES

Partner *Activity: Mirroring*

Directions

1. Pair up with a partner. Spouses may not partner with each other!

2. Choose who will be the first Talker and the first Listener.

3. Talkers, talk about whatever you like. Here are some suggested topics:

   - How did you come to be a good money manager? Were you always good at managing money, or did you learn the hard way? Explain to your listener your spiritual relationship to money.

   - We all have those days when nothing seems to go right. Somehow, the day gets off to the wrong start-we burn the toast, get a ticket for speeding, and then the computer network's down when we really need it. Recall such a day and tell your listener about it.

   - Think of a personal relationship-current or past-that has been challenging. This relationship can be with a friend, coworker, family member, or anyone. Describe the relationship to the listener.

4. Listeners, your job is to respond to the Talkers by mirroring their words and reflecting what you think they're feeling about what they're saying.

5. The only rule for Listeners is that they cannot ask any questions. This will be harder than it sounds!

Silence can serve an important and productive purpose. If the client is silent, it's as if he or she is at a stop sign, wondering whether to turn right or left or to go straight. If the counselor asks a question, the counselor may be essentially telling the client where to turn. If the counselor remains silent, the client can decide which way to turn. This is the purpose of mirroring—to let the client direct the conversation. Rather than get the information you would have wanted, you will get the information that your client wants to tell you. This is a much more productive way to establish rapport.

Did anyone feel like their conversation was going around in circles?

Pause for responses.

If you feel like this is happening, you can try saying something like "Let me summarize what I hear you saying. You said A, B, and C. Now, was there anything else affecting the problem?"

One other thing I'd like to mention is that word choice can be critical to a comfortable exchange. For example, would you rather be told "You seem out of sorts," or "You're really angry"? The term "out of sorts" is a much gentler way of acknowledging angry feelings. If you're looking for the right word to describe a feeling, it's better to choose a soft word.

There is a list of feeling words on page 114 in your Appendix that you may wish to review later.

Now let's focus on the Talkers. Describe how it felt to have someone focus on you and reflect your feelings.

NOTES

Partner *Activity: Mirroring*

Directions

1. Pair up with a partner. Spouses may not partner with each other!

2. Choose who will be the first Talker and the first Listener.

3. Talkers, talk about whatever you like. Here are some suggested topics:

    *   How did you come to be a good money manager? Were you always good at managing money, or did you learn the hard way? Explain to your listener your spiritual relationship to money.

    *   We all have those days when nothing seems to go right. Somehow, the day gets off to the wrong start-we burn the toast, get a ticket for speeding, and then the computer network's down when we really need it. Recall such a day and tell your listener about it.

    *   Think of a personal relationship-current or past-that has been challenging. This relationship can be with a friend, coworker, family member, or anyone. Describe the relationship to the listener.

4. Listeners, your job is to respond to the Talkers by mirroring their words and reflecting what you think they're feeling about what they're saying.

5. The only rule for Listeners is that they cannot ask any questions. This will be harder than it sounds!

Possible responses:

- I didn't realize I was projecting a certain feeling, but when the Listener picked it up, it really fit.

- It felt great to have someone's complete attention and response.

You can see the power of mirroring. It will take some practice, but it can have a dramatic effect on helping you build a relationship with your client. Again, building a relationship is key to your success as a counselor.

As you begin to use mirroring with clients—and you'll have a chance to do this in the next session—you may have more questions about handling specific situations. Pages 109 to 111 in the Appendix cover many of the commonly asked questions about building rapport with your client.

1 minute

SESSION SUMMARY

In this session, you have had the opportunity to practice your listening skills. In the next session, we will move back to the counseling process and focus on the first meeting. You will have a chance to apply these listening skills as you practice the first meeting steps.

CONDUCT THE
FIRST MEETING

SESSION SNAPSHOT

OVERVIEW

In Session 4, we explore the first client meeting in depth, providing tools, tips, and practice for that important initial contact with a new client. The first meeting is where clients get their first impression of the counselor. That impression should be of a helper who is confident, skilled, and compassionate. We'll watch video segments that allow us to observe portions of a first meeting. A role play gives participants an opportunity to try out the process themselves.

OBJECTIVES

In this session, participants will:

1. Practice the opening steps of the first meeting
2. Fill out a Spending Record
3. Review a Client Profile

OUTLINE

I. Introduction

II. Pointers for the First Meeting

III. Overview of the First Meeting

IV. First Meeting: Steps 1-4

    A. Video: *Opening of a First Meeting*

V. First Meeting: Steps 5-7

    A. Step 5: Sign the Good $ense Budget Counseling Covenant

    B. Step 6: Review the Client Profile

    C. Video: *Review the Client Profile*

    D. Step 7: Explain the Spending Record

    E. Individual Activity: *Complete a Spending Record*

VI. First Meeting: Steps 8-11

    A. Step 8: Assign Action Items for the Next Meeting

    B. Step 9: Set up the Next Meeting

    C. Step 10: Pray

    D. Step 11: Complete the Client Progress Report

VII. Partner Activity: *Role Play of the First Meeting*

VIII. Session Summary

CONDUCT THE FIRST MEETING

TIME & MEDIA	CONTENTS

2 minutes

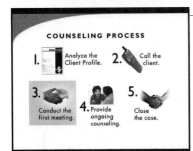

INTRODUCTION

> Participant's Guide, page 53.

Remember where we left off in the counseling process?

We've analyzed the Client Profile and called the client.

Now, that we are equipped with some counseling skills, we are ready to conduct the first meeting.

➤ In this session, we will practice the opening steps of this meeting, fill out a Spending Record, and review a Client Profile.

Turn to page 54.

> Participant's Guide, page 54.

➤ Just to clarify: The focus of the first meeting is to get the relationship with your client off to a great start.

As we've discussed, gaining rapport with your clients is a key to helping them develop good money habits and grow spiritually.

NOTES

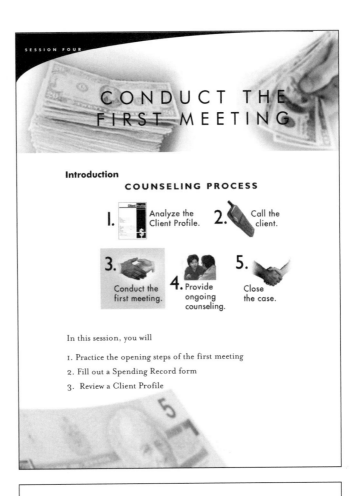

SESSION FOUR

CONDUCT THE FIRST MEETING

Introduction

COUNSELING PROCESS

1. Analyze the Client Profile.

2. Call the client.

3. Conduct the first meeting.

4. Provide ongoing counseling.

5. Close the case.

In this session, you will

1. Practice the opening steps of the first meeting

2. Fill out a Spending Record form

3. Review a Client Profile

Focus of the First Meeting

- Get the relationship off to a great start.

- Gain a better understanding of the client's financial situation.

- Teach the client how to begin keeping _____.

Pointers for the First Meeting

Typical Time Frame

$1\frac{1}{2}$ to 2 hours

Recommended Meeting Place

Church or other neutral location like a reserved room in a library

Other Considerations

Insure that a couple has a babysitter so they can focus on the meeting.

Arrival Time

10 to 15 minutes before the appointed time

What You Need to Bring

- Client Profile
- Completed Client Profile Analysis Chart
- Good $ense Budget Counseling Covenant
- Calculator
- Pen or pencil

What You Need to Tell the Client to Bring

Any items you wrote at the end of the Client Profile Analysis Chart

Other objectives of this meeting are to:

Gain a better understanding of the client's financial situation, and to teach the client how to begin keeping RECORDS.

2 minutes

POINTERS FOR THE FIRST MEETING

Here are some pointers for the first meeting.

The first item concerns the time frame.

You'll probably want to allow 1 1/2 to 2 hours for the first meeting.

This way, you'll have time to start building rapport and probably still have an opportunity to clarify questions you have about their profile.

Take a moment and read the remainder of the list.

> Pause.

Any questions?

> Pause.

Okay, now let's talk about the steps involved in the first meeting.

NOTES

Focus of the First Meeting

- Get the relationship off to a great start.

- Gain a better understanding of the client's financial situation.

- Teach the client how to begin keeping _____.

Pointers for the First Meeting

Typical Time Frame

$1\frac{1}{2}$ to 2 hours

Recommended Meeting Place

Church or other neutral location like a reserved room in a library

Other Considerations

Insure that a couple has a babysitter so they can focus on the meeting.

Arrival Time

10 to 15 minutes before the appointed time

What You Need to Bring

- Client Profile
- Completed Client Profile Analysis Chart
- Good $ense Budget Counseling Covenant
- Calculator
- Pen or pencil

What You Need to Tell the Client to Bring

Any items you wrote at the end of the Client Profile Analysis Chart

1 minute

OVERVIEW OF THE FIRST MEETING

Participant's Guide, page 55.

Although there is a sequence of steps that make sense during a first meeting, I want to be clear that your meetings won't always flow along this prescribed path! We want to present to you the "ideal" flow for a first meeting with a client, but these steps should serve as a guideline, not a drill that you must get through.

There are eleven steps that we will cover:

Step 1: Greet your clients.

Step 2: Pray.

Step 3: Explain your ministry and budgeting background.

Step 4: Get to know your clients.

Step 5: Sign the Good $ense Budget Counseling Covenant.

Step 6: Review the Client Profile.

Step 7: Explain the Spending Record.

Step 8: Assign action items for the next meeting.

Step 9: Set up the next meeting.

Step 10: Pray.

Step 11: Complete the Client Progress Report.

Turn to page 56.

Conduct the First Meeting

▌ Step 1: Greet your clients.
▌ Step 2: Pray.
▌ Step 3: Explain your ministry and budgeting background.
▌ Step 4: Get to know your clients.
▌ Step 5: Sign the Good $ense Budget Counseling Covenant.

Conduct the First Meeting

▌ Step 6: Review the Client Profile.
▌ Step 7: Explain the Spending Record.
▌ Step 8: Assign action items for the next meeting.
▌ Step 9: Set up the next meeting.
▌ Step 10: Pray.
▌ Step 11: Complete the Client Progress Report.

NOTES

Overview of the First Meeting

- Step 1: Greet clients.

- Step 2: Pray.

- Step 3: Explain your ministry and budgeting background.

- Step 4: Get to know your clients.

- Step 5: Sign the Good $ense Budget Counseling Covenant.

- Step 6: Review the Client Profile.

- Step 7: Explain the Spending Record form.

- Step 8: Assign action items for the next meeting.

- Step 9: Set up the next meeting.

- Step 10: Pray.

- Step 11: Complete the Client Progress Report.

20 minutes

FIRST MEETING: STEPS 1-4

> Participant's Guide, page 56.

First, let's watch the opening of the first meeting, Steps 1 through 4, with Mark and Carol Olsen. You'll be able to get a feel for how the first meeting typically begins.

Video: *Opening of a First Meeting*

> View video: *Opening of a First Meeting.*

Wrap-up
We just saw Steps 1 through 4 of the first meeting. As we discuss how Roger covered these steps with the Olsens, you may wish to follow along beginning on page 57.

> Participant's Guide, page 57.

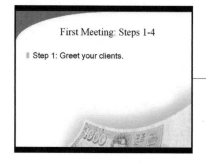

First Meeting: Steps 1-4

▌ Step 1: Greet your clients.

Let's begin with Step 1: Greet your clients. How did Roger make Mark and Carol feel comfortable?

> Possible responses:
>
> • He shook their hands.
>
> • He offered them something to drink.
>
> • He took their jackets and offered them a seat.

▶ Next, in Step 2, Roger prayed with them. Prayers should be brief and should not be disguised as "teaching lessons" but simply a sincere appeal for God's presence and wisdom along with thanksgiving for the client's presence. We've provided a sample prayer that you can refer to.

▶ Next, for Step 3, Roger explained his ministry and budgeting background.

NOTES

_____
_____
_____
_____
_____
_____
_____
_____
_____
_____
_____
_____
_____
_____
_____
_____
_____
_____
_____
_____
_____
_____

First Meeting: Steps 1-4

 Video: _Opening of a First Meeting_

> Notes

First Meeting: Steps 1-4

Step 1: Greet your clients.

Step 2: Pray.

Sample Prayer:

> _Gracious Father, thank you for _____ (name/s) having taken this step to seek to understand how to manage their finances in a way that will be wise and honor you. Thanks for the privilege of being of service to him/her/them. Bless our time together, and I pray for your guidance and wisdom. In Christ's name, amen._

Step 3: Explain your budgeting and ministry background.

- Your budgeting background

- Your history with your church

- How you became a Good $ense counselor

- Ask, "Is there anything else you'd like to know about me?"

This step is important because the clients may be curious about you, you'll want to establish budget counseling credibility with them, and this may give them a chance to get more comfortable with you before revealing any information about themselves.

Tell the clients about:

➤ Your budgeting background, your history with your church, and how you became a Good $ense counselor.

Don't be shy about sharing your budgeting background. If you're a homemaker, your skill set is different than that of a mortgage banker but is no less valuable. Whatever your background, it may create the perfect inspiration and comfort level for the client.

If the clients are your very first, be up front about that. In order to establish budget counseling credibility with them, tell them that you've been trained in budget counseling and that you have learned about proven tools to help them improve their financial situation.

➤ After you've finished telling the clients about yourself, ask, "Is there anything else you'd like to know about me?"

They may ask a few questions that enable them to get a little more comfortable with you.

Turn to page 58.

➤ The other thing that Roger did was Step 4: Get to know your clients.

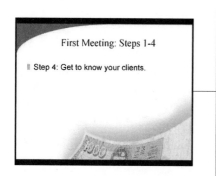

First Meeting: Steps 1-4

Step 4: Get to know your clients.

Participant's Guide, page 58.

Let's talk about how he did this.

NOTES

_____

_____

_____

_____

_____

_____

_____

_____

_____

_____

_____

_____

_____

_____

_____

_____

_____

_____

_____

_____

_____

_____

First Meeting: Steps 1-4

Step 1: Greet your clients.

Step 2: Pray.

Sample Prayer:

Gracious Father, thank you for _____ (name/s) having taken this step to seek to understand how to manage their finances in a way that will be wise and honor you. Thanks for the privilege of being of service to him/her/them. Bless our time together, and I pray for your guidance and wisdom. In Christ's name, amen.

Step 3: Explain your budgeting and ministry background.

- Your budgeting background

- Your history with your church

- How you became a Good $ense counselor

- Ask, "Is there anything else you'd like to know about me?"

Step 4: Get to Know Your Clients.

- State that you would like to get to know your clients better.

- Use open-ended questions and mirroring to build rapport.

  Sample questions:

  ○ How do you spend a typical day at your job?

  ○ Tell me about your family.

  ○ How did you select this church as your church home?

  ○ How do you like to spend your weekends?

  ○ Remember: After each question, look for opportunities to mirror back the client's feelings.

- Transition to a more focused conversation about finances.
  For example: "Now, let's talk about your financial situation."

- Ask appropriate open-ended questions about finances.
  Sample questions*:

  ○ What led you to apply for Good $ense counseling?

  ○ What would you like to see happen as a result of our working together?

* Look for opportunities to use your mirroring skills.

He started by transitioning from a discussion about his own background to a discussion about Mark and Carol.

▶ Do this by stating that you would like to get to know your clients better.

Rather than delving into financial topics right away, notice that Roger found out who Mark and Carol are. Often you can identify something on the profile that you can ask about, such as their children or job. Other topics may include the church or hobbies. Don't forget to include questions for both spouses if you are counseling a couple. Often one of the spouses is more reticent about being there than the other. Work hard to draw them out.

▶ Use open-ended questions and mirroring to build this rapport.

An open-ended question is a question that requires the person to give more than a simple one-word response.

The following sample questions and statements may help you.

How do you spend a typical day at your job?

Tell me about your family.

How did you select this church as your church home?

How do you do like to spend your weekends?

Remember, after each question, look for opportunities to mirror back the client's feelings.

Once you've established rapport, transition to a more focused conversation about finances.

For example, you may say, "Now, let's talk about your financial situation."

Then, follow up this statement with an appropriate, open-ended question about their finances.

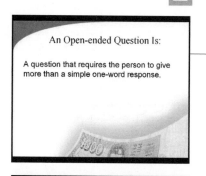

An Open-ended Question Is:

A question that requires the person to give more than a simple one-word response.

Sample Questions and Statements*

▪ How do you spend a typical day at your job?
▪ Tell me about your family.
▪ How did you select this church as your church home?
▪ How do you like to spend your weekends?

* Remember: After each question, look for opportunities to mirror back the client's feelings.

Step 4: Get to Know Your Client

▪ Transition to a more focused conversation about finances.
▪ Follow up with an appropriate, open-ended question about their finances.

NOTES

Step 4: Get to Know Your Clients.

- State that you would like to get to know your clients better.

- Use open-ended questions and mirroring to build rapport.

  Sample questions:

  ○ How do you spend a typical day at your job?

  ○ Tell me about your family.

  ○ How did you select this church as your church home?

  ○ How do you like to spend your weekends?

  ○ Remember: After each question, look for opportunities to mirror back the client's feelings.

- Transition to a more focused conversation about finances.

  For example: "Now, let's talk about your financial situation."

- Ask appropriate open-ended questions about finances.

  Sample questions*:

  ○ What led you to apply for Good $ense counseling?

  ○ What would you like to see happen as a result of our working together?

* Look for opportunities to use your mirroring skills.

Here are some sample questions:

➤ What led you to apply for Good $ense counseling?

What would you like to see happen as a result of our working together?

Listen carefully to the answers to these types of questions because they let you know what the client really wants to be working on during your counseling sessions. This is where the client may begin to reveal their goals. Note that pages 125–130 in the Appendix contain additional information on goal setting that you might find useful.

➤ Again, look for opportunities to use your mirroring skills.

This is a key time when your client needs a good listener.

At this point, we have covered the first four steps of the first meeting.

- Step 1: Greet your clients.

- Step 2: Pray.

- Step 3: Explain your ministry and budgeting background.

- Step 4: Get to know your clients.

Before we move on, I want to briefly mention that Steps 3 and 4 are often intertwined. You may first ask questions about the client before sharing about yourself. However you choose to approach it is fine as long as you cover both steps. Also let me caution against rushing through Steps 3 and 4. As we have stated, building rapport and trust with your client is key to the ultimate success of the counseling relationship.

NOTES

Step 4: Get to Know Your Clients.

- State that you would like to get to know your clients better.

- Use open-ended questions and mirroring to build rapport.

  Sample questions:
  - How do you spend a typical day at your job?

  - Tell me about your family.

  - How did you select this church as your church home?

  - How do you like to spend your weekends?

  - Remember: After each question, look for opportunities to mirror back the client's feelings.

- Transition to a more focused conversation about finances.

  For example: "Now, let's talk about your financial situation."

- Ask appropriate open-ended questions about finances.

  Sample questions*:
  - What led you to apply for Good $ense counseling?

  - What would you like to see happen as a result of our working together?

* Look for opportunities to use your mirroring skills.

In many cases, those of us who are Good $ense counselors are more comfortable working with the client's profile and discussing numbers with them than we may be with spending time getting to know them. However, the client must feel we are more interested in them as a person than we are with the numbers on their profile. Take your time!

3 minutes

FIRST MEETING: STEPS 5-7

Participant's Guide, page 59.

Now, let's continue on to Steps 5 through 7.

These steps include:

 Step 5: Sign the Good $ense Budget Counseling Covenant.

Step 6: Review the Client Profile.

Step 7: Explain the Spending Record.

Let's cover each of these steps in depth.

Step 5: Sign the Good $ense Budget Counseling Covenant.

Step 5 is, Sign the Good $ense Budget Counseling Covenant, which is a form that clearly states the responsibilities of each person within the counseling relationship: the client and the counselor.

Review each item on the front of the form with the clients, then have them sign it. Finally, you sign the covenant, make a copy for yourself, and give the original to the client.

Participant's Guide, pages 60–61.

NOTES

First Meeting: Steps 5-7

- Step 5: Sign the Good $ense Budget Counseling Covenant.

- Step 6: Review the Client Profile.

- Step 7: Explain the Spending Record.

Step 5: Sign the Good $ense Budget Counseling Covenant.

See sample form on pages 60 and 61.

There's a sample Good $ense Budget Counseling Covenant on pages 60 and 61. Take a moment to briefly review it.

Pause for 1 minute while participants review the form.

The front side of the covenant is divided into three sections:

- The responsibilities/commitments of the client

- The responsibilities/commitments of the counselor

- A signature area to sign when all have agreed to their responsibilities

How does setting the conditions of the counseling relationship help both you and the client?

Possible response:

Structure helps us feel more comfortable because we know what's expected.

The back side of the form contains a summary of the Biblical Financial Principles for the Good $ense Ministry. Briefly review these principles with your client and ask them if they have any questions.

Turn to page 62.

Step 6: Review the Client Profile.

Participant's Guide, page 62.

If relationship building has gone well and the client seems eager to get working, and sufficient time remains before the close of your time together, you may begin to go over their profile with them.

NOTES

GOOD $ENSE
BUDGET COUNSELING COVENANT

As a Good $ense client, you are asked to commit to the following:

1. A *significant effort* to develop better financial habits.

2. Regular *prayer* for learning and adopting new financial practices.

3. *Honesty* and openness—no financial surprises two months down the road.

4. An *honest effort* to act upon the counselor's guidance.

5. A consistent commitment of *time*, more at first but then tapering off gradually.

6. A willingness on your part to *be accountable* to the budget you and your counselor design for you.

As a counselor, I commit to you:

1. *Encouragement.*

2. Regular thoughts and *prayers* for you and your situation.

3. Respect for your *privacy.* All information you convey to me is kept *confidential.*

4. *Time* to meet with you.

5. *Training* seminars to sharpen my skills and knowledge.

6. My *skills* and expertise in budget counseling and the application of the Biblical Financial Principles to my own life.

7. *Ideas* to challenge you in your spiritual growth in the financial area of your life.

_____   _____
Client Signature   Counselor Signature

_____
Spouse Signature

BIBLICAL FINANCIAL PRINCIPLES

Steward's Mindset

    God created everything. (Genesis 1:1)
    God owns everything. (Psalms 24:1; 50:10, 12b)
    We are trustees. (1 Corinthians 4:1-2)

Earning

    Be diligent. (Colossians 3:23)
    Be purposeful. (Colossians 3:23; 1 Timothy 5:8)
    Be grateful. (Deuteronomy 8:18)

Giving

Giving is a key to a satisfied and fulfilled life. We are to give:

    As a response to God's goodness. (James 1:17)
    To focus on God as our source of security. (Matthew 6:19-20a; 23b-33)
    To achieve economic justice.
    To bless others. (Genesis 12:2-3)
    To break the hold of money.

Saving

    It is wise to save. (Proverbs 6:8; 21:20)
    It is sinful to hoard. (Luke 12:16-21)

Debt

    Repay debt. (Psalm 37:21)
    Avoid debt. (Proverbs 22:7)

Spending

    Beware of idols. (Deuteronomy 5:8; Romans 1:25)
    Guard against greed. (Luke 12:15)
    Be content. (Philippians 4:12)

Step 6: Review the Client Profile.

- Affirm the client by referring to the "+" items on the Client Profile Analysis Chart.

- Raise some of the questions you noted by checking the "?" side of the Client Profile Analysis Chart.

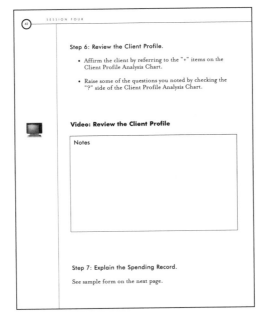

Video: Review the Client Profile

> Notes

Step 7: Explain the Spending Record.

See sample form on the next page.

This will provide the opportunity to affirm the client by referring to the plus items on your Client Profile Analysis Chart, and to raise with them at least some of the questions you have noted on the chart.

Reviewing the Client Profile provides data for assigning action steps and creates a sense of accomplishment at the end of that first meeting—but don't consider the meeting a failure if you don't get to the Client Profile.

To review the Client Profile, refer to the Client Profile Analysis Chart that you developed back in part one of the counseling process when you analyzed the Client Profile. You will walk through the profile with the client, covering the issues you checked as questions on the Client Profile Analysis Chart and affirming all the items you checked as pluses.

When discussing costs that seem high with the client, approach the topic with sensitivity, seeking information without being judgmental. For example, one of the questions on our chart for the Olsens dealt with food costs that appear higher than normal. One of the reasons for the high food costs may be special dietary needs.

Let's take a look at a video showing how this is done. We are going to watch Roger review a portion of the Client Profile with Mark and Carol Olsen.

16 minutes

Video: *Review the Client Profile*

View video: *Review the Client Profile.*

Wrap-up
How did Roger affirm the Olsens?

NOTES

Step 6: Review the Client Profile.

- Affirm the client by referring to the "+" items on the Client Profile Analysis Chart.

- Raise some of the questions you noted by checking the "?" side of the Client Profile Analysis Chart.

Video: Review the Client Profile

Notes

Step 7: Explain the Spending Record.

See sample form on the next page.

Possible responses:

- He affirmed their desire to get out of debt. He also affirmed that they were asking good questions.

- He affirmed their 401k savings.

How did Roger keep the discussion from feeling like an interrogation?

Possible responses:

- He was encouraging.

- He focused on creating a plan and taking action steps.

- He took an interest in Ben.

- His responses were hopeful.

Now that we've reviewed the Client Profile, the next step in the process is to explain the Spending Record form.

5 minutes

Step 7: Explain the Spending Record.

The Spending Record will help the client begin to record their expenses so that more data will be available with which to develop their budget.

The Spending Record is a two-sided form—one side for recording monthly fixed expenses like rent and debt payments, and the other side for keeping a journal of daily variable expenditures.

Let's walk through a sample form.

Look at page 63.

Daily Variable Expenses

Participant's Guide, pages 63–64.

NOTES

Step 6: Review the Client Profile.

- Affirm the client by referring to the "+" items on the Client Profile Analysis Chart.

- Raise some of the questions you noted by checking the "?" side of the Client Profile Analysis Chart.

Video: **Review the Client Profile**

Notes

Step 7: Explain the Spending Record.

See sample form on the next page.

You can see a sample of the "Spending Record—Daily Variable Expenses" side of the form.

Initially this form is used to gather spending data to develop the client's budget or Spending Plan. Once the Spending Plan has been developed, the Spending Record is used to track expenses and compare them to the plan. Line 1 is where the Spending Plan numbers are entered. The example shows this section left blank because the client will fill these in when the budget has been developed. We'll cover this in Session 5.

At the top of the sheet are the categories that vary each month, have multiple transactions, and are generally the hardest to control. These categories are expenses the client is tracking.

The lines in the middle of the form are to record what is spent. In order to fill these lines in, the clients need to save each of their receipts as they make purchases. It is helpful to save them in an accessible, consistent place. This may be a pants pocket, or a certain section of a purse, or even a special envelope labeled "Receipts."

Then, when they come home at the end of the day, they write the amount of each receipt under the proper column. Amounts are rounded off to the nearest dollar to simplify record keeping.

In this example, look at the first column, which is transportation/gas. The family bought gas five different days that month and each time recorded the amount spent: $14, $23, $19, $21, and $11. Now, move over to the household/groceries column. You can see that they purchased groceries seven times and recorded each purchase: $9, $87, $43, etc.

At the bottom of the sheet are numbers from 1 to 31. When the clients finish recording their expenses each day, they should cross out the number corresponding to the date, so they'll know that they didn't forget a day.

NOTES

Month ___May___

Spending Record

	Transportation		Household						Professional Services	Entertainment		
	Gas, etc.	Maint/ Repair	Groceries	Clothes	Gifts	Household Items	Personal	Other		Going Out	Travel	Other
(1) Spending Plan	(Fill in this line when the Spending Plan has been completed.)											
	14	21	9	89	17	14	16	25		22	70	22
	23		87	6	55	22	18			46		(utter)
	19		43			9				19		
	21		106			31						
	11		21									
			7									
			13									
(2) Total	88	21	286	95	72	76	34	25		87	70	22
(3) (Over)/Under												
(4) Last Month YTD												
(5) Total Year to Date												

- Use this page to record expenses that tend to be daily, variable expenses—often the hardest to control.
- Keep receipts throughout the day and record them at the end of the day.
- Total each category at the end of the month (line 2) and compare to the Spending Plan (line 1). Subtracting line 2 from line 1 gives you an (over) or under the budget figure for that month (line 3).
- To verify that you have made each day's entry, cross out the number at the bottom of the page that corresponds to that day's date.
- Optional: If you wish to monitor your progress as you go through the year, you can keep cumulative totals in lines 4 and 5.

Toward the bottom of the sheet, there's a line marked "(2) Total." At the end of the month, the clients total what they spent in each category and record it on this line.

You can see that the total for transportation—gas is $88 and the total for household—groceries is $286.

The line below, "(3) (Over)/Under," then shows how much they're over or under for the month—the difference between lines 1 and 2. This cannot be completed until the budget is set on line 1.

There are two optional rows at the bottom of your sheet—lines 4 and 5. These are year-to-date totals they can use to keep track of their progress through the year as they get more comfortable with record keeping. An explanation of these lines is on page 136 in the Appendix.

Turn to page 64.

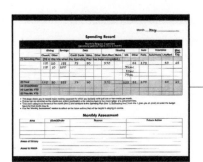

Monthly Regular Expenses
The "Monthly Regular Expenses" side of the form is used to record the client's fixed monthly expenses. These types of expenses typically fall into the categories shown. Again, all amounts entered should be rounded to the nearest dollar.

The last column, "Miscellaneous Cash Expenditures," is used to record a total amount that is used like a "petty cash" fund. It's a monthly lump sum that covers all of the little miscellaneous expenses so that clients don't have to record the small amounts paid for every pack of gum, cup of coffee, newspaper, etc.

At the very bottom of the sheet, notice that there's a section for a monthly assessment. If your client takes a couple moments each month to record the areas they need to watch more carefully and to note the areas where they had victories, it could be very helpful to them.

NOTES

Month ___May___

Spending Record

	Transportation		Household						Professional Services	Entertainment		
Daily Variable Expenses	Gas, etc.	Maint/ Repair	Groceries	Clothes	Gifts	Household Items	Personal	Other		Going Out	Travel	Other
(1) Spending Plan	(Fill in this line when the Spending Plan has been completed.)											
	14	21	9	89	17	14	16	25		22	70	22
	23		87	6	55	22	18			46		(utter)
	19		43			9				19		
	21		106			31						
	11		21									
			7									
			13									
(2) Total	88	21	286	95	72	76	34	25		87	70	22
(3) (Over)/Under												
(4) Last Month YTD												
(5) Total Year to Date												

~~X X X X X X X X X X X X X X X X X X X X X X X X X X X X X X X~~

- Use this page to record expenses that tend to be daily, variable expenses—often the hardest to control.
- Keep receipts throughout the day and record them at the end of the day.
- Total each category at the end of the month (line 2) and compare to the Spending Plan (line 1). Subtracting line 2 from line 1 gives you an (over) or under the budget figure for that month (line 3).
- To verify that you have made each day's entry, cross out the number at the bottom of the page that corresponds to that day's date.
- Optional: If you wish to monitor your progress as you go through the year, you can keep cumulative totals in lines 4 and 5.

Month ___May___

Spending Record

	Giving		Savings	Debt			Housing				Auto	Insurance		Misc. Cash Exp.
Monthly Regular Expenses (generally paid by check once a month)	Church	Other		Credit Cards	Educ.	Other	Mort./Rent	Maint.	Util.	Other	Pmts.	Auto/Home	Life/Med.	
(1) Spending Plan	(Fill in this line when the Spending Plan has been completed.)													
	110	20	155	75	50		970			44	270		40	65
	110	10	200						95(elec)					
									31(gas)					
									79(wt)					
(2) Total	220	30	355	75	50		970		205	44	270		40	65
(3) (Over)/Under														
(4) Last Mo. YTD														
(5) This Mo. YTD														

- This page allows you to record major monthly expenses for which you typically write just one or two checks per month.
- Entries can be recorded as the checks are written (preferably) or by referring back to the check ledger at a convenient time.
- Total each category at the end of the month (line 2) and compare to the Spending Plan (line 1). Subtracting line 2 from line 1 gives you an (over) or under the budget figure for that month (line 3).
- Use the "Monthly Assessment" section to reflect on the future actions that will be helpful in staying on course.

Monthly Assessment

Area	(Over)/Under	Reason	Future Action

Areas of Victory _____

Areas to Watch _____

When introducing your client to this form, remember that for some people, math and record keeping are very difficult tasks. Even if this form seems completely simple and self-explanatory to you, it may not be so for your clients! Always take the time to walk them through the form, showing them exactly how to complete it.

Here are the key points to remember when teaching clients how to complete the Spending Record.

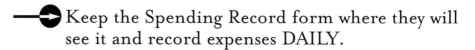

Participant's Guide, page 65.

Keep the Spending Record form where they will see it and record expenses DAILY.

 Keep it simple! Round all amounts to the nearest dollar.

 If a receipt contains several small items that belong in different categories, don't worry about calculating sales tax for each SMALL ITEM. Just round each item to the nearest dollar.

 For higher-priced items that appear on the same receipt and belong in different categories, include the sales tax by estimating the tax for each individual item.

 Remember that when small items such as a newspaper or a pack of gum are purchased separately, they get lumped into the "Miscellaneous Cash Expense" category.

6 minutes

Individual Activity: *Complete a Spending Record*

In order for you to coach your clients on how to use the Spending Record, it's best if you've worked with it yourself. You should use it for at least a month so that you are familiar with any situations your client may ask about.

NOTES

Key Points for Completing the Spending Record

- Keep the Spending Record where you will see it and record expenses _____.

- Round all amounts to the nearest dollar.

- Don't calculate sales tax for each _____.

- For higher-priced items, include the sales tax by estimating the tax for each individual item.

- Use a "Miscellaneous Cash Expense" category.

Individual Activity: *Complete a Spending Record*

Directions
Assume it's the end of the day, and you've made some purchases. Using the receipts shown on the next page, fill out the Spending Record form on page 67.

Individual Activity:

Complete a
Spending Record

Now, we're going to take just a few minutes to let you begin practicing with this form. We're going to focus only on the Daily Variable Expenses side of the form. The daily variable expenses are the ones most people have trouble controlling.

> Objective:
> For participants to become familiar with using the Spending Record.

Directions
Assume it's the end of the day, and you've made some purchases. Using the receipts shown on the next page, fill out the Spending Record on page 67.

> Call the group back together after about 2 minutes. Be sure to keep track of how much time you actually gave them to complete the exercise because you will refer to it in a moment. Note the time here: _____.

Wrap-up
Let's look at each receipt. Tell me where you logged it.

Where did you log the $18.00 fuel receipt?

> Answer: In the "Gas/Etc." column under the "Transportation" heading.

What about the paint store receipt?

> Answer: "Household Items." Rounded to $38.

The Neighborhood Foods total obviously goes into "Groceries," and you round the amount to $17.00.

NOTES

Key Points for Completing the Spending Record

- Keep the Spending Record where you will see it and record expenses _____.

- Round all amounts to the nearest dollar.

- Don't calculate sales tax for each _____.

- For higher-priced items, include the sales tax by estimating the tax for each individual item.

- Use a "Miscellaneous Cash Expense" category.

Individual Activity: Complete a Spending Record

Directions
Assume it's the end of the day, and you've made some purchases. Using the receipts shown on the next page, fill out the Spending Record form on page 67.

Sample Receipts

```
MAIN STREET GAS

DLR# 9485588
GURNEE IL

5/15/00
AUTH# 72109
PUMP #2
SPECIAL                9.579G
PRICE/GAL    $1.879

FUEL TOTAL             $18.00
```

```
ABC Department Store

DEPT 196 CL 8
KNIT JACKET            98.00
 PLU DISC 30%          29.40–
 NET ITEM PRICE        68.60

DEPT 209 LS 2
KING LINEN             58.00
 PLU DISC 30%          17.40–
 NET ITEM PRICE        40.60

SUBTOTAL              109.20
TX IL 8.25%             9.55

TOTAL                 118.75

501502000          11:27 AM
```

MASON'S PAINTS		126870	
	DATE	5/15/00	
NAME	Carol Larson		
QTY	DESCRIPTION	PRICE	AMT
1	Gal. B. Moore Flat Color #124	$17.99	$17.99
1	Gal. B. Moore Flat Color #643	$17.99	$17.99
	Subtotal		$35.98
		Tax	1.98
	Total		$37.96

.70 soft drink from a machine

```
Neighborhood Foods
Libertyville

TUE    5/15/00    10:25AM

B. Don Water Gal        1.09
BE Chop Spinach          .83
BE Chop Spinach          .83
Flav Broc-Cau           1.49
Salad Bar               1.50
Carr's Lemon Cremes     2.45
Classico De Napoli      2.79
Sarg Ricotta            2.29
Bays SD Muffins         2.08
Barrilla Lasagna        1.49

Tax 1                    .38
Total                  17.22
```

Month _____

Spending Record

	Transportation		Household						Professional Services	Entertainment		
	Gas, etc.	Maint/ Repair	Groceries	Clothes	Gifts	Household Items	Personal	Other		Going Out	Travel	Other
(1) Spending Plan												
(2) Total												
(3) (Over)/Under												
(4) Last Month YTD												
(5) Total Year–to–Date												

Daily Variable Expenses

1 2 3 4 5 6 7 8 9 10 11 12 13 14 15 16 17 18 19 20 21 22 23 24 25 26 27 28 29 30 31

- Use this page to record expenses that tend to be daily, variable expenses—often the hardest to control.
- Keep receipts throughout the day and record them at the end of the day.
- Total each category at the end of the month (line 2) and compare to the Spending Plan (line 1). Subtracting line 2 from line 1 gives you an (over) or under the budget figure for that month (line 3).
- To verify that you have made each day's entry, cross out the number at the bottom of the page that corresponds to that day's date.
- Optional: If you wish to monitor your progress as you go through the year, you can keep cumulative totals in lines 4 and 5.

What about the soft drink?

> Answer: It doesn't get recorded.

Such small cash expenses should not be logged—our goal is to simplify record keeping as much as possible. A key way to do that is to eliminate having to make a lot of entries for small expenses for which there often are not even receipts. Remember, the strategy is to set aside one lump sum every month for "Miscellaneous Cash Expenses" and take the soft drink money out of that. Clients can cash a check for the estimated amount, then tuck the cash into an envelope or separate coin purse.

If the client runs out of this cash before the month is up, they need to reevaluate their spending or alter the miscellaneous cash amount. The key point is that if a client spends $40 per month on small items averaging 75 cents each, use of the cash account for such items saves recording over fifty different expenditures.

The department store receipt has one clothing item and one household item—linens. What amounts did you write in each of those categories?

> Answer: Take the net item price for each item and estimate the approximate tax to add to that amount. For the jacket, you could write about $74 or $75 and for the bed linens, write $44 or $45.

Let me now call your attention to a very important point. I noted the time it took you to make those entries, and it was only _____ minutes.

> Insert the time you kept track of on page 190 in the blank above.

NOTES

Sample Receipts

MAIN STREET GAS

DLR# 9485588
GURNEE IL

5/15/00
AUTH# 72109
PUMP #2
SPECIAL   9.579G
PRICE/GAL $1.879

FUEL TOTAL $18.00

ABC Department Store

DEPT 196 CL 8
KNIT JACKET   98.00
    PLU DISC 30%   29.40–
    NET ITEM PRICE   68.60

DEPT 209 LS 2
KING LINEN   58.00
    PLU DISC 30%   17.40–
    NET ITEM PRICE   40.60

SUBTOTAL   109.20
TX IL 8.25%   9.55

TOTAL   118.75

501502000   11:27 AM

MASON'S PAINTS   126870

DATE   5/15/00

NAME	Carol Larson		
QTY	DESCRIPTION	PRICE	AMT
1	Gal. B. Moore Flat Color #124	$17.99	$17.99
1	Gal. B. Moore Flat Color #643	$17.99	$17.99
	Subtotal		$35.98
		Tax	1.98
	Total		$37.96

.70 soft drink from a machine

Neighborhood Foods
Libertyville

TUE   5/15/00   10:25AM

B. Don Water Gal   1.09
BE Chop Spinach   .83
BE Chop Spinach   .83
Flav Broc-Cau   1.49
Salad Bar   1.50
Carr's Lemon Cremes   2.45
Classico De Napoli   2.79
Sarg Ricotta   2.29
Bays SD Muffins   2.08
Barrilla Lasagna   1.49

Tax 1   .38
Total   17.22

Month _____

Spending Record

	Transportation		Household						Professional Services	Entertainment		
	Gas, etc.	Maint/ Repair	Groceries	Clothes	Gifts	Household Items	Personal	Other		Going Out	Travel	Other
Daily Variable Expenses												
(1) Spending Plan												
(2) Total												
(3) (Over)/Under												
(4) Last Month YTD												
(5) Total Year–to–Date												

1 2 3 4 5 6 7 8 9 10 11 12 13 14 15 16 17 18 19 20 21 22 23 24 24 26 27 28 29 30 31

- Use this page to record expenses that tend to be daily, variable expenses—often the hardest to control.
- Keep receipts throughout the day and record them at the end of the day.
- Total each category at the end of the month (line 2) and compare to the Spending Plan (line 1). Subtracting line 2 from line 1 gives you an (over) or under the budget figure for that month (line 3).
- To verify that you have made each day's entry, cross out the number at the bottom of the page that corresponds to that day's date.
- Optional: If you wish to monitor your progress as you go through the year, you can keep cumulative totals in lines 4 and 5.

And if you didn't finish it, I'm sure it would only be a matter of practicing a time or two until you could complete this daily task in less than 2 minutes. Point this out to your client.

Turn to page 68.

Here's a key question to have your clients ask themselves:

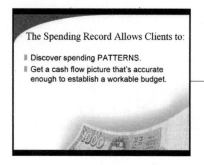

➜ Is it worth 2 minutes a day to bring this crucial area of my life under control?

The reality is, record keeping can be much simpler and take much less time than most people believe. Strongly encourage your client to understand that the idea with the Spending Record is not for them to start counting nickels and dimes!

It allows clients to:

➜ Discover spending PATTERNS so that behavior can be modified.

Get a cash flow picture that's accurate enough to be able to establish a workable budget.

A few dollars more or less won't make or break the budget, so our rounding and estimating to keep this simple won't matter.

▶ ➜ Finally, the simple act of beginning to record their expenses will, in and of itself, begin to CHANGE their spending habits.

Just being reminded of what we've spent by writing it down will have a significant impact. Be sure to share this with your client.

We have now completed the first seven steps of the first meeting.

NOTES

_____
_____
_____
_____
_____
_____
_____
_____
_____
_____
_____
_____
_____
_____
_____
_____
_____
_____
_____
_____
_____
_____
_____

Question:

Is it worth two minutes a day to bring this crucial area of my life under control?

The Spending Record form allows clients to:

- Discover spending _____
- Get a cash flow picture that's accurate enough to establish a workable budget
- Begin to _____ their spending habits

First Meeting: Steps: 1-7

- Step 1: Greet Clients.

- Step 2: Pray.

- Step 3: Explain your ministry and budgeting background.

- Step 4: Get to know your clients.

- Step 5: Sign the Good $ense Budget Covenant.

- Step 6: Review the _____.

- Step 7: Explain the Spending Record.

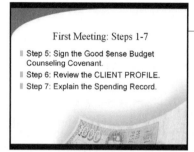

They are:

Step 1: Greet your clients.

Step 2: Pray.

Step 3: Explain your ministry and budgeting background.

Step 4: Get to know your clients.

Step 5: Sign the Good $ense Budget Counseling Covenant.

Step 6: Review the CLIENT PROFILE.

Step 7: Explain the Spending Record.

Now, it is time to conclude the meeting. Let's cover the remaining steps.

FIRST MEETING: STEPS 8-11

Participant's Guide, page 69.

Steps 8-11 include:

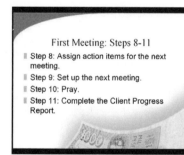

5 minutes

Step 8: Assign action items for the next meeting.

Step 9: Set up the next meeting.

Step 10: Pray.

Step 11: Complete the Client Progress Report.

Let's talk about each of these steps.

Step 8: Assign Action Items for the Next Meeting.

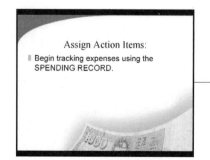

Step 8 is "Assign action items for the next meeting."

Normally, counselors will ask clients to begin tracking their expenses using the SPENDING RECORD to prepare for the next meeting.

NOTES

_____

_____

_____

_____

_____

_____

_____

_____

_____

_____

_____

_____

_____

_____

_____

_____

_____

_____

_____

_____

_____

Question:

Is it worth two minutes a day to bring this crucial area of my life under control?

The Spending Record form allows clients to:

- Discover spending _____
- Get a cash flow picture that's accurate enough to establish a workable budget
- Begin to _____ their spending habits

First Meeting: Steps: 1-7

- Step 1: Greet Clients.
- Step 2: Pray.
- Step 3: Explain your ministry and budgeting background.
- Step 4: Get to know your clients.
- Step 5: Sign the Good $ense Budget Covenant.
- Step 6: Review the _____.
- Step 7: Explain the Spending Record.

First Meeting: Steps 8-11

Steps 8-11 include:

- Step 8: Assign action items for the next meeting.
- Step 9: Set up the next meeting.
- Step 10: Pray.
- Step 11: Complete the Client Progress Report.

Step 8: Assign Action Items for the Next Meeting.

Possible action items include:

- Begin tracking expenses using the _____
- Borrow or charge no more!
- Review the current budget for expenses to cut, and prioritize the spending cuts
- Complete other items specific to the case

Purposes of completing action items:

- Helps determine the client's skill level (or lack of skill) in this area

- Shows their _____ to making the counseling work

- Gives you, the counselor, additional information to work with

- Helps clients develop _____

If clients already have been successfully tracking their expenses, you can consider additional assignments such as:

▶ ➤ Borrow or charge no more!

Clients can note instances where they were tempted and report how they overcame the temptation.

▶ ➤ Review the current budget for expenses to cut and prioritize the spending cuts.

➤ Complete other items specific to the case.

For example, you may assign clients to find out the current cash value of their life insurance policy, or have the clients search through their home to determine if there are unused items that can be sold to raise cash.

Completing action items for the next meeting serves several purposes:

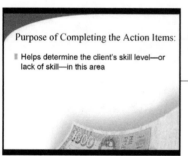

Purpose of Completing the Action Items:

▌ Helps determine the client's skill level—or lack of skill—in this area

➤ It helps determine the client's skill level—or lack of skill—in this area.

For some people, record keeping requires a tremendous amount of effort. For example, some people have never balanced a checkbook or don't have basic math skills.

▶ ➤ If the assignments are getting done, it shows their COMMITMENT to making the counseling work.

Completed homework offers the counselor multiple opportunities for praise and encouragement of the client's efforts.

▶ ➤ It gives you, the counselor, additional information to work with.

➤ It helps clients develop GOOD HABITS.

NOTES

First Meeting: Steps 8-11

Steps 8-11 include:

- Step 8: Assign action items for the next meeting.

- Step 9: Set up the next meeting.

- Step 10: Pray.

- Step 11: Complete the Client Progress Report.

Step 8: Assign Action Items for the Next Meeting.

Possible action items include:

- Begin tracking expenses using the _____

- Borrow or charge no more!

- Review the current budget for expenses to cut, and prioritize the spending cuts

- Complete other items specific to the case

Purposes of completing action items:

- Helps determine the client's skill level (or lack of skill) in this area

- Shows their _____ to making the counseling work

- Gives you, the counselor, additional information to work with

- Helps clients develop _____

Once they get into the habit of tracking expenses and performing other such homework, they'll most likely continue such habits in the future. Action items help produce an awareness of behaviors that might otherwise never be examined.

Turn to page 70.

Step 9: Set Up the Next Meeting.

First Meeting: Steps 8-11

Step 8: Assign action items for the next meeting.
Step 9: Set up the next meeting.
  Ideally takes place within TWO weeks of the first meeting

Participant's Guide, page 70.

Step 9 is "Set up the next meeting."

The second meeting ideally takes place within TWO weeks of the first meeting.

Waiting too long may cause the case to lose momentum, while meeting too soon won't allow adequate time for the client to really begin taking those first few steps toward their goal.

Step 10: Pray.

Step 10 is "Pray."

Just as you opened the meeting, close it with a prayer of thanks for:

The progress made during the meeting, and the client's continued commitment to counseling.

Step 11: Complete the Client Progress Report.

Step 11 is "Complete the Client Progress Report."

Right after the meeting is the best time to jot down your meeting notes on the Client Progress Report.

NOTES

Step 9: Set Up the Next Meeting.

- Ideally takes place within _____ weeks of the first meeting

Step 10: Pray.

Thank God for:

- The progress made during the meeting

- The client's continued commitment to counseling

Step 11: Complete the Client Progress Report.

It contains:

- Results of previous action items

- _____ about the client's behavior and attitudes

- Thoughts on the client's progress

- Action items assigned for the next meeting

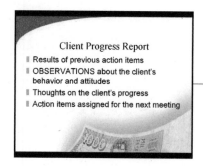

This form will help you keep a diary of sorts regarding the progress of the case. It's not intended to be an in-depth analysis, but rather a summarized record of your meetings.

It contains:

Results of previous assignments, OBSERVATIONS about the client's behavior and attitudes, thoughts on the client's progress and action items assigned for the next meeting.

Participant's Guide, page 71.

On the next page is a sample Client Progress Report that Roger completed after the first meeting with the Olsens. Take a moment to review it.

Pause until most participants are finished.

After each meeting, you'll write your report and file it in the client's file. Review the report briefly before the next meeting.

Turn to page 72.

Partner Activity: *Role Play of the First Meeting*

60 minutes

Participant's Guide, page 72.

We're now going to role-play a portion of the first meeting. This activity is designed to simulate the experience of a first counseling meeting. It will give you an opportunity to practice the tools and techniques involved in the first meeting steps. It will also simulate the anxiety level you'll feel in real life. But now is the time to practice, as opposed to practicing when you're with a client. Take advantage of this safe environment.

NOTES

_____

_____

_____

_____

_____

_____

_____

_____

_____

_____

_____

_____

_____

_____

_____

_____

_____

_____

_____

_____

_____

_____

_____

_____

_____

Step 9: Set Up the Next Meeting.

• Ideally takes place within _____ weeks of the first meeting

Step 10: Pray.

Thank God for:

• The progress made during the meeting

• The client's continued commitment to counseling

Step 11: Complete the Client Progress Report.

It contains:

• Results of previous action items

• _____ about the client's behavior and attitudes

• Thoughts on the client's progress

• Action items assigned for the next meeting

Client Progress Report
Good $ense Ministry

Counselor: _Roger Liston_   Case No. _178_

Client: _Mark and Carol Olsen_

Instructions: This report serves as a summarized record of meetings with your client. Include the results of previous action items, observations about your client's behavior and attitudes, thoughts on your client's progress, and action items assigned for the next meeting. At the completion of this case, all progress reports should be forwarded to the ministry office.

Meeting Date: _3/31_   Next Meeting Date: _6/15_

Time: _10:00 – 11:30 A.M._   Time: _7:00 – 9:00 P.M._

Results of previous action items:

N/A – first meeting

Observations about the client's behavior and attitudes:

– _Somewhat stressed due to child's situation and lack of time alone as a couple_
– _Seem committed to working on financial situation and grateful for help. Mark is a little harder to involve than Carol but he seemed to be opening up._

Thoughts on the client's progress:

N/A – first meeting

Action Items assigned for the next meeting:

– _Prioritize goals_
– _Pray about giving_
– _Begin using Spending Record_
– _Estimate amount spent on gifts, other blank categories, and miscellaneous small cash items_
– _Call the church about a program for Ben_

Observations about the client's spiritual condition:

Partner Activity: *Role Play of First Meeting*

Directions

1. Refer to the Client Profile Analysis Chart that you developed during the activity back in Session 2 on pages 233–236. If you analyzed the Client Profile for Sharlene and Chris Moore, pair up with someone who analyzed the profile for Barb Leonard.

2. Those who analyzed the Moores' profile will begin as their counselor. Use the worksheet on pages 73 and 74 to prepare for the first meeting. We will have time to cover steps 1–4, which focus on getting the relationship off to a good start, and step 6, which is "Review the Client Profile." Remember to use your mirroring skills. One final note: This is your opportunity to practice in a safe place before you actually meet a client.

3. The other partner will role-play one of the Moores. Spend this preparation time preparing for your role. Carefully read the Client Profile on pages 225–228 and put yourself into this client's shoes. Please treat your role seriously. It's okay to give the counselor a bit of a hard time, but make it realistic and productive.

   When the instructor calls "time" for the end of the first round, the counselor and the client should walk through the Feedback Checklist on pages 75 and 76, with the client giving the counselor feedback.

4. Each round of this activity will last for 25 minutes:
   • 5 minutes for preparation
   • 15 minutes for the actual role-playing
   • 5 minutes for feedback

5. When the first round has been completed, we will switch roles. The partner who analyzed Barb Leonard's profile in Session 2 will prepare for their role as counselor by completing the worksheet on pages 73 and 74. The other partner will read the Client Profile on pages 229–232 and put themselves in the shoes of the client.

We'll do this by pairing up and having some of you play the role of the client so that your classmates can practice counseling you. Of course, we'll do a role reversal so everyone gets an opportunity to try out the first meeting in the role of a Good $ense counselor.

> Objective:
> For participants to practice the tools and techniques involved in the steps of the first meeting.
>
> As you read the directions, pause to allow participants time to locate the appropriate pages.

Directions

1. Refer to the Client Profile Analysis Chart you developed during the activity back in Session 2 on pages 233–236. If you analyzed the Client Profile for Sharlene and Chris Moore, pair up with someone who analyzed the profile for Barb Leonard.

2. Those who analyzed the Moores' profile will begin as the Moores' counselor.

> Pause.

Raise your hand if you are the Moores' counselor.

Use the worksheet on pages 73 and 74 to prepare for the first meeting. We will have time to cover Steps 1 through 4, which focus on getting the relationship off to a good start, and Step 6, which is "Review the Client Profile." Remember to use your mirroring skills. One final note: This is your opportunity to practice in a safe place before you actually meet a client.

The other partner will role-play one of the Moores. Spend this preparation time preparing for your role. Carefully read the Client Profile on pages 225–228 and put yourself into this client's shoes. Please treat your role seriously. It's okay to give the counselor a bit of a hard time, but make it realistic and productive.

NOTES

Partner Activity: *Role Play of First Meeting*

Directions

1. Refer to the Client Profile Analysis Chart that you developed during the activity back in Session 2 on pages 233–236. If you analyzed the Client Profile for Sharlene and Chris Moore, pair up with someone who analyzed the profile for Barb Leonard.

2. Those who analyzed the Moores' profile will begin as their counselor. Use the worksheet on pages 73 and 74 to prepare for the first meeting. We will have time to cover steps 1-4, which focus on getting the relationship off to a good start, and step 6, which is "Review the Client Profile." Remember to use your mirroring skills. One final note: This is your opportunity to practice in a safe place before you actually meet a client.

3. The other partner will role-play one of the Moores. Spend this preparation time preparing for your role. Carefully read the Client Profile on pages 225–228 and put yourself into this client's shoes. Please treat your role seriously. It's okay to give the counselor a bit of a hard time, but make it realistic and productive.

   When the instructor calls "time" for the end of the first round, the counselor and the client should walk through the Feedback Checklist on pages 75 and 76, with the client giving the counselor feedback.

4. Each round of this activity will last for 25 minutes:
   - 5 minutes for preparation
   - 15 minutes for the actual role-playing
   - 5 minutes for feedback

5. When the first round has been completed, we will switch roles. The partner who analyzed Barb Leonard's profile in Session 2 will prepare for their role as counselor by completing the worksheet on pages 73 and 74. The other partner will read the Client Profile on pages 229–232 and put themselves in the shoes of the client.

3. When I call time for the end of the first round, the counselor and the client should walk through the feedback checklist on pages 75 and 76, with the client giving the counselor feedback.

4. Each round of this activity will last for 25 minutes:

   • 5 minutes for preparation

   • 15 minutes for the actual role playing

   • 5 minutes for feedback

5. When the first round has been completed, we will switch roles. The partner who analyzed Barb Leonard's profile in Session 2 will prepare for their role as counselor by completing the worksheet on pages 73 and 74. The other partner will read the Client Profile on pages 229–232 and put themselves in the shoes of the client.

Any question on the directions?

Pause.

Raise your hand if you are the first client, the Moores.

Pause.

Begin your 5-minute prep period *now*.

• After 5 minutes, instruct participants to begin the role play.

• After 10 minutes, mention that the counselor should move on to reviewing the Client Profile.

• After 5 more minutes have elapsed, call "time." You will allow 15 minutes total for each role play.

NOTES

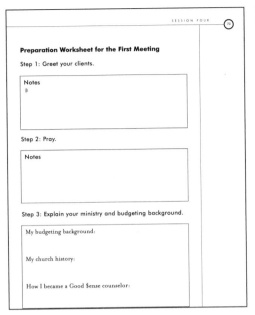

- Allow 5 minutes for the counselor and the client to walk through the Feedback Checklist together, with the client giving the counselor feedback.

- Repeat the entire process again with the partners switching roles.

- Call the group back together after a total of 60 minutes.

Wrap-up

Think about when you were playing the role of client.

What did your counselor do to make a good first impression and to help you feel comfortable?

Possible responses:

- He asked me to take off my coat and offered me coffee.

- She greeted me warmly with a firm handshake.

- She was friendly and acted genuinely happy to see me.

How well did your counselor use mirroring skills during this scenario?

Possible responses:

- She did a good job. First she asked me to tell about my family. Then, rather than asking more questions, she restated the stress I was feeling about my hearing-impaired child.

- I was surprised at how much information my counselor drew out of me when he asked me what led me to apply for Good $ense counseling, but then he didn't ask a single follow-up question.

- My counselor actually seemed to overdo it with mirroring. I was waiting for him to move on, and he kept just stating my same feelings over and over again.

NOTES

_____

_____

_____

_____

_____

_____

_____

_____

_____

_____

_____

_____

_____

_____

_____

_____

_____

_____

_____

_____

_____

_____

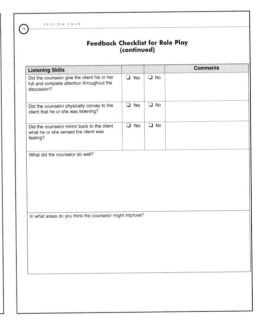

What did your counselor do particularly well?

Possible responses:

- He seemed to really listen to me.

- She did an exceptional job using mirroring skills.

- He did a good job covering the Client Profile without making me feel interrogated.

Now, consider your role as a counselor.

What did the first 5 minutes of this meeting feel like?

Possible responses:

- It seemed uncomfortable because I was nervous.

- I was surprised by how quickly the time seemed to go.

- The time seemed to drag by because my client didn't want to open up.

How do you think you might improve?

Possible responses:

- I need to use a better balance of mirroring and asking questions.

- I need to let the conversation proceed a little bit more slowly rather than hurrying the client along.

- I need to practice the process more, so I am more comfortable with where to go next.

Was this easier or more difficult than you imagined? Why?

NOTES

_____

_____

_____

_____

_____

_____

_____

_____

_____

_____

_____

_____

_____

_____

_____

_____

_____

_____

_____

_____

_____

_____

_____

Preparation Worksheet for the First Meeting

Step 1: Greet your clients.

Notes

Step 2: Pray.

Notes

Step 3: Explain your ministry and budgeting background.

My budgeting background:

My church history:

How I became a Good $ense counselor:

Step 4: Get to know your clients.

State that I would like to get to know my client better:

Use open-ended questions to build rapport:

Transition to a more focused conversation about finances:

Ask appropriate questions about finances:

Step 6: Review the Client Profile (you may use the Client Profile Analysis Chart you completed on pages 38–41.

Notes

Feedback Checklist for Role Play

			Comments
Step 1: Greet your clients.			
Did the counselor warmly greet the client and make the client feel comfortable?	❑ Yes	❑ No	
Step 2: Pray.			
Did the counselor pray with the client, offering an appeal for God's presence and wisdom along with thanksgiving for the client's presence?	❑ Yes	❑ No	
Step 3: Explain your ministry and budgeting background.			
Did the counselor describe his or her budgeting background?	❑ Yes	❑ No	
Did the counselor talk about his or her history with the church?	❑ Yes	❑ No	
Did the counselor tell how he or she became a Good $ense counselor?	❑ Yes	❑ No	
Did the counselor allow the client to ask questions about his or her background?	❑ Yes	❑ No	
Step 4: Get to know your clients.			
Did the counselor state that he or she would like to get to know the client better?	❑ Yes	❑ No	
Did the counselor use open-ended questions to build rapport?	❑ Yes	❑ No	
Did the counselor transition to a more focused conversation about the client's finances?	❑ Yes	❑ No	
Did the counselor ask appropriate questions about finances?	❑ Yes	❑ No	
Step 6: Review the Client Profile.			
Did the counselor clarify the issues he or she had questions about?	❑ Yes	❑ No	

Feedback Checklist for Role Play
(continued)

Listening Skills			Comments
Did the counselor give the client his or her full and complete attention throughout the discussion?	❑ Yes	❑ No	
Did the counselor physically convey to the client that he or she was listening?	❑ Yes	❑ No	
Did the counselor mirror back to the client what he or she sensed the client was feeling?	❑ Yes	❑ No	

What did the counselor do well?

In what areas do you think the counselor might improve?

Possible responses:

- I found it a little bit more difficult since my client didn't want to open up.

- I was actually surprised to find that once I got into it, it was much easier than I expected.

- I found it harder because I had trouble sensing when I should move to the next step.

Note that this was a one-on-one role play. The clients in the first role play were actually a couple. You will encounter many couples. Page 115 in the Appendix provides some advice for working with spouses.

0 minutes

SESSION SUMMARY

We have now conducted the first meeting, and you had the opportunity to experience what a counseling session feels like. Once again, take your time to build the relationship.

In the next session, we will cover ongoing counseling.

ONGOING
COUNSELING

SESSION SNAPSHOT

OVERVIEW

In Session 5 we cover the key forms that need to be completed during ongoing counseling. We discuss Good $ense's recommended order for helping our red-case clients use their income and Good $ense strategies for making adjustments to the Spending Plan. We explore how the Biblical Financial Principles can be incorporated throughout the counseling process. Finally, we briefly cover how to close a case.

OBJECTIVES

In this session, participants will:

1. Use the Spending Plan worksheet
2. Complete a Debt Reduction Plan
3. Revisit applying the Biblical Financial Principles into their counseling meeting
4. Review when and how to close a case

OUTLINE

I. Introduction

II. Goals of Ongoing Counseling

III. Spending Plan

IV. Recommended Order for the Use of Income

V. Completing the Spending Plan

VI. Adjust the Spending Plan

VII. Debt Reduction

    A. Video: *Out of Debt*

    B. Debt Reduction Plan

    C. Individual Activity: *Debt Reduction Plan*

VIII. Transfer the Budget to the Spending Record

IX. Envelope System

X. Applying the Biblical Financial Principles

    A. Video: *Applying the Biblical Financial Principles*

XI. Close the Case

XII. Counseling Process Summary

ONGOING COUNSELING

TIME & MEDIA

1 minute

CONTENTS

INTRODUCTION

Participant's Guide, page 77.

Let's review the counseling process for a moment.

We have:

➤ Analyzed the Client Profile.

Called the client.

Conducted the first meeting.

We have two parts remaining:

➤ Provide ongoing counseling, and

Close the case.

In this final session, we will cover these two last steps.

➤ We will use the Spending Plan, complete a Debt Reduction Plan, revisit applying the Biblical Financial Principles into your counseling meetings, and then discuss when and how to close a case.

Turn to page 78.

NOTES

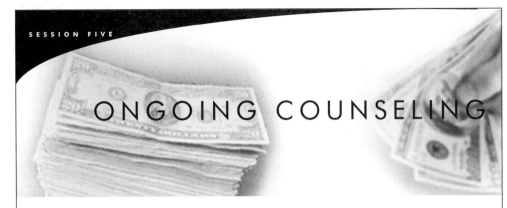

SESSION FIVE

ONGOING COUNSELING

Introduction

COUNSELING PROCESS

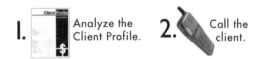

1. Analyze the Client Profile.

2. Call the client.

3. Conduct the first meeting.

4. Provide ongoing counseling.

5. Close the case.

In this session, you will

1. Use the Spending Plan worksheet

2. Complete a Debt Reduction Plan

3. Revisit applying the Biblical Financial Principles into your counseling meetings

4. Review when and how to close a case

1 minute

GOALS OF ONGOING COUNSELING

Participant's Guide, page 78.

Goals of Ongoing Counseling

| Complete the client's financial picture
| Develop a BUDGET and a Debt Reduction Plan
| Provide encouragement and affirmation
| Provide correction where necessary
| Encourage the client's SPIRITUAL growth

The goals of ongoing counseling are to:

Complete the client's financial picture.

Develop a BUDGET and a Debt Reduction Plan.

Provide encouragement and affirmation.

Provide correction where necessary.

Encourage the client's SPIRITUAL growth.

Ongoing meetings will include the opening steps that we used in the first meeting: greeting the client and praying to open the meeting, as well as the closing steps: assign action items, set up next meeting, pray, and complete the Client Progress Report.

Keeping in mind that the pace of ongoing meetings will vary tremendously with the client, we will focus in this session on the three forms we want to complete during these meetings:

Forms to Complete During Ongoing Meetings

| The Spending Plan
| The Debt Reduction Plan
| The Spending Record

The Spending Plan

The Debt Reduction Plan

The Spending Record

It is likely that it will take two or three meetings, and sometimes more, to complete these items.

Let's talk about each of these items in depth and discuss the tools we'll need.

NOTES

Goals of Ongoing Counseling

- Complete the client's financial picture

- Develop a _____ and a debt reduction plan

- Provide encouragement and affirmation

- Provide correction where necessary

- Encourage the client's _____ growth

Forms to Complete During Ongoing Meetings:

- Spending Plan

- Debt Reduction Plan

- Spending Record

1 minute

SPENDING PLAN

Participant's Guide, page 79.

It's assumed that all of you here today are pretty good at budgeting your money. You wouldn't be here if you weren't. So, your skills in budgeting will clearly benefit your clients. The tool we will use to set up a budget is the Spending Plan form that you have on page 79.

You'll notice that this form looks like the "What I Spend" section from the Client Profile. However, the change in title is significant. The intent is for the client to move from what *is*—what I spend—to a *plan*, the Spending Plan, based on their goals.

Let's take a look at the order in which the form is organized. Remember the five financial areas we talked about in Session 1? These areas are represented on the form. You can see that earning is at the top, followed by giving, saving, debt, and then the various spending categories.

This form is consistent with Good $ense's recommended approach for using our income.

Let's move away from the form for a moment and talk about this order and how it is applied in red cases. Turn to page 80.

4 minutes

RECOMMENDED ORDER FOR THE USE OF INCOME FOR RED CASES

Participant's Guide, page 80.

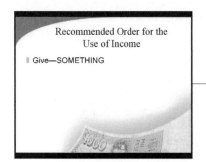

Recommended Order for the Use of Income

Give—SOMETHING

→ The Good $ense Ministry's recommended order for the use of income begins with giving.

And the word associated with giving is SOMETHING.

NOTES

SPENDING PLAN

EARNINGS/INCOME PER MONTH		TOTALS
Salary #1 (net take-home)	_____	
Salary #2 (net take-home)	_____	
Other (less taxes)	_____	
TOTAL MONTHLY INCOME		$ _____

% GUIDE

1. GIVING $ _____
- Church _____
- OTHER CONTRIBUTIONS _____

2. SAVING   5–10% $ _____
- EMERGENCY _____
- REPLACEMENT _____
- LONG TERM _____

3. DEBT   0–10% $ _____
- CREDIT CARDS:
  - VISA _____
  - Master Card _____
  - Discover _____
  - American Express _____
  - Gas Cards _____
  - Department Stores _____
- EDUCATION LOANS _____
- OTHER LOANS:
  - Bank Loans _____
  - Credit Union _____
  - Family/Friends _____
  - OTHER _____

4. HOUSING   25–38% $ _____
- MORTGAGE/TAXES/RENT _____
- MAINTENANCE/REPAIRS _____
- UTILITIES:
  - Electric _____
  - Gas _____
  - Water _____
  - Trash _____
  - Telephone/Internet _____
  - Cable TV _____
  - OTHER _____

5. AUTO/TRANSP.   12–15% $ _____
- CAR PAYMENTS/LICENSE _____
- GAS & BUS/TRAIN/PARKING _____
- OIL/LUBE/MAINTENANCE _____

* This is a % of total monthly income. These are guidelines only and may be different for individual situations. However, there should be good rationale for a significant variance.

6. INSURANCE (Paid by you)   5% $ _____
- AUTO _____
- HOMEOWNERS _____
- LIFE _____
- MEDICAL/DENTAL _____
- Other _____

7. HOUSEHOLD/PERSONAL   15–25% $ _____
- GROCERIES _____
- CLOTHES/DRY CLEANING _____
- GIFTS _____
- HOUSEHOLD ITEMS _____
- PERSONAL:
  - Liquor/Tobacco _____
  - Cosmetics _____
  - Barber/Beauty _____
- OTHER:
  - Books/Magazines _____
  - Allowances _____
  - Music Lessons _____
  - Personal Technology _____
  - Education _____
  - Miscellaneous _____

8. ENTERTAINMENT   5–10% $ _____
- GOING OUT:
  - Meals _____
  - Movies/Events _____
  - Baby-sitting _____
- TRAVEL (VACATION/TRIPS) _____
- OTHER:
  - Fitness/Sports _____
  - Hobbies _____
  - Media Rental _____
  - OTHER _____

9. PROF. SERVICES   5–15% $ _____
- CHILD CARE _____
- MEDICAL/DENTAL/PRESC. _____
- OTHER
  - Legal _____
  - Counseling _____
  - Professional Dues _____

10. MISC. SMALL CASH EXPENDITURES   2–3% $ _____

TOTAL EXPENSES $ _____

TOTAL MONTHLY INCOME	$ _____
LESS TOTAL EXPENSES	$ _____
INCOME OVER/(UNDER) EXPENSES	$ _____

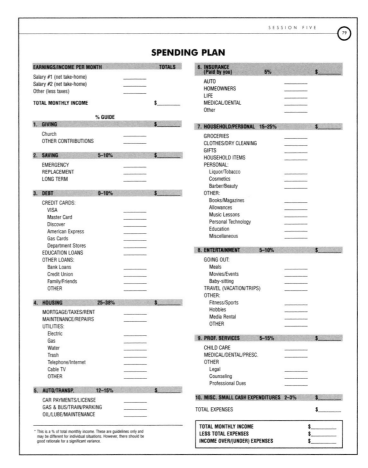

Recommended Order for the Use of Income for Red Cases

- Give— _____

  A Christian should:
  - Desire to be at (or even beyond) the tithe

  If they aren't at the tithe, they should:
  - Begin giving something

  - Begin to develop a plan for getting there

- Save—a little

- Debt— _____ repayment

- Lifestyle—spartan

Completing the Spending Plan Worksheet

Use:

- Information obtained when you reviewed the Client Profile
- New data obtained from the Spending Record

Look at the Spending Record and ask the client:

- What categories do they seem to be managing well?
- In what areas can they exert a little more control?

We are called to give, so each of us must wrestle with the question of "how much?" The answer to that question is a matter of the heart; for a Christian it is a matter between them and God. The biblical benchmark for giving is the tithe. Many of our clients come to us in great financial pain, and we do not take the position that they should immediately begin the full tithe.

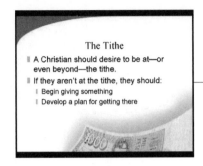

Our position is that a Christian should desire to be at—or even beyond—the tithe.

If they aren't at the tithe, then our stance is that they should:

Begin giving something.

At this point, it may not be a whole lot, because of their circumstances, but it should be something . . . a regular, proportionate, and cheerfully given amount based on gratitude for what they do have and not discontentment for what they don't have. Attitude is more important than amount.

In addition, they should begin to develop a plan for getting to the tithe.

There is more information on tithing in the Appendix on page 117.

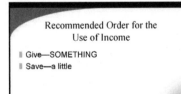

After giving, the next use of income in our recommended order is saving. A red case should begin by saving a little.

As long as they're in the red, it will not be much because debt reduction will be the top priority. But even if it's just a little, encourage your clients to begin the savings habit now.

Third, pay debt. The words associated with debt are "MAXIMIZE repayment."

NOTES

Recommended Order for the Use of Income for Red Cases

- Give— _____

  A Christian should:
  - Desire to be at (or even beyond) the tithe

  If they aren't at the tithe, they should:
  - Begin giving something

  - Begin to develop a plan for getting there

- Save—a little

- Debt— _____ repayment

- Lifestyle—spartan

Completing the Spending Plan Worksheet

Use:

- Information obtained when you reviewed the Client Profile
- New data obtained from the Spending Record

Look at the Spending Record and ask the client:

- What categories do they seem to be managing well?
- In what areas can they exert a little more control?

224

Our clients need to pay the maximum amount that they can to get out of debt as soon as possible. We will talk more about this shortly.

▶ ➡ The final priority is lifestyle. For red cases, the word associated with lifestyle in the short-term is "spartan."

By spartan, we mean taking drastic short-term steps to reduce lifestyle expenses in order to maximize the amount of money to pay off debt. For example, rather than the client spending what they currently do on entertainment—going to the movies, eating out, etc.—they choose to rent a video for a few dollars, or perhaps even borrow one free from the library. Walks in the park and evenings spent playing board games with friends replace more expensive activities.

In a similar fashion, rather than spending hundreds of dollars on clothing for the latest seasonal change, they make a commitment to buy only the basic necessities and go back to the closet and dresser drawers for last year's clothing.

A spartan lifestyle involves looking at all the categories of the Spending Plan and identifying every possible area where short-term cutbacks can be made in order to take a big step toward debt reduction.

Now that you understand Good $ense's recommended order for our red-case clients and how the Spending Plan supports this order, let's talk about how to complete the Spending Plan.

NOTES

Recommended Order for the Use of Income for Red Cases

- Give— _____

  A Christian should:
  ○ Desire to be at (or even beyond) the tithe

  If they aren't at the tithe, they should:
  ○ Begin giving something

  ○ Begin to develop a plan for getting there

- Save—a little

- Debt— _____ repayment

- Lifestyle—spartan

Completing the Spending Plan Worksheet

Use:

- Information obtained when you reviewed the Client Profile
- New data obtained from the Spending Record

Look at the Spending Record and ask the client:

- What categories do they seem to be managing well?
- In what areas can they exert a little more control?

4 minutes

COMPLETING THE SPENDING PLAN

In order to complete the Spending Plan with the client, you can use:

➤ Some of the information obtained when you reviewed the Client Profile with your client, and the new data obtained from your client's action item from the first meeting, the Spending Record.

Look at the Spending Record with your client and ask them what they've discovered about their expenses.

➤ What categories do they seem to be managing well?

In what areas can they exert a little more control?

Let's look at a Spending Record begun by the Olsens on pages 81 and 82.

Participant's Guide, pages 81–82.

Notice that this form contains two weeks of spending information that they have collected since the first meeting.

What categories do they appear to be managing well?

Answer: Going out, which is zero.

Remember from their profile and the first meeting that they really needed some time alone? Their counselor would ask them if they are accomplishing this without spending money. If so, he would want to really affirm them.

In what areas does it appear that they need to exert a little more control?

NOTES

SESSION FIVE

Recommended Order for the Use of Income for Red Cases

- Give—_____

  A Christian should:
  - Desire to be at (or even beyond) the tithe

  If they aren't at the tithe, they should:
  - Begin giving something

  - Begin to develop a plan for getting there

- Save—a little

- Debt—_____ repayment

- Lifestyle—spartan

Completing the Spending Plan Worksheet

Use:

- Information obtained when you reviewed the Client Profile

- New data obtained from the Spending Record

Look at the Spending Record and ask the client:

- What categories do they seem to be managing well?

- In what areas can they exert a little more control?

Olsens' Spending Record (2 Weeks of Data)

Spending Record

Month __May__

	Transportation		Household						Professional Services	Entertainment		
	Gas, etc.	Maint/ Repair	Groceries	Clothes	Gifts	Household Items	Personal	Other		Going Out	Travel	Other
(1) Spending Plan												
	24	400	87	65	35	14	9	40	316			15
	17		63	45	40	22	16					5
			110			19	45					
			90									
			15									
(2) Total												
(3) (Over)/Under												
(4) Last Month YTD												
(5) Total Year to Date												

Daily Variable Expenses

| ✗ | ✗ | ✗ | ✗ | ✗ | ✗ | ✗ | ✗ | ✗ | ✗ | ✗ | ✗ | ✗ | ✗ | 15 | 16 | 17 | 18 | 19 | 20 | 21 | 22 | 23 | 24 | 26 | 27 | 28 | 29 | 30 | 31 |

- Use this page to record expenses that tend to be daily, variable expenses—often the hardest to control.
- Keep receipts throughout the day and record them at the end of the day.
- Total each category at the end of the month (line 2) and compare to the Spending Plan (line 1). Subtracting line 2 from line 1 gives you an (over) or under the budget figure for that month (line 3).
- To verify that you have made each day's entry, cross out the number at the bottom of the page that corresponds to that day's date.
- Optional: If you wish to monitor your progress as you go through the year, you can keep cumulative totals in lines 4 and 5.

Olsens' Spending Record (2 Weeks of Data)

Spending Record

Month __May__

	Giving		Savings	Debt			Housing				Auto	Insurance		Misc. Cash Exp.
	Church	Other		Credit Cards	Educ.	Other	Mort./Rent	Maint.	Util.	Other	Pmts.	Auto/Home	Life/Med.	
(1) Spending Plan														
				137		20	1236	100	85 (elec.)			62		150
				18					135 (gas)					100
									13 (water)					
(2) Total														
(3) (Over)/Under														
(4) Last Mo. YTD														
(5) This Mo. YTD														

Monthly Regular Expenses (generally paid by check once a month)

- This page allows you to record major monthly expenses for which you typically write just one or two checks per month.
- Entries can be recorded as the checks are written (preferably) or by referring back to the check ledger at a convenient time.
- Total each category at the end of the month (line 2) and compare to the Spending Plan (line 1). Subtracting line 2 from line 1 gives you an (over) or under the budget figure for that month (line 3).
- Use the "Monthly Assessment" section to reflect on the future actions that will be helpful in staying on course.

Monthly Assessment

Area	(Over)/Under	Reason	Future Action

Areas of Victory _____

Areas to Watch _____

Possible responses:

- Auto repair is an area in which they ran into trouble. This is an area about which you'd want to ask and show sympathy for the client.

- Groceries appear high for a family of three.

- Clothes may be high, but it's hard to tell after just two weeks.

- Miscellaneous Cash Expenditures seems high. It looks like they started with $150 but had to go back and get an additional $100.

Now that we've begun to collect some data on the Olsens' spending, let's look at page 83 and discuss their Spending Plan. In many cases we'll need more than two weeks of data; but for illustrative purposes let's move ahead and draft a plan for the Olsens.

Here is the first draft of their Spending Plan. Their counselor, Roger, coached them on how to complete it, but he had them fill it out. Be sure that you do the same with your clients so that they understand and take ownership of their budget.

Once they have filled out all the expenses on the worksheet, they should complete the box at the bottom right-hand corner of the form. Looking at Mark and Carol's form, you can see from this box that their monthly expenses exceed income by $211.

For many clients, their expenses will initially exceed their income. Let's look at how we can help them adjust the Spending Plan.

Turn to page 84.

NOTES

Olsens' First-Draft Spending Plan
SPENDING PLAN

EARNINGS/INCOME PER MONTH		TOTALS
Salary #1 (net take-home)	4494	
Salary #2 (net take-home)		
Other (less taxes)		
TOTAL MONTHLY INCOME		$ 4494

% GUIDE

1. GIVING		$ 50
Church	50	
OTHER CONTRIBUTIONS		

2. SAVING	5–10%	$ 200
EMERGENCY	200	
REPLACEMENT		
LONG TERM		

3. DEBT	0–10%	$ 357
CREDIT CARDS:		
VISA		
Master Card	137	
Discover	18	
American Express		
Gas Cards		
Department Stores		
EDUCATION LOANS		
OTHER LOANS:		
Bank Loans	182	
Credit Union		
Family/Friends		
Other	20 (Hospital)	

4. HOUSING	25–38%	$ 1622
MORTGAGE/TAXES/RENT	1236	
MAINTENANCE/REPAIRS	50	
UTILITIES:		
Electric	80	
Gas	100	
Water	13	
Trash	13	
Telephone/Internet	100	
Cable TV	30	
Other		

5. AUTO/TRANSP.	12–15%	$ 228
CAR PAYMENTS/LICENSE	8	
GAS & BUS/TRAIN/PARKING	120	
OIL/LUBE/MAINTENANCE	100	

6. INSURANCE (Paid by you)	5%	$ 212
AUTO	62	
HOMEOWNERS		
LIFE	42	
MEDICAL/DENTAL	108	
Other		

7. HOUSEHOLD/PERSONAL	15–25%	$ 1090
GROCERIES	550	
CLOTHES/DRY CLEANING	100	
GIFTS	110	
HOUSEHOLD ITEMS	80	
PERSONAL:		
Liquor/Tobacco		
Cosmetics	40	
Barber/Beauty	75	
OTHER:		
Books/Magazines	30	
Allowances		
Music Lessons		
Personal Technology	30	
Education	35	
Miscellaneous	40	

8. ENTERTAINMENT	5–10%	$ 330
GOING OUT:		
Meals	40	
Movies/Events	20	
Baby-sitting	25	
TRAVEL (VACATION/TRIPS)	200	
OTHER:		
Fitness/Sports	25	
Hobbies		
Media Rental	20	
Other		

9. PROF. SERVICES	5–15%	$ 316
CHILD CARE		
MEDICAL/DENTAL/PRESC.	316	
OTHER		
Legal		
Counseling		
Professional Dues		

10. MISC. SMALL CASH EXPENDITURES	2–3%	$ 300
TOTAL EXPENSES		$ 4705

TOTAL MONTHLY INCOME	$ 4494
LESS TOTAL EXPENSES	$ 4705
INCOME OVER/(UNDER) EXPENSES	$ (211)

* This is a % of total monthly income. These are guidelines only and may be different for individual situations. However, there should be good rationale for a significant variance.

5 minutes

ADJUST THE SPENDING PLAN

Participant's Guide, page 84.

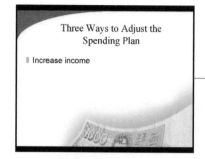

Three Ways to Adjust the Spending Plan

▌ Increase income

There are three ways to adjust the Spending Plan.

➤ The client can increase income.

Under most circumstances, this isn't the recommended approach. Taking on a second job or asking another family member to begin working may provide some extra money in the short term. But it might also add stress and fatigue to an already tense situation. In addition, one would have to make a relatively large amount with that second salary to have a little net income after taxes and additional expenses. More importantly, simply increasing income does not, in most cases, deal with the root issue of why spending is exceeding income. Until that issue has been solved, having more income will probably only lead to more spending and not solve the problem.

➤ The second way to adjust the Spending Plan is to sell assets to pay off some debt.

It's a short-term approach that may give the client a jump-start toward balancing the budget and reducing debt, but it's not a long-term solution. Again, it doesn't get to the root of why spending is exceeding income. If that doesn't change, then debt will soon build back up.

Note that, occasionally, a financial burden can be eased by drawing on the cash value of a life insurance policy or retirement plan. These options should be approached with caution and are explained in more detail in the "Drawing on Assets" article in the Appendix on page 171.

NOTES

Adjust the Spending Plan

Three ways to adjust:

- Increase income

- Sell assets

- Reduce _____

Reducing Expenses:

- Is this an optional expense that can be eliminated? Look in:

  ○ Household/personal

  ○ Entertainment

  ○ Professional services

- Is this a _____ expense that can be controlled and reduced? Look at:

  ○ Utilities

  ○ Groceries

  ○ Other household items.

- Is this an expense that has wrongly been assumed as being "fixed"? Consider:

  ○ Mortgage or rent

  ○ Car payments

The final way, and our recommended approach, is to reduce EXPENSES.

The key is for the client to live within their existing income.

To have your clients reduce expenses, they need to make adjustments to the Spending Plan. Work through the plan with your client, carefully looking at each category.

In reviewing the spending categories, ask the following questions:

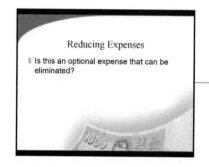

Reducing Expenses

- Is this an optional expense that can be eliminated?

Is this an optional expense that can be eliminated? Good places to look for these are in the household/personal, entertainment, and professional services categories.

Is this a VARIABLE expense that can be controlled and reduced? Look at utilities, groceries, and other household items.

Is this an expense that has wrongly been assumed as being "fixed"? Costs such as mortgage or rent and car payments are "fixed" only if the client continues to live where they are and drive what they do.

They may need to consider downsizing living quarters or renting out a room. Is there a way to eliminate the "fixed" cost of two cars by finding a creative way to get by with one?

In the case of the Olsens, they agreed that a number of expenses could be lowered. You can see this reflected on their adjusted Spending Plan on page 85.

Look at groceries under Household/Personal. Although their child requires a special diet, they still determined that they could cut down on the cost of groceries for themselves by doing more meal planning.

NOTES

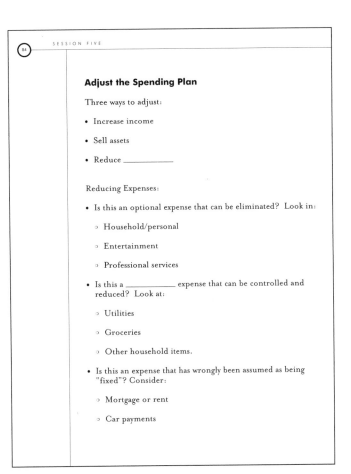

Adjust the Spending Plan

Three ways to adjust:

- Increase income

- Sell assets

- Reduce _____

Reducing Expenses:

- Is this an optional expense that can be eliminated? Look in:

  ○ Household/personal

  ○ Entertainment

  ○ Professional services

- Is this a _____ expense that can be controlled and reduced? Look at:

  ○ Utilities

  ○ Groceries

  ○ Other household items.

- Is this an expense that has wrongly been assumed as being "fixed"? Consider:

  ○ Mortgage or rent

  ○ Car payments

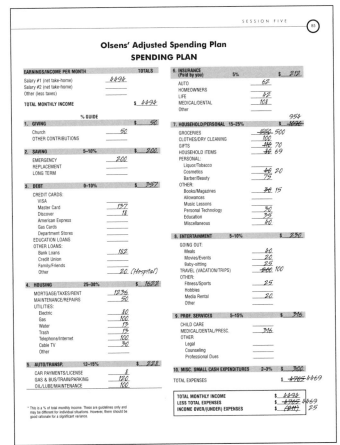

Olsens' Adjusted Spending Plan
SPENDING PLAN

EARNINGS/INCOME PER MONTH		TOTALS
Salary #1 (net take-home)	4494	
Salary #2 (net take-home)		
Other (less taxes)		
TOTAL MONTHLY INCOME		$ 4494

	% GUIDE	
1. GIVING		$ 50
Church	50	
OTHER CONTRIBUTIONS		
2. SAVING	5–10%	$ 200
EMERGENCY	200	
REPLACEMENT		
LONG TERM		
3. DEBT	0–10%	$ 357
CREDIT CARDS:		
VISA		
Master Card	137	
Discover	18	
American Express		
Gas Cards		
Department Stores		
EDUCATION LOANS		
OTHER LOANS:		
Bank Loans	182	
Credit Union		
Family/Friends		
Other	20 (Hospital)	
4. HOUSING	25–38%	$ 1622
MORTGAGE/TAXES/RENT	1236	
MAINTENANCE/REPAIRS	50	
UTILITIES:		
Electric	80	
Gas	100	
Water	13	
Trash	13	
Telephone/Internet	100	
Cable TV	30	
Other		
5. AUTO/TRANSP.	12–15%	$ 228
CAR PAYMENTS/LICENSE	8	
GAS & BUS/TRAIN/PARKING	120	
OIL/LUBE/MAINTENANCE	100	

6. INSURANCE (Paid by you)	5%	$ 212
AUTO	62	
HOMEOWNERS		
LIFE	42	
MEDICAL/DENTAL	108	
Other		
		954
7. HOUSEHOLD/PERSONAL	15–25%	$ ~~1096~~
GROCERIES	~~550~~ 500	
CLOTHES/DRY CLEANING	100	
GIFTS	~~110~~ 70	
HOUSEHOLD ITEMS	~~80~~ 69	
PERSONAL:		
Liquor/Tobacco		
Cosmetics	~~40~~ 20	
Barber/Beauty	75	
OTHER:		
Books/Magazines	~~30~~ 15	
Allowances		
Music Lessons		
Personal Technology	30	
Education	35	
Miscellaneous	60	
8. ENTERTAINMENT	5–10%	$ 230
GOING OUT:		
Meals	60	
Movies/Events	20	
Baby-sitting	25	
TRAVEL (VACATION/TRIPS)	~~200~~ 100	
OTHER:		
Fitness/Sports	25	
Hobbies		
Media Rental	20	
Other		
9. PROF. SERVICES	5–15%	$ 316
CHILD CARE		
MEDICAL/DENTAL/PRESC.	316	
OTHER		
Legal		
Counseling		
Professional Dues		
10. MISC. SMALL CASH EXPENDITURES	2–3%	$ 300
TOTAL EXPENSES		$ ~~4705~~ 4469

TOTAL MONTHLY INCOME	$ 4494
LESS TOTAL EXPENSES	$ ~~4705~~ 4469
INCOME OVER/(UNDER) EXPENSES	$ ~~(211)~~ 25

* This is a % of total monthly income. These are guidelines only and may be different for individual situations. However, there should be good rationale for a significant variance.

SESSION FIVE

Under Household/Personal they also determined that they could better control their spending on gifts, household items, cosmetics, and books and magazines.

Another area they decided was high was travel—under Entertainment. Although the client had not indicated any travel expenses on their profile or Spending Record form, they had determined that their annual vacation was one cause of their credit card debt. They had decided to budget money for travel on a monthly basis. Although this is a good strategy, after further discussion they agreed that they could take a less lavish vacation this year.

After the Olsens made these changes, which actually lowered expenses to $25 less than income, the counselor had one more important recommendation.

Although it was admirable for the Olsens to set a savings goal of $200, they would be much farther ahead by moving some of that savings money into debt repayment.

Before we consider the counselor's recommendation about that, let's take a little bit of time and talk about debt reduction.

Turn to page 86.

4 minutes

DEBT REDUCTION

Participant's Guide, page 86.

It is very helpful to educate your clients about what happens if they make only the minimum monthly payments on their debts. This information can have a dramatic impact on our clients and serve as a great motivator for them!

NOTES

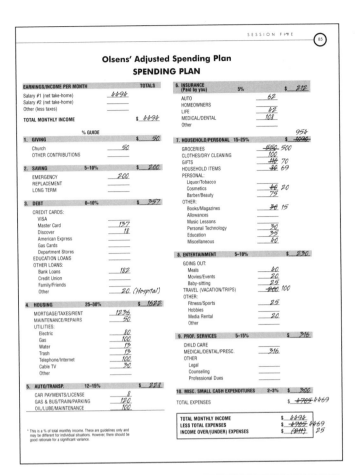

Olsens' Adjusted Spending Plan
SPENDING PLAN

EARNINGS/INCOME PER MONTH		TOTALS
Salary #1 (net take-home)	4494	
Salary #2 (net take-home)		
Other (less taxes)		
TOTAL MONTHLY INCOME		$ 4494

% GUIDE

1. GIVING — $ 50
Church	50
OTHER CONTRIBUTIONS	

2. SAVING 5–10% — $ 200
EMERGENCY	200
REPLACEMENT	
LONG TERM	

3. DEBT 0–10% — $ 357
CREDIT CARDS:	
VISA	
Master Card	137
Discover	18
American Express	
Gas Cards	
Department Stores	
EDUCATION LOANS	
OTHER LOANS:	
Bank Loans	182
Credit Union	
Family/Friends	
Other	20 (Hospital)

4. HOUSING 25–38% — $ 1622
MORTGAGE/TAXES/RENT	1236
MAINTENANCE/REPAIRS	50
UTILITIES:	
Electric	80
Gas	100
Water	13
Trash	13
Telephone/Internet	100
Cable TV	30
Other	

5. AUTO/TRANSP. 12–15% — $ 228
CAR PAYMENTS/LICENSE	8
GAS & BUS/TRAIN/PARKING	120
OIL/LUBE/MAINTENANCE	100

6. INSURANCE (Paid by you) 5% — $ 212
AUTO	62
HOMEOWNERS	
LIFE	42
MEDICAL/DENTAL	108
Other	

7. HOUSEHOLD/PERSONAL 15–25% — $ 1096 / 956
GROCERIES	550 / 500
CLOTHES/DRY CLEANING	100
GIFTS	110 / 70
HOUSEHOLD ITEMS	56 / 69
PERSONAL:	
Liquor/Tobacco	
Cosmetics	46 / 20
Barber/Beauty	75
OTHER:	
Books/Magazines	30 / 15
Allowances	
Music Lessons	
Personal Technology	30
Education	35
Miscellaneous	40

8. ENTERTAINMENT 5–10% — $ 230
GOING OUT:	
Meals	60
Movies/Events	20
Baby-sitting	25
TRAVEL (VACATION/TRIPS)	200 / 100
OTHER:	
Fitness/Sports	25
Hobbies	
Media Rental	20
Other	

9. PROF. SERVICES 5–15% — $ 316
CHILD CARE	
MEDICAL/DENTAL/PRESC.	316
OTHER	
Legal	
Counseling	
Professional Dues	

10. MISC. SMALL CASH EXPENDITURES 2–3% — $ 300

TOTAL EXPENSES — $ 4705 / 4469

TOTAL MONTHLY INCOME	$	4494
LESS TOTAL EXPENSES	$	4705 / 4469
INCOME OVER/(UNDER) EXPENSES	$	(211) / 25

* This is a % of total monthly income. These are guidelines only and may be different for individual situations. However, there should be good rationale for a significant variance.

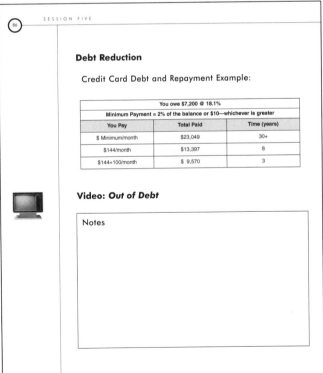

Debt Reduction

Credit Card Debt and Repayment Example:

You owe $7,200 @ 18.1%		
Minimum Payment = 2% of the balance or $10—whichever is greater		
You Pay	Total Paid	Time (years)
$ Minimum/month	$23,049	30+
$144/month	$13,397	8
$144+100/month	$ 9,570	3

Video: *Out of Debt*

Notes

Unfortunately, some people believe that if they're making the minimum monthly payments on their credit cards or other debts, they are keeping up with their debt. Nothing could be further from the truth! The minimum monthly payment is a calculation guaranteed to keep interest payments flowing into the hands of the lenders, with only a tiny fraction of the payment applied to the debt's principal.

Let's look at a debt payment example from both a time and money perspective. This example shows the potential long-term bondage that can result from credit card debt.

Debt Example

You owe $7200 @ 18.1%
(Minimum Payment = 2% of the balance or
$10/month - whichever is greater)

According to the Consumer Federation of America, this represents the average credit card debt owed per family in the United States in 1998, which was $7,200 with an average interest on that debt of 18.1 percent. This example assumes a fairly common minimum payment per month of 2 percent of the balance or $10, whichever is greater.

▶ Let's assume your client follows the credit card company's plan and pays only the minimum payment each month. The first month they pay 2 percent of $7,200 or $144. Over time, as they make some progress on reducing the $7,200, the minimum payment decreases somewhat . . . to $140, then $135, etc.

Following that plan, their repayment will take over thirty years and amount to over $23,000.

▶ On the other hand, let's look at what happens if they pay $144 a month until the loan is completely repaid. That is, they don't decrease their payments when the credit card company says they can. It might take some discipline, but their repayment drops to a little more than $13,000 and the debt gets paid off in ninety-four months or a little under eight years! That's a huge step in the right direction . . . but let's look at an even better possibility.

NOTES

Debt Reduction

Credit Card Debt and Repayment Example:

You owe $7,200 @ 18.1%		
Minimum Payment = 2% of the balance or $10—whichever is greater		
You Pay	Total Paid	Time (years)
$ Minimum/month	$23,049	30+
$144/month	$13,397	8
$144+100/month	$ 9,570	3

Video: *Out of Debt*

Notes

If they are able to pay an extra $100 a month, on top of the $144, the total repayment drops to $9,570 and is done in only forty months, a little over three years.

There are two important comparisons in this illustration. First is the $9,500 repayment vs. $23,000, which is pretty significant. The second and even more important one, however, is getting out from the bondage of debt in only three years vs. thirty-plus years!

8 minutes

Video: *Out of Debt*

Let's stop for a moment and take a look at what some Good $ense clients have to say. This video goes beyond the numbers and helps us truly understand the power of debt reduction in helping our clients achieve financial freedom.

View video: *Out of Debt*

Wrap-up
Powerful, isn't it? Open your clients' eyes to the truth about just making minimum payments. Just making minimum payments will keep them in bondage for a long, long time. Motivate them to accelerate their debt repayment.

5 minutes

Debt Reduction Plan

Participant's Guide, page 87.

Now, let's talk about how to help people become debt free by developing a Debt Reduction Plan.

The Debt Reduction Plan we use is designed to pay more than the minimum monthly payment for reasons we've just discussed.

NOTES

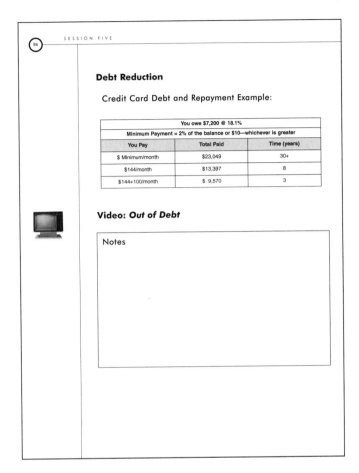

Debt Reduction

Credit Card Debt and Repayment Example:

You owe $7,200 @ 18.1%		
Minimum Payment = 2% of the balance or $10—whichever is greater		
You Pay	Total Paid	Time (years)
$ Minimum/month	$23,049	30+
$144/month	$13,397	8
$144+100/month	$ 9,570	3

Video: *Out of Debt*

Notes

Sample Debt Reduction Plan

Item	Amount Owed	Interest	Minimum Monthly Payment	Additional Payment $ 150	Payment Plan and Pay-off Dates				
					3 Months	6 Months	15 Months	22 Months	26 Months
Sears	$372	18.0	$15	$165	Paid!				
Doctor	$550	0	$20	$20	$185	Paid!			
Visa	$1980	19.0	$40	$40	$40	$225	Paid!		
Master	$2369	16.9	$50	$50	$50	$50	$275	Paid!	
Auto	$7200	6.9	$259	$259	$259	$259	$259	$534	Paid!
Total	$12,471		$384	$534	$534	$534	$534	$534	0

- The first and second columns list to whom the debt is owed and the amount owed. Debts are listed in the order of lowest to highest amount.
- The third and fourth columns list the interest rate and the minimum monthly payment for each debt.
- The fifth column indicates the amount of additional payment above the minimum that can be made and adds that amount to the minimum payment for the first (smallest) debt listed.
- The remaining columns show how, as each debt is paid, the payment for it is rolled down to the next debt. Pay-off dates can be calculated in advance or simply recorded as they are achieved.

Our plan attacks the debts from smallest to largest—regardless of the interest rate. By attacking the smallest debt first, we can retire some debt quickly. Your clients can celebrate a victory sooner rather than later. This victory is of enormous psychological value and becomes a strong motivator for continuing the plan. The differential in total interest paid is minimal in most cases.

Let's look at the sample Debt Reduction Plan on page 87.

First, it is helpful to understand that this plan is a bit more complex than the other forms we've used. Note that the counselor, rather than the client, should complete this form.

Let's walk through this sample, and then you'll have a chance to complete a plan.

Here's how it's done:

- First, list all creditors in the first column. Include all debt except mortgage. You want to list these in order from the lowest balance owed to the highest balance owed. Remember, we attack the smallest debt first. If there are many creditors, use two worksheets, or draw a horizontal line to split each row in half.

- List the total amount owed and the interest rate for each debt in the next two columns.

- In the next column write in the minimum monthly payment required by each creditor.

- Total the "Amount Owed" and the "Minimum Monthly Payment" columns and write the results in the "Total" row.

- Now, after analyzing their monthly spending habits, your clients should have a pretty good idea of how much extra money per month they can put toward debt retirement. Write this amount in the blank under "additional payment."

NOTES

_____

_____

_____

_____

_____

_____

_____

_____

_____

_____

_____

_____

_____

_____

_____

_____

_____

_____

_____

_____

_____

_____

_____

Sample Debt Reduction Plan

Item	Amount Owed	Interest	Minimum Monthly Payment	Additional Payment $ 150	Payment Plan and Pay-off Dates				
					3 Months	6 Months	15 Months	22 Months	26 Months
Sears	$372	18.0	$15	$165	Paid!				
Doctor	$550	0	$20	$20	$185	Paid!			
Visa	$1980	19.0	$40	$40	$40	$225	Paid!		
Master	$2369	16.9	$50	$50	$50	$50	$275	Paid!	
Auto	$7200	6.9	$259	$259	$259	$259	$259	$534	Paid!
Total	$12,471		$384	$534	$534	$534	$534	$534	0

- The first and second columns list to whom the debt is owed and the amount owed. Debts are listed in the order of lowest to highest amount.
- The third and fourth columns list the interest rate and the minimum monthly payment for each debt.
- The fifth column indicates the amount of additional payment above the minimum that can be made and adds that amount to the minimum payment for the first (smallest) debt listed.
- The remaining columns show how, as each debt is paid, the payment for it is rolled down to the next debt. Pay-off dates can be calculated in advance or simply recorded as they are achieved.

- Add this extra amount to the minimum monthly payment amount for the first debt, and write the result in the "Additional Payment" column. In the sample, the clients are putting up an extra $150 per month, so when we add that to the $15 minimum monthly payment for the department store account, that equals $165. This debt is currently in what we call "acceleration mode."

- Each time a debt is retired, add that entire payment amount to the next debt.

- Let's see how this affects the second debt in our sample. Once the Sears debt is paid off (in less than three months), we roll that $165 payment into the doctor's debt, paying $185 per month until that debt is gone.

- Can you see what's going to happen as we move forward? As we retire each debt, the amount freed up rolls into the next debt, creating an amazing snowball effect!

- The approximate pay-off times can be estimated by arithmetic or more precisely by using a computer spreadsheet. This spreadsheet is available at the Good $ense web site at www.GoodSenseMinistry.com.

Now you get to try creating a Debt Reduction Plan on your own. Please turn to page 88.

Individual Activity: *Debt Reduction Plan*

Participant's Guide, page 88.

Objective:
For participants to practice creating a Debt Reduction Plan for the Olsens.

16 minutes

Individual Activity:

Debt Reduction Plan

NOTES

_____

_____

_____

_____

_____

_____

_____

_____

_____

_____

_____

_____

_____

_____

_____

_____

_____

_____

_____

_____

_____

_____

Sample Debt Reduction Plan

Item	Amount Owed	Interest	Minimum Monthly Payment	Additional Payment $ 150	Payment Plan and Pay-off Dates				
					3 Months	6 Months	15 Months	22 Months	26 Months
Sears	$372	18.0	$15	$165	Paid!				
Doctor	$550	0	$20	$20	$185	Paid!			
Visa	$1980	19.0	$40	$40	$40	$225	Paid!		
Master	$2369	16.9	$50	$50	$50	$50	$275	Paid!	
Auto	$7200	6.9	$259	$259	$259	$259	$259	$534	Paid!
Total	$12,471		$384	$534	$534	$534	$534	$534	0

- The first and second columns list to whom the debt is owed and the amount owed. Debts are listed in the order of lowest to highest amount.
- The third and fourth columns list the interest rate and the minimum monthly payment for each debt.
- The fifth column indicates the amount of additional payment above the minimum that can be made and adds that amount to the minimum payment for the first (smallest) debt listed.
- The remaining columns show how, as each debt is paid, the payment for it is rolled down to the next debt. Pay-off dates can be calculated in advance or simply recorded as they are achieved.

SESSION FIVE

87

Individual Activity: *Debt Reduction Plan*

Directions

Complete a Debt Reduction Plan for the Olsens assuming they decided to move $150 out of their goal for savings—as well as use the $50 they squeezed out of expenses—to apply an additional $200 toward debt repayment. Use the blank worksheet on the following page. Don't worry about calculating the approximate pay-off dates at this time.

The Olsens have the following debts:

- A loan from relatives of $3,400 at no interest and no monthly payments.

- A hospital debt of $1,000 at no interest and monthly payments of $20.

- A Mastercard with a $4,417 balance at 17.65 percent interest and minimum monthly payments of $137.

- An bank loan of $7,954 at 13 percent interest and a minimum monthly payment of $182.

- A Discover card with a $265 balance at 19.8 percent interest and a minimum monthly payment of $18.

Directions:

Complete a Debt Reduction Plan for the Olsens assuming they decided to move $150 out of their goal for savings—as well as use the $50 they squeezed out of expenses—to apply an additional $200 toward debt repayment. Use the blank worksheet on the following page. Don't worry about calculating the approximate pay-off dates at this time.

The Olsens have the following debts:

- A loan from relatives of $3,400 at no interest and no required monthly payments.

- A hospital debt of $1,000 at no interest and monthly payments of $20.

- A MasterCard with a $4,417 balance at 17.65 percent interest and minimum monthly payments of $137.

- A bank loan of $7,954 at 13 percent and a minimum monthly payment of $182.

- A Discover card with a $265 balance at 19.8 percent interest and a minimum monthly payment of $18.

You'll have 10 minutes to do this exercise.

Call the group back together after 10 minutes.

Wrap-up

Let's compare your Debt Reduction Plans to the answer key.

In this activity, we did not calculate the approximate pay-off dates due to limited time. To calculate pay-off dates, use the spreadsheet on the Good $ense web site at www.GoodSenseMinistry.com.

NOTES

Individual Activity: *Debt Reduction Plan*

Directions

Complete a Debt Reduction Plan for the Olsens assuming they decided to move $150 out of their goal for savings—as well as use the $50 they squeezed out of expenses—to apply an additional $200 toward debt repayment. Use the blank worksheet on the following page. Don't worry about calculating the approximate pay-off dates at this time.

The Olsens have the following debts:

- A loan from relatives of $3,400 at no interest and no monthly payments.

- A hospital debt of $1,000 at no interest and monthly payments of $20.

- A Mastercard with a $4,417 balance at 17.65 percent interest and minimum monthly payments of $137.

- An bank loan of $7,954 at 13 percent interest and a minimum monthly payment of $182.

- A Discover card with a $265 balance at 19.8 percent interest and a minimum monthly payment of $18.

Debt Reduction Plan for the Olsens

Item	Amount Owed	Interest	Minimum Monthly Payment	Additional Payment $____	Payment Plan and Pay-off Dates				
Total									

- The first and second columns list to whom the debt is owed and the amount owed. Debts are listed in the order of lowest to highest amount.
- The third and fourth columns list the interest rate and the minimum monthly payment for each debt.
- The fifth column indicates the amount of additional payment above the minimum that can be made and adds that amount to the minimum payment for the first (smallest) debt listed.
- The remaining columns show how, as each debt is paid, the payment for it is rolled down to the next debt. Pay-off dates can be calculated in advance or simply recorded as they are achieved.

Item	Amount Owed	Interest	Minimum Monthly Payment	Additional Payment $ 200	Approximate Pay-off Date				
					1 Months	5 Months	17 Months	18 Months	30 Months
Discount	265	19.8	18	218	Paid				
Hospital	1000	–	20	20	234	Paid			
MC	4417	17.65	137	137	137	375	Paid		
Bank	7954	13.0	192	192	192	192	557	Paid	
Relatives	3400	–	–	–	–	–	–	557	PAID!
Total	17,08	–	357	557	$554	$554	$554	$554	0

If you have Internet access in your training room, you may wish to demonstrate the use of the spreadsheet.

Strictly following the rule of first paying lowest to highest debt, this is the proper Debt Reduction Plan. However, let's look at an exception to the rule that Ralph made in the Olsens' situation.

Looking at the plan Ralph developed, you'll notice that one of the interest-free debts was of such magnitude—$3,400—that paying it off before MasterCard and the bank would not have resulted in a significantly quicker payoff and would have resulted in a fair amount of additional interest being paid on the other debts. Thus, it was relegated to last on the list. On the other hand, a smaller interest-free debt of $1,000 was not moved since it was able to be paid off in just four months after the debt before it.

Turn to page 90.

Before we look at the Olsens' final adjusted Spending Plan, I'd like to point out some other keys to debt reduction that you can share with your client:

Participant's Guide, page 90.

Other Keys to Debt Reduction

▌ Be sure the plan is realistic.

➤ Be sure the plan is realistic.

That's why it's important for clients to get a grip on their monthly cash flow before you spend the time creating the Debt Reduction Plan. We need to know that the extra amount we're applying is doable for the clients and that the minimum monthly payments can be made on the accounts that are not in acceleration mode.

 ➤ Incur no NEW debt!

NOTES

_____

_____

_____

_____

_____

_____

_____

_____

_____

_____

_____

_____

_____

_____

_____

_____

_____

_____

_____

_____

_____

_____

_____

Debt Reduction Plan for the Olsens

Item	Amount Owed	Interest	Minimum Monthly Payment	Additional Payment $_____	Payment Plan and Pay-off Dates					
Total										

- The first and second columns list to whom the debt is owed and the amount owed. Debts are listed in the order of lowest to highest amount.
- The third and fourth columns list the interest rate and the minimum monthly payment for each debt.
- The fifth column indicates the amount of additional payment above the minimum that can be made and adds that amount to the minimum payment for the first (smallest) debt listed.
- The remaining columns show how, as each debt is paid, the payment for it is rolled down to the next debt. Pay-off dates can be calculated in advance or simply recorded as they are achieved.

Other Keys to Debt Reduction:

- Be sure the plan is realistic.

- Incur no _____ debt!

- Modify the plan when unexpected windfalls or pay raises come into play.

- As each debt is retired, _____!

The plan assumes that no more debt is incurred. Point out to the client both how important this is and what a huge achievement in and of itself it will represent. If they do no more than stop going further into debt and make just small progress in reducing existing debt, they will have made a 180-degree turn . . . and that is huge!

 ● Modify the plan as necessary when unexpected windfalls or pay raises come into play.

Encourage your clients to apply all such bonuses toward debt repayment. A single big payment can knock years off the debt repayment schedule!

 ● As each debt is retired, CELEBRATE!

Record the dates on the Debt Reduction Plan grid, and congratulate your clients. Say a prayer of thanks and rejoice!

You may also want to give your clients a small, tangible token of the occasion: a card, a personal note, or a small gift, perhaps a "Payday" candy bar!

Here's one final note on debt reduction. In a few extreme cases, clients are not able to make even minimum payments due to situations like loss of a job or family illness. If this applies to your client, they may need assistance in communicating with creditors. There is information on this topic in the Appendix on page 147.

Now, let's return to the Olsens' Spending Plan for a moment. On page 90 you can see their "final" plan.

Participant's Guide, page 90.

It reflects the additional changes we discussed for savings and debt and a $25 reduction in "Miscellaneous Small Cash Expenditures."

NOTES

_____

_____

_____

_____

_____

_____

_____

_____

_____

_____

_____

_____

_____

_____

_____

_____

_____

_____

_____

_____

_____

_____

_____

_____

_____

_____

_____

Other Keys to Debt Reduction:

- Be sure the plan is realistic.

- Incur no _____ debt!

- Modify the plan when unexpected windfalls or pay raises come into play.

- As each debt is retired, _____!

Olsens' "Final" Spending Plan
SPENDING PLAN

EARNINGS/INCOME PER MONTH	TOTALS
Salary #1 (net take-home)	4494
Salary #2 (net take-home)	
Other (less taxes)	
TOTAL MONTHLY INCOME	$ 4494

% GUIDE		
1. GIVING		$ 50
Church	50	
OTHER CONTRIBUTIONS		
		50
2. SAVING 5–10%		$ 800 50
EMERGENCY	800 50	
REPLACEMENT		
LONG TERM		
		557
3. DEBT 0–10%		$ 557
CREDIT CARDS:		
VISA		
Master Card	137	
Discover	16 218	
American Express		
Gas Cards		
Department Stores		
EDUCATION LOANS		
OTHER LOANS:		
Bank Loans	182	
Credit Union		
Family/Friends		
Other	20 (Hospital)	
4. HOUSING 25–38%		$ 1622
MORTGAGE/TAXES/RENT	1236	
MAINTENANCE/REPAIRS	50	
UTILITIES:		
Electric	80	
Gas	100	
Water	13	
Trash	13	
Telephone/Internet	100	
Cable TV	30	
Other		
5. AUTO/TRANSP. 12–15%		$ 228
CAR PAYMENTS/LICENSE	8	
GAS & BUS/TRAIN/PARKING	120	
OIL/LUBE/MAINTENANCE	100	

6. INSURANCE (Paid by you) 5%		$ 212
AUTO	62	
HOMEOWNERS		
LIFE	42	
MEDICAL/DENTAL	108	
Other		
		954
7. HOUSEHOLD/PERSONAL 15–25%		$ 1096
GROCERIES	550 500	
CLOTHES/DRY CLEANING	100	
GIFTS	16 70	
HOUSEHOLD ITEMS	50 69	
PERSONAL:		
Liquor/Tobacco		
Cosmetics	16 20	
Barber/Beauty	75	
OTHER:		
Books/Magazines	30 15	
Allowances		
Music Lessons		
Personal Technology	30	
Education	35	
Miscellaneous	40	
8. ENTERTAINMENT 5–10%		$ 230
GOING OUT:		
Meals	60	
Movies/Events	20	
Baby-sitting	25	
TRAVEL (VACATION/TRIPS)	800 100	
OTHER:		
Fitness/Sports	25	
Hobbies		
Media Rental	20	
Other		
9. PROF. SERVICES 5–15%		$ 316
CHILD CARE		
MEDICAL/DENTAL/PRESC.	316	
OTHER		
Legal		
Counseling		
Professional Dues		
10. MISC. SMALL CASH EXPENDITURES 2–3%		$ 300 275
TOTAL EXPENSES		$ 4705 4469 4494

TOTAL MONTHLY INCOME	$ 4494
LESS TOTAL EXPENSES 4494	$ 4705 4469
INCOME OVER/(UNDER) EXPENSES –0–	$ (211) 25

* This is a % of total monthly income. These are guidelines only and may be different for individual situations. However, there should be good rationale for a significant variance.

At this point in the process, Mark and Carol have a balanced Spending Plan and a Debt Reduction Plan in hand.

Turn to page 92.

1 minute

TRANSFER THE BUDGET TO THE SPENDING RECORD

Participant's Guide, pages 93–94.

➡ Once the Spending Plan is in balance, the budget needs to be transferred to the Spending Record.

Notice that line 1 on page 93 says "Spending Plan." The counselor had the Olsens fill in the amounts their Spending Plan calls for, both monthly variable and monthly regular expenses.

You'll notice that the Spending Record combines some Spending Plan categories. For example, look at the "Going Out" category, which is under "Entertainment." This category combines the Spending Plan categories of Meals, Movies and Events, and Baby-Sitting. This was done to reduce the number of columns so that the plan would fit on one sheet.

The Olsens filled in $120 for Gas, $100 for Maintenance/Repair, $500 for Groceries, $100 for Clothes, $70 for Gifts, $69 for Household Items, etc.

Turn to page 95.

NOTES

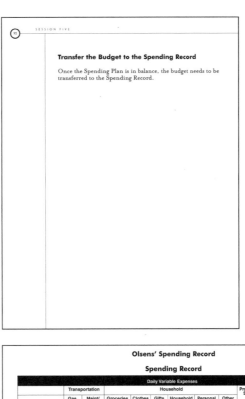

Transfer the Budget to the Spending Record

Once the Spending Plan is in balance, the budget needs to be transferred to the Spending Record.

Olsens' Spending Record

Spending Record

Month_____

Daily Variable Expenses											
	Transportation		Household						Professional Services	Entertainment		
	Gas, etc.	Maint/ Repair	Groceries	Clothes	Gifts	Household Items	Personal	Other		Going Out	Travel	Other
(1) Spending Plan	120	100	500	100	70	69	95	120	316	85	100	45
(2) Total												
(3) (Over)/Under												
(4) Last Month YTD												
(5) Total Year to Date												

1 2 3 4 5 6 7 8 9 10 11 12 13 14 15 16 17 18 19 20 21 22 23 24 25 26 27 28 29 30 31

- Use this page to record expenses that tend to be daily, variable expenses—often the hardest to control.
- Keep receipts throughout the day and record them at the end of the day.
- Total each category at the end of the month (line 2) and compare to the Spending Plan (line 1). Subtracting line 2 from line 1 gives you an (over) or under the budget figure for that month (line 3).
- To verify that you have made each day's entry, cross out the number at the bottom of the page that corresponds to that day's date.
- Optional: If you wish to monitor your progress as you go through the year, you can keep cumulative totals in lines 4 and 5.

Olsens' Spending Record

Spending Record

Month_____

Monthly Regular Expenses (generally paid by check once a month)													
	Giving		Savings	Debt			Housing				Auto	Insurance		Misc. Cash Exp.
	Church	Other		Credit Cards	Educ.	Other	Mort./Rent	Maint.	Util.	Other	Pmts.	Auto/Home	Life/Med.	
(1) Spending Plan				355	–	202	1236	50	336	–	8	62	150	275
(2) Total														
(3) (Over)/Under														
(4) Last Mo. YTD														
(5) This Mo. YTD														

- This page allows you to record major monthly expenses for which you typically write just one or two checks per month.
- Entries can be recorded as the checks are written (preferably) or by referring back to the check ledger at a convenient time.
- Total each category at the end of the month (line 2) and compare to the Spending Plan (line 1). Subtracting line 2 from line 1 gives you an (over) or under the budget figure for that month (line 3).
- Use the "Monthly Assessment" section to reflect on the future actions that will be helpful in staying on course.

Monthly Assessment

Area	(Over)/Under	Reason	Future Action

Areas of Victory _____

Areas to Watch _____

1 minute

1 minute

ENVELOPE SYSTEM

Participant's Guide, page 95.

Up to this point, we have assumed that the client will use the Spending Record form to continue keeping records. Some clients work better with the envelope record-keeping system.

In this system, envelopes are designated for monthly variable expense categories such as Groceries, Clothes, Household, Entertainment, etc. All income is deposited into a master account and, each payday, an amount of cash based upon the Spending Plan is placed in each envelope. Expenditures are then made with that cash. The amount of money in the envelope provides tangible feedback of how well the person is sticking to each expense category. For many people who have never budgeted before, this may be a good place for them to start. There is more information on the envelope system in the Appendix on page 133. Please review this system so you can share it with your clients as an alternate method of record keeping. It has worked extremely well for many individuals.

Turn to page 96.

APPLYING THE BIBLICAL FINANCIAL PRINCIPLES

Participant's Guide, page 96.

Before we move to the last step of the counseling process, we want to revisit the Biblical Financial Principles.

In discussing both the first meeting and ongoing counseling, we have focused on the strategy and the forms. Although it is difficult to fit the Biblical Financial Principles into one clear step during the counseling process, it is important to keep them in mind throughout your meetings. Our whole objective is to have the client understand and incorporate sound Biblical Financial Principles.

NOTES

_____

_____

_____

_____

_____

_____

_____

_____

_____

_____

_____

_____

_____

_____

_____

_____

_____

_____

_____

_____

_____

Envelope System

ENVELOPE SYSTEM

All Income

Master Checking Account

Checks (Fixed Expenses)

Cash

Envelopes (Variable Expenses)

Notes

Applying the Biblical Financial Principles

When a person is in crisis, they are often open to God and spiritual transformation.

Video: _Applying the Biblical Financial Principles_

Notes

Applying the Biblical Financial Principles

When a person is in crisis, he or she is often open to God and spiritual transformation.

In addition, when a person is in crisis, he or she is often open to God and spiritual transformation.

Therefore, look for opportunities to share your faith journey as well as opportunities to bring the Biblical Financial Principles into the discussion.

Let's take a look at a video and observe how Roger uses a natural opening to introduce Biblical Financial Principles into the discussion.

6 minutes

Video: *Applying the Biblical Financial Principles*

View video: *Applying the Biblical Financial Principles.*

Wrap-up

You've now seen how one counselor found openings to interject the Biblical Financial Principles into his counseling meetings. It is important to be aware of these potential opportunities as you work with your clients.

Let's now move back to the counseling process.

5 minutes

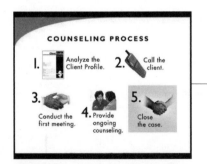

COUNSELING PROCESS

1. Analyze the Client Profile.
2. Call the client.
3. Conduct the first meeting.
4. Provide ongoing counseling.
5. Close the case.

CLOSE THE CASE

Participant's Guide, page 97.

We are at the final part of the process, close the case.

All cases, successful or not, require a Case Completion Report to close the case.

There are four criteria for pronouncing a case a success:

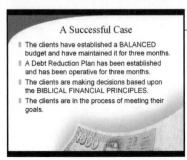

A Successful Case

- The clients have established a BALANCED budget and have maintained it for three months.
- A Debt Reduction Plan has been established and has been operative for three months.
- The clients are making decisions based upon the BIBLICAL FINANCIAL PRINCIPLES.
- The clients are in the process of meeting their goals.

The clients have established a BALANCED budget and have maintained it for three months.

A Debt Reduction Plan has been established and has been operative for three months.

NOTES

_____

_____

_____

_____

_____

_____

_____

_____

_____

_____

_____

_____

_____

_____

_____

_____

_____

_____

_____

_____

_____

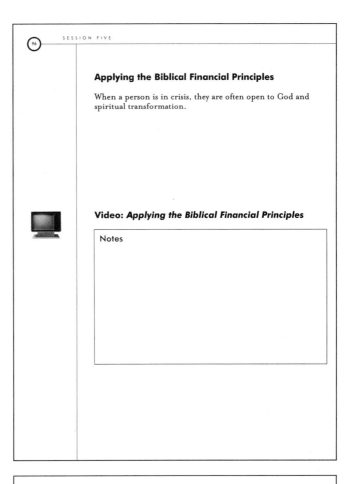

Applying the Biblical Financial Principles

When a person is in crisis, they are often open to God and spiritual transformation.

Video: _Applying the Biblical Financial Principles_

Notes

Close the Case

COUNSELING PROCESS

1. Analyze the Client Profile.

2. Call the client.

3. Conduct the first meeting.

4. Provide ongoing counseling.

5. Close the case.

The criteria for calling a case a success:

• The clients have established a _____ budget and have maintained it for three months.

• A Debt Reduction Plan has been established and has been operative for three months.

• The clients are making decisions based upon

_____ .

• The clients are in the process of meeting their goals.

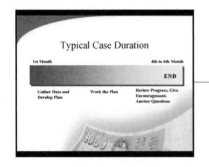

The clients are making decisions based upon the BIBLICAL FINANCIAL PRINCIPLES.

The clients are in the process of meeting their goals.

Turn to page 98.

The actual point at which a case reaches completion is decided on a case-by-case basis but typically is no longer than four to six months.

Participant's Guide, page 98.

This includes:

One to two months to gather data and get the plan in place;

One to two months to work the plan in place;

One to two months to review progress, give encouragement, and answer questions.

When the criteria we discussed are met and you feel the clients' attitudes and behaviors are on target, you may express to them your confidence that they are ready to continue on their own.

It is often very difficult for a person to make the necessary changes—often perceived as sacrifices in their mind—to get their financial house in order. As we have pointed out, it takes not only external discipline but an internal work of the Holy Spirit. As a result, it is not uncommon for more than a majority of cases to fail to meet the criteria for success as we have defined it.

NOTES

Close the Case

COUNSELING PROCESS

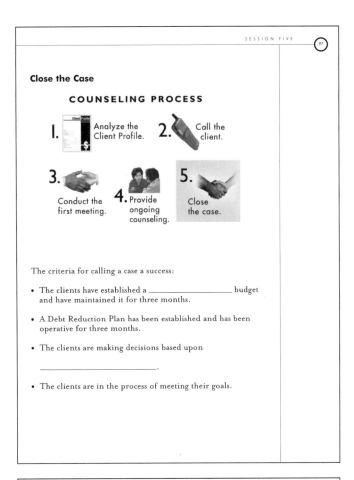

1. Analyze the Client Profile.
2. Call the client.
3. Conduct the first meeting.
4. Provide ongoing counseling.
5. Close the case.

The criteria for calling a case a success:

• The clients have established a _____ budget and have maintained it for three months.

• A Debt Reduction Plan has been established and has been operative for three months.

• The clients are making decisions based upon

_____.

• The clients are in the process of meeting their goals.

Typical Case Duration

1st Month		4th to 6th Months
Gather data and develop plan.	Work the plan.	Review progress, give encouragement, answer questions.

The typical case duration is no longer than four to six months. This includes:

• 1 to 2 months to gather data and get the plan in place

• 1 to 2 months to work the plan

• 1 to 2 months to review progress, give encouragement, and answer questions

To close a case:

• Complete the Case Completion Report

• Submit all of your Client Progress Reports to your ministry administrator along with the Case Completion Report.

When a case is not successful, you should not feel you have been a failure. You are simply confronting a very difficult situation that does not always result in success. Should that happen, we encourage you to continue to pray for the client. There have been many instances in which an unsuccessful case returns to the ministry for another try at counseling a year or more later, and at that point the client has the additional motivation to become a successful case.

Once a decision has been reached on a case, there is an additional mission you can help your clients with. Find out whether they are connected somewhere in the church. If not, provide them with information on ways to get involved so that they will have ongoing support and encouragement.

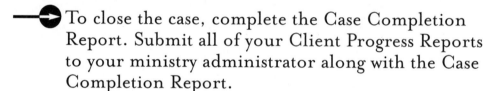 To close the case, complete the Case Completion Report. Submit all of your Client Progress Reports to your ministry administrator along with the Case Completion Report.

You may want to keep copies of your Client Progress Reports—perhaps you'll encounter a similar case in the future and will find your notes helpful at that time.

Let's take a look at a sample Case Completion Report on page 99.

Participant's Guide, page 99.

This form was completed by Roger, when the case with the Olsens was complete. The form is pretty self-explanatory. I'll give you a minute to look it over.

Pause for 1 minute or until most participants have finished reading this report.

NOTES

_____

_____

_____

_____

_____

_____

_____

_____

_____

_____

_____

_____

_____

_____

_____

_____

_____

_____

_____

_____

_____

_____

_____

_____

_____

Typical Case Duration

1st Month		4th to 6th Months
Gather data and develop plan.	Work the plan.	Review progress, give encouragement, answer questions.

The typical case duration is no longer than four to six months. This includes:

- 1 to 2 months to gather data and get the plan in place

- 1 to 2 months to work the plan

- 1 to 2 months to review progress, give encouragement, and answer questions

To close a case:

- Complete the Case Completion Report

- Submit all of your Client Progress Reports to your ministry administrator along with the Case Completion Report.

CASE COMPLETION REPORT
Good $ense Ministry

Instructions: At the completion of a case, this form should be forwarded with the Client Progress Reports to the Good $ense administrator.

Date _9/8_   Client Name _Mark and Carol Olsen_

Last date of contact _9/7_   Counselor _Roger Liston_

How terminated: ☒ In person   ☐ By telephone   ☐ No contact

Who decided: ☒ Mutual   ☐ Counselor   ☐ Client

In view of counselor:
Original problem that brought about referral : _Lack of budget, debt_
_____
_____

Is this problem now: ☐ Resolved   ☒ Improved   ☐ Unchanged   ☐ Worse

Additional problems worked on: Is each problem:

Communication   ☐ Resolved   ☒ Improved   ☐ Unchanged   ☐ Worse

_____   ☐ Resolved   ☐ Improved   ☐ Unchanged   ☐ Worse

Counseling Results:
Success is judged by the following criteria: 1) the client is embracing the Biblical Financial Principles and making decisions based upon these principles; 2) the client has a Spending Plan in place and has been following it for at least three months; 3) the client has a Debt Reduction Plan in place and has been following it for at least three months; 4) the client has met his/her goals.

☒ Successful   ☐ Partial   ☐ Unsuccessful
(met all criteria)   (met some criteria)   (met no criteria)

Comments:
They worked hard! They are on the right track, and I believe they
will stay there.

NOTE: Upon completion of a case—successful or unsuccessful—the goal is to have the client connected to a church ministry that can provide additional help and/or to a small group that can help them grow. Please indicate the results of your efforts in this regard: Client ☒ Is ☐ Is NOT connected elsewhere. Explain:

Carol joined the family ministry. I encouraged Mark to join her there or
to contact Tom Smith about the sports ministry in which he had
expressed some interest.

Is there something about this case that could help and/or encourage other counselors or clients? If so, what?
_____
_____
_____
_____

The Case Completion Report may be used by your ministry administrator to calculate simple statistics such as the total number of successful cases. The form also provides a one-page overview of a case in the event a former client contacts the ministry again.

Turn to page 100.

COUNSELING PROCESS SUMMARY

2 minutes

Participant's Guide, page 100.

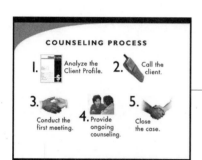

We have now completed the five parts of the counseling process.

➤ Analyze the Client Profile.

Call the client.

Conduct the first meeting.

Provide ongoing counseling, and

Close the case.

We've come a long way since we began this workshop. You've seen the vision of Good $ense, practiced counseling skills, learned the budget counseling process through video and practice, and have learned to use the tools that Good $ense has to offer you and your clients.

I would like to take this time to encourage you to review the Appendix after today's course. It contains the answers to questions like, "What do I do if the client isn't making any progress?" and "What do I do if the client wants me to make their decisions for them or do their work?" There are also articles on a variety of topics that you can study to enhance your budget counseling skills, as well as a list of additional resources.

NOTES

Counseling Process Summary

COUNSELING PROCESS

1. Analyze the Client Profile.

2. Call the client.

3. Conduct the first meeting.

4. Provide ongoing counseling.

5. Close the case.

- Analyze the Client Profile.

- Call the client.

- Conduct the first meeting.

- Provide ongoing counseling.

- Close the case.

The *Good $ense Implementation Guide* strongly recommends that counselors form a group or groups that meet regularly to discuss the issues counselors face in their work. It also recommends the formation of a mentoring program for new counselors. If these programs are planned or already in existence at your ministry, take a moment to discuss them now.

5 minutes

CLOSING

Participant's Guide, page 101.

"Those of us who are strong and able in the faith need to step in and lend a hand to those who falter, and not just do what is most convenient for us. Strength is for service, not status. Each one of us needs to look after the good of the people around us, asking ourselves, 'How can I help?'"
Romans 15:1 (MSG)

There are two passages from Eugene Peterson's *The Message* that I'd like to leave you with as we close.

> *"Those of us who are strong and able in the faith need to step in and lend a hand to those who falter, and not just do what is most convenient for us. Strength is for service, not status. Each one of us needs to look after the good of the people around us, asking ourselves, 'How can I help?'"* Romans 15:1 (MSG).

God is pleased that you, who are strong and able in financial matters, are willing to lend a hand to those who falter. Thanks for recognizing your strength in this area and stepping forward to help those who struggle. As you do so, keep in mind the words of this second verse:

"Summing up: Be agreeable, be sympathetic, be loving, be compassionate, be humble. That goes for all of you, no exceptions. No retaliation. No sharp-tongued sarcasm. Instead, bless—that's your job, to bless. You'll be a blessing and also get a blessing."
1 Peter 3:8-9 (MSG)

> *"Summing up: Be agreeable, be sympathetic, be loving, be compassionate, be humble. That goes for all of you, no exceptions. No retaliation. No sharp-tongued sarcasm. Instead, bless—that's your job, to bless. You'll be a blessing and also get a blessing."* 1 Peter 3:8-9 (MSG).

I think those words have real significance for a Good $ense counselor. God made us to be a blessing to others. You will bless others in your role as a counselor, and you will be blessed as you are a blessing.

NOTES

Closing

Those of us who are strong and able in the faith need to step in and lend a hand to those who falter, and not just do what is most convenient for us. Strength is for service, not status. Each one of us needs to look after the good of the people around us, asking ourselves, "How can I help?"

Romans 15:1 (MSG)

Summing up: Be agreeable, be sympathetic, be loving, be compassionate, be humble. That goes for all of you, no exceptions. No retaliation. No sharp-tongued sarcasm. Instead, bless—that's your job, to bless. You'll be a blessing and also get a blessing.

1 Peter 3:8-9 (MSG)

Let's close in prayer.

Please stand, form a circle, and join hands. I will begin with a single word that sums up my feelings about the day. Then, I'd like each of you to do the same thing. When it comes around to me, I'll close.

> Begin by saying one single word that sums up your feelings about the day. For example, "hope," or "compassion." Ask the person on your right to go next, and then continue around the circle. You may want to go around the circle more than once. End by saying a short prayer of thanks for the day of learning and fellowship.

A P P E N D I X

APPENDIX CONTENTS

Relationship Issues

Additional Biblical Financial Principles

Budgeting Tools and Issues

Financial and Legal Issues

Miscellaneous Articles

Recommended Resources

Pre-Reading for the *Good $ense Counselor Training Workshop*

Forms

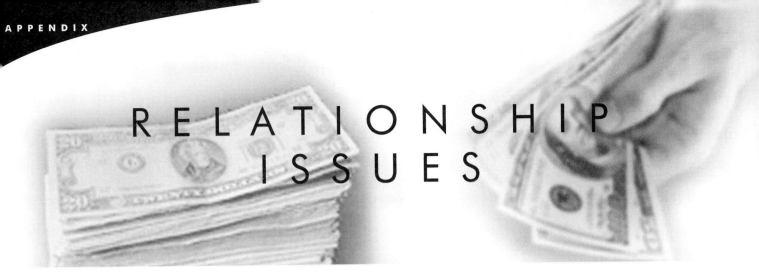

RELATIONSHIP ISSUES

LACK OF CLIENT PROGRESS

Warning Signs

There are several warning signs that indicate your client is not making progress:

- The client does not do the action items.

- By the end of the fourth meeting, attitudes and behavior have not changed.

- The client is not listening to you (after you have listened to him/her).

- In conversations, the client frequently changes the subject and/or talks a lot.

- The client cuts you off when you are speaking.

- Spouses continue to disagree and do not cooperate.

- The client is dishonest or withholds information.

- The client misses meetings without a reasonable explanation.

Handling Lack of Progress

- Refer back to client goals at each meeting, and ask how the client is doing in their efforts to achieve them.

- Don't spend a great deal of time trying to turn around a client who won't put forth an effort.

No-shows

- If the client misses more than two meetings in a short time span, try to discover the cause of the problem

- If you can't get an honest response, consider closing the case.

Terminating a Case

Before terminating a case, discuss the situation with your ministry leader(s) so they are aware of the problem.

When terminating a case:

- Be gracious and professional.

- Leave the door open for the client to return in the future.

COMMON QUESTIONS ABOUT BUILDING RAPPORT

Building a relationship of empathy and trust with the client is key to being able to help them. One barrier new counselors sometimes experience in developing a good relationship is the shock they experience in seeing how poorly their client has handled their financial affairs. By definition, however, you are the counselor because you have done well in this area, and they are the client because they need help. Your role is not to confront the foolishness or unbiblical nature of their past actions but to affirm their request for help and to use your strengths to give that help.

How do I strike the right balance between mirroring and asking questions?

In the early stages you are trying to build rapport. You want the client to do the talking. If need be, get them to talk about anything they're willing to talk about. It may be necessary at first to ask some questions. Avoid questions that can be answered with one or two words. Start with open-ended statements or questions such as "Tell me about your work," or "What do you like to do to relax?" As they begin to talk, focus on mirroring their feelings.

Is it okay to tell the client that I relate to their feelings?

The difficulty with talking about your own feelings is that you turn the attention to yourself. The purpose of mirroring is to keep the attention on the person talking. If you want to say something, say it concisely and then turn the attention back toward the client with a "tell me more about that" statement.

You want to let the client direct the conversation. That's one of the quickest ways to build rapport. Let them decide what they want to reveal to you. You are a guest in their "house." They are "showing you around." If you say, "I like this room," chances are they will stop there, when perhaps they really wanted to show you another room.

What if the conversation seems to circle around the same topic without going anywhere?

You can interrupt your client with a short summary sentence and the question, "Did I get that right?" That sort of interruption is welcome. You are not saying, "Stop talking about this because I want to talk about something else." You are saying, "I want to make sure I'm with you, and I understand." Often when they realize you understand the point they are making, it frees them to move on to other topics.

What if my client is not communicative?

Ask the client a question you know they can answer—choose one of their interests. Another approach is to focus on the here and now by reading their nonverbal cues. You could say, "Looks like you're feeling nervous about our meeting. Was it hard to come today?" If they admit it was, follow up with an open-ended statement like, "Tell me about that," or ask a question, "Why did you come today?"

As our relationship develops, is it okay for me to ask additional questions about their financial situation?

Don't hesitate or be embarrassed about asking additional clarifying questions. Your interest in getting the whole picture and getting to the bottom of the matter will more likely be perceived as an indication of your interest and desire to help than as an offense.

What if I encounter a long stretch of silence with a client who had been talking?

When you encounter silence, it's like coming to a stop sign. The person is thinking about which direction they want to go. Let them make that decision. Let them take their time, and give them the freedom and privilege of determining what they want to tell you. Read their body language. You can usually tell if someone is thinking something through. Your silence and body language (not sighing or shifting in your chair) tells them, "I will wait patiently until you let me know whether you have more to say or not." If they are looking at you and seem to be asking,

"What do we do now?" you can simply say, "You looked as though you were thinking something. Were you?" If they say no, move on, but if they say yes, then ask them, "Would you like to tell me what you're thinking?"

A Note about Listening

Matthew 12:34 states, "Out of the overflow of the heart the mouth speaks. "Sometimes people don't mean what they say, but sometimes they mean a lot more than what they say. Matthew 12:34 suggests we listen not only to the words but listen to the heart as well. When someone says they just can't manage their money, their heart may be saying, "I need you to believe in me and encourage me."

In his book *Connecting,* Larry Crabb describes the thoughts and feelings of a person coming for help:

> When you see me struggling, realize that my worst fear is that I'm nothing more than a struggler, that nobody can see anything deeper in me than my sin and pain, because that's all there is, that my only hope is to sin less and to somehow feel better. When you see me filled with doubt, when you observe me during my worst seasons of discouragement and failure, I want you to be filled with both anguish (weep with me as I weep) and hope, not the empty hope that says trite things like "It'll all work out" or "Just hang in there—I'm sure you'll feel better soon," but a hope that exists because it sees something in me that is absolutely terrific. Believe that there is life in me. I want to catch the gleam in your eye that tells me you know there is more to me than my problems and that you're confidently hopeful that the good will emerge. I want you to ache when you see the good buried beneath so much bad, but I want you to be passionately convinced that, by the grace of God, the good is there waiting to be released. Don't be intrusive. Build a bridge of trust before you pass weighty things out of your heart into mine.

For information on building rapport when working with spouses, see page 277.

MIRRORING EXAMPLE

Following is a portion of the video script from the mirroring video used in the course.

Ann: (the counselor): Well, Susan, I see you've brought all your paper work.

Susan: Oh my goodness. I don't know if I have everything or not. I tried to get everything you asked for, but, of course, when you want something you can't find it, so I spent most of last night searching through every desk drawer, box and pile trying to find all my receipts and all my bills. I don't have a very organized plan right now, which is why I need to see you. I hope this is ok.

Ann: Sounds like you're a little overwhelmed.

Susan: Yes. I've never done anything like this before. Well, I've never needed to do anything like this before. Well, maybe that's not true. I have needed to; just have never been at this point before.

Ann: Where you're feeling a little desperate.

Susan: Oh yeah. You see, my parents don't think I can do this—live on my own. They think I'm irresponsible.

Ann: And you want to show them otherwise.

Susan: Yes. Thank you. I do. I can. I just need someone to get me on track. Because I don't have money and I'm drowning in debt and the last place I want to go is to my parents and prove them right.

Ann: So you are here making a responsible adult decision in getting help before it's too late.

Susan: (relaxes) Yes. I am. I am being a responsible adult, aren't I?

Ann: Yes, you sure are and your parents are going to be very proud of how you are going to handle your finances from here on out.

Susan: Yes, they are. Thank you. Thank you.

Ann: And you're ready to get started.

Susan: You betcha. Let's go.

FEELING WORDS

Here is a list of feeling words that may be useful when using mirroring with your clients.

HAPPY
festive
contented
relaxed
calm
complacent
satisfied
serene
comfortable
peaceful
joyous
ecstatic
enthusiastic
inspired
glad
pleased
grateful
excited
cheery
lighthearted
buoyant
carefree
surprised
optimistic
spirited
vivacious
brisk
sparkling
merry
generous
hilarious
exhilarated
jolly
playful
elated
jubilant
thrilled
restful
silly
giddy

EAGER
keen
earnest
intent
zealous
ardent
avid
enthusiastic
proud
excited
desirous

SAD
sorrowful
unhappy
depressed
melancholy
gloomy
somber
dismal
heavy-hearted
quiet
mournful
dreadful
dreary
flat
blah
dull
in the dumps
sullen
moody
sulky
out of sorts
low
discontented
discouraged
disappointed
concerned
sympathetic
compassionate
choked up
embarrassed
shameful
ashamed
useless
worthless
ill at ease
weepy
vacant

HURT
injured
isolated
offended
distressed
pained
suffering
afflicted
worried
aching
crushed
heartbroken
cold
upset
lonely
despairing
tortured
pathetic
wounded

ANGRY
contemptuous
resentful
irritated
enraged
furious
annoyed
inflamed
provoked
offended
sullen
indignant
irate
wrathful
cross
sulky
bitter
frustrated
boiling
grumpy
fuming
stubborn
belligerent
confused
awkward
bewildered

FEARLESS
encouraged
courageous
confident
secure
independent
reassured
bold
brave
daring
heroic
hardy
determined
loyal
proud
impulsive

INTERESTED
concerned
fascinated
engrossed
intrigued
absorbed
excited
curious
inquisitive
inquiring
creative
sincere

DOUBTFUL
unbelieving
skeptical
distrustful
suspicious
dubious
uncertain
questioning
evasive
wavering
hesitant
perplexed
indecisive
hopeless
powerless
helpless
defeated
pessimistic
confused

PHYSICAL
taut
uptight
immobilized
paralyzed
tense
stretched
hollow
empty
frisky
strong
weak
sweaty
breathless
nauseated
sluggish
weary
repulsed
tired
alive
firm
hard
light
fragile

AFFECTIONATE
soft
close
loving
sexy
tender
seductive
warm
open
appealing
aggressive
passionate

AFRAID
fearful
frightened
timid
wishy-washy
shaky
apprehensive
terrified
panicky
tragic
hysterical
alarmed
cautious
shocked
horrified
insecure
impatient
nervous
dependent
fidgety
anxious
pressured
worried
suspicious
hesitant
awed
dismayed
scared
cowardly
threatened
appalled
petrified
gutless
edgy

MISCELLANEOUS
humble
torn
mixed-up
envious
jealous
preoccupied
cruel
distant
bored
hypocritical
phoney
two-faced
cooperative
burdened
played out
hopeful

COUNSELING SPOUSES

When the client is a married couple, it is vital that both husband and wife are involved in the counseling. In rare situations where one spouse is genuinely desirous of understanding how to manage their finances and the other spouse refuses to attend, you may decide to accommodate the lone spouse. However, it must be recognized that family financial problems will not be solved unless both partners cooperate.

It is also wise to recognize that in many cases one spouse may express reluctance. It is helpful to acknowledge this up front by saying something like, "Thanks for being honest. I'm glad you came because I think it takes both of you to resolve the problem and I hope that after a few times together you'll be glad you came."

A good question to ask in the first session is what the individuals believe the problem is. The spouse with the dominant personality will usually be the first to offer a response. Always allow one spouse to complete their comments before allowing interruptions from the other. It is equally important to get both spouses' responses. How they respond and the differences in their responses will often give helpful insight into how they communicate with one another and what the real problem may be.

In his *Counselor Self-Study Course Manual,* Larry Burkett gives the following illustration:

> One husband, when asked what he thought their financial problem was, responded, "Even with both of us working we never seem to make enough to meet our bills." When the wife was asked she responded, "I don't want to work. It seems I work just to support our boat, vacations, and new cars."
>
> The husband identified the symptoms (a lack of money) while his wife focused on their problem (indulgence or greed).

If one spouse is very quiet, you may have to make an extra effort to direct questions to them. If the other spouse answers or interrupts, stop them from talking by saying, "I'll be eager to hear your thoughts later. Right now I just want to see what he/she has to say." If you do not engage the quiet spouse in the first meeting, they may not return to subsequent meetings, or they may sabotage efforts to make progress.

If arguing between the spouses should occur, let it go on for thirty to sixty seconds at most. Interrupt with, "I bet you've had this discussion before. How about if we continue with my questions and return to this later?" Be sure to write down the area of conflict as a reminder. Prayer may be an effective tool to calm tempers if things have temporarily gotten out of control. If conflict emerges as a pattern, ask the couple if they have considered talking to a professional counselor who can provide them with tools for resolving conflict.

Never side with one partner against the other. Your goal is to find areas where they agree, and to build on these agreements.

ADDITIONAL BIBLICAL FINANCIAL PRINCIPLES

TITHING

Few financial issues cause as much controversy and discussion among Christian churches today as the issue of tithing (giving 10 percent of one's income back to God). Spiritual leaders and biblical teachers differ greatly on whether or not tithing is applicable to today's believer. For those who advocate its relevancy, a host of secondary questions arise. From what base is the tithe computed? Who is eligible to receive it? Since this can be perplexing for the client who is serious about honoring God with his/her finances, the Good $ense counselor needs to be equipped to address this issue.

A quick review of the Bible reveals many Old Testament references to tithing but few New Testament references. Many people believe that the tithe originated with the Mosaic laws, but the giving of a tenth to honor God first appears in Genesis 14:20. Abraham (Abram), in apparent recognition of God's help in defeating his enemies and capturing their material possessions, gives a tenth of the wealth to Melchizedek, a "priest of God Most High." His action can be interpreted as giving back to God a portion (one-tenth) of what God allowed him to acquire. He realized that God was the source of his ability to be victorious in battle.

A second reference to tithing prior to the Mosaic laws occurs in Genesis 28:22. Here Jacob vows to give a tenth to God of all that God gives to him. Up until this point there has been no official commandment to tithe. But, apparently, a way to honor God as provider of material gain was to tithe or give from the "first fruits," as Abel did in Genesis 4.

When God instituted the law through Moses several centuries after Abraham, the tithe on income became a commandment. In fact, a strong case can be made for there being as many as three tithes (Deuteronomy 14:22–23; Numbers 18:21–26; Deuteronomy 14:28–39). Whether one tithe or three, God took the tithe very seriously. In Malachi 3:8–12, God tells Israel that the nation is robbing him by not bringing the whole tithe into God's house. The result of this disobedience was economic disaster for Israel.

The New Testament is somewhat vague on the subject of tithing. Jesus mentions tithing only once in Matthew 23:23. In this reference, Christ challenges the religious leaders of this day about the depth of their devotion to God:

> "Woe to you, teachers of the law and Pharisees, you hypocrites! You give a tenth of your spices—mint, dill and cummin. But you have neglected the more important matters of the law—justice, mercy and faithfulness. You should have practiced the latter without neglecting the former."

Jesus' final word of rebuke is that they should have tithed as well as practiced justice, mercy, and faithfulness. Speaking in the past tense makes it difficult to use this verse convincingly to support a New Testament commandment to tithe. Was he saying they should have done both in the past, while under the law, without necessarily stating a tithing obligation for the future? As Paul informs us, we are no longer under the law. It was merely there to serve as a tutor to lead us to Christ (Galatians 3:24–25). If the law on tithing is no longer binding on the believer, then what? Paul states that the Spirit, not the law, should be our guide (Galatians 5:18). Second Corinthians 9:7 supports giving with enthusiasm, and teaches that our desire to accomplish God's work should dictate the amount.

God expects Spirit-led giving from a totally surrendered follower (Romans 12:1). Except for the portion that is to be kept to provide for oneself and needy relatives, with reasonable safeguards for the future, the rest should be dispersed to God's work. Whether that is or should be 90 percent or 10 percent of one's income is irrelevant.

Tithing can become a starting point for a new believer, based on Old Testament guidelines, but should yield to Spirit-directed guidance as the believer matures.

How Much to Give

For counseling purposes, stress the importance of giving as a requirement of the totally surrendered believer. Allow the client to begin slowly if their faith is weak or if past financial mistakes have reduced available income to subsistence living. Giving only 1 to 2 percent of income can be an acceptable beginning, as long as the proper attitude is present. It is appropriate to suggest putting a plan in place to move toward the biblical benchmark of a tithe (10 percent) in the future. For those who tithe comfortably without any desire to move above that amount, encourage them to acknowledge that their giving does not stop with a tithe. Growing spiritually results in an increased desire to see God's work accomplished, often at the expense of increasing lifestyle comfort. This is a highly personal issue that is ultimately a matter of conscience and heart.

Where to Give

Galatians 6:6 and I Corinthians 9:11–14 stipulate that those who minister spiritually through the local church are to be taken care of materially. Matthew 25:14–30 also calls believers to choose the recipients of giving carefully and support those enterprises and outreaches that have maximum effectiveness in achieving God's purposes. If the local church is faithfully carrying out God's work, then it is deserving of a believer's generous support.

A Closing Thought on Giving

There is another often overlooked reason that giving is very important. The reality is that there is an eternal feud between God and money, and we cannot serve both. Where our treasure is, our heart will be. Money is a powerful thing! Some would say money is the chief rival god and is powerfully attempting to gain our allegiance and exercise control over us. In the midst of these sobering thoughts, it is good to realize that the act of giving money away (a very "unnatural" act since money is a medium of exchange for which we are supposed to get something tangible of equal or greater value) is probably the most effective way to be sure we control it rather than allow it to control us.

The act of generous giving, and the joy and blessing that accompany it, leads to freedom from anxiety and worry about money. That in turn leads to growing contentment with what one has. You are giving a great gift to your clients when you help them understand and experience that truth.

WHEN IS ENOUGH, ENOUGH?

The Bible doesn't give absolute guidelines for deciding when enough is enough, but the following nine principles can provide guidance for making wise financial decisions or evaluating a desire to purchase something.

1. Start with the right attitude: everything you have was created by God, is owned by God, and is to be used for God's purposes.

2. If the desire seems reasonable to mature Christian brothers and sisters whose discernment you respect, it is usually wise.

3. If the desire arises from pain over the plight of the poor, the unfortunate, or the disenfranchised, it is likely to be Spirit led and honoring to God.

4. If the desire involves the well-being of children, it is often right.

5. If the desire is primarily one of wanting to improve your own living conditions or lifestyle, you should not automatically assume it is wrong.

6. Consider whether the desire springs from an incompleteness in your relationship with Christ. Are you trying to fill with purchases an empty place in your heart?

7. Consider whether the resources of God's creation would be adequate to provide for all of his children the thing you desire for yourself.

8. Evaluate how important your desire seems in the context of your own mortality. Ask, "How important will this purchase seem to me when I am on my deathbed?"

9. Ask, "What would Jesus do in my situation?"

If we try to answer the question, "When is enough, enough?" on the basis of what someone else has, enough will never be enough. And if we love money, Ecclesiastes 5:10 warns, "Whoever loves money never has money enough."

Points two through six adapted from *Freedom of Simplicity,* Richard J. Foster (HarperCollins, San Francisco, 1981), pages 88-89.

BANKRUPTCY

There are a wide variety of opinions about whether or not Christians should ever declare bankruptcy. On one side of the spectrum, bankruptcy is never perceived as an option for a Christian who can pay debts at an agreed-upon schedule. Support for this stance is found in Psalm 37:21, "The wicked borrow and do not repay, but the righteous give generously." Borrowing constitutes an obligation to repay regardless of legal options. Ecclesiastes 5:4–5 says, "When you make a vow to God, do not delay in fulfilling it. He takes no pleasure in fools; fulfill your vow. It is better not to vow than to make a vow and not fulfill it."

A vow, whether made to God, a spouse, or creditor, is treated seriously by God and should not be made without consideration of the consequences. Proverbs 3:27 states, "Do not withhold good from those who deserve it, when it is in your power to act." Declaring bankruptcy to protect personal property when assets are available to be applied to legally or morally binding debt obligations is perceived as abusing a creditor.

The ramification of debt is slavery, as warned in Scripture. Proverbs 22:7 says, "The rich rule over the poor and the borrower is servant to the lender." This can be emotional as well as literal slavery. In bankruptcy, the creditor may be released from receiving full repayment, but is the debtor free from pangs of conscience by leaving a vow unfulfilled? The obligation to repay debts and fulfill promises is strongly affirmed in Scripture.

On the other end of the spectrum, some argue that legally accepted options offered in the bankruptcy laws are available to the believer despite the arguments above. The biblical evidence primarily centers around the Mosaic laws as described in Deuteronomy 15 and Leviticus 25. Deuteronomy 15:1–2 states, "At the end of every seventh year you must cancel your debts. This is how it must be done. Creditors must cancel the loans they have made to their fellow Israelites. They must not demand payment from their neighbor or relatives, for the Lord's time of release has arrived" (NLT). Leviticus 25:10–17 speaks of the Year of Jubilee. This, too, released a debtor from a creditor in that land, and properties were returned to original owners every fifty years.

The argument for the validity of bankruptcy is not based on the theory that Old Testament laws are still in force today, but that the principle behind the law applies today. God does not want his people, or anyone else for that matter, to live in never-ending servitude to lenders based on an economic situation beyond their control, or even including a poor economic decision willfully made in the past (getting into too much debt). Therefore, the argument goes, bankruptcy laws are in some ways a contemporary application of Old Testament statutes. This stance carries some credence in that God is gracious, forgiving, and expects societies to imitate him. One also hears stories of debtors whose overaggressiveness in collecting obligations may tend to make bankruptcy options more justifiable. In fact, the original intent of bankruptcy laws was to protect individuals from creditors who made unreasonable demands despite the debtor's best efforts to repay the debt.

Both perspectives carry elements of truth.

In reflecting upon God's Word and the bankruptcy options, under certain conditions bankruptcy can be a plausible alternative for the Christian. This option should be viewed as a last resort and never taken without much thought and prayer. Perhaps the most important aspect to consider is the attitude of the debtor. Is the debtor willing to:

- Morally and ethically satisfy the creditor's legal demands, if given the chance?

- Do what is necessary to keep any roadblocks from interfering with a creditor's perspective of Christianity?

- Make significant cutbacks in lifestyle to cooperate with creditors?

- Allow God an opportunity to provide the funds at a later date to pay the debts completely?

- Receive grace from a creditor who could agree to a reduced payment?

When the answer to these questions is yes, bankruptcy may be appropriate for the believer.

Bankruptcy should not be viewed as a quick fix or a way to avoid moral obligations. It should not be viewed as a way to avoid losing assets or income in order to sustain a lifestyle above the basic needs of life and at the expense of creditors. The obligation of the budget counselor is to present the alternatives to the client. The choice to file bankruptcy cannot be made by the counselor.

For more information on bankruptcy laws, see page 337.

BUDGETING TOOLS AND ISSUES

SETTING ACHIEVABLE GOALS

A critical skill in counseling of any kind is the ability to help the client set achievable goals. A goal can be simply defined as a "desired state." The counselor's job is to help a client reach the desired state through teaching and coaching. There are several types of goals counselors can help clients define:

- An overall goal for counseling. What is the desired outcome of the counseling process? What is the most important outcome they are trying to achieve?

- A goal for the next meeting

- Smaller goals that help achieve a larger goal

- Daily or weekly goals that slowly chip away at bad habits and behaviors

- Spending or savings goals that quantify progress.

Goals are fluid and changeable. Don't be afraid to assist clients in modifying their goals. You might want to encourage them to write their goals in pencil!

What Makes a Goal Achievable?

There are four criteria that help make goals achievable. They are:

- State goals in positive terms.

- Make sure goals are measurable.

- Keep goals realistic.

- Keep goals action oriented.

State Goals in Positive Terms

When helping a client set goals, being *for* something instead of *against* something puts the idea into a positive framework. Consider the two examples below.

Negative Goal	"I won't go to the mall."
Positive Goal	"When I go to the mall, I'll buy only what's on my list."

Negative Goal	"I want to stop going out every Friday after work; I always spend too much buying my friends pizza."
Positive Goal	"I want to find ways to continue to spend time with my friends and show them I care without spending money."

Make Sure Goals Are Measurable

A good goal can be measured easily. You can measure time and you can measure amounts. If the goal is to pay off all debt, what is the amount of the debt and what amount will be applied toward it? How frequently will this amount be applied? In how many weeks or months will the debt be paid off?

Frequency is another measure. Say a couple spends too much on groceries because they don't plan ahead and are always running to the grocery store at the last minute. This costs them a lot of time and certainly more money. They may set as their goal a single, weekly shopping trip at which they purchase all items for the week. That is, the frequency of their grocery store trips will be reduced to once weekly.

Another example might be: "I will figure out five ways to reduce my clothing expenses." "Five" is the number to measure against.

Keep Goals Realistic

One need not set lofty goals—a lofty goal may be achieved through a series of smaller goals. If a client is having trouble setting smaller goals, you might try stating their larger goal and then ask them, "What will be the very first sign that you're moving in the right direction?" Their answer becomes the first, smaller goal.

Achieving a series of small goals gives clients confidence and helps establish a pattern of success.

Goals Should Be Action Oriented

Goals should state specific actions that will be taken to accomplish the desired outcome. For example, "I will reduce my expenses by taking the bus to work instead of driving and by packing my lunch," indicates specific actions that will be taken.

The Goals Analysis Practice Exercise

It often helps clients to have a written record of the goals they establish so they can check their goals periodically to see how they're progressing. One of the activities you can use with clients is the Goals Analysis Practice Exercise on page 291. It is an optional exercise but may be one you find useful for quickly helping them understand how to establish goals.

Target Questions for Goal-Setting

If clients still seem stuck on defining goals, use the following questions to help them articulate their desires.

- What do you want? (Stated in positive terms.)

- When do you want it?

- Where and with whom do you want it?

- How will you know that you have it?

- When you get what you want, what else in your life will improve?

- What resources do you have to help you?

- What can you begin to do now to get what you want?

- What things have you tried already?

- What obstacles are in the way?

GOALS ANALYSIS PRACTICE EXERCISE

For each goal shown below, determine whether it meets the four criteria listed. If it meets a criteria, check the box. A goal that meets all four criteria is a well-defined goal. Answers appear on the following page.

1. I want to get out of debt.
    ☐ Positive ☐ Measurable ☐ Realistic ☐ Action/Solution Oriented

2. I will wait forty-eight hours before buying an item costing over $20 to make sure I really need it.
    ☐ Positive ☐ Measurable ☐ Realistic ☐ Action/Solution Oriented

3. I want to pay off all of my debt in two years by disconnecting my cable television service, retiring my cell phone, and putting the money I save on these items toward debt.
    ☐ Positive ☐ Measurable ☐ Realistic ☐ Action/Solution Oriented

4. I want to save money by packing my lunch until my debt is paid off.
    ☐ Positive ☐ Measurable ☐ Realistic ☐ Action/Solution Oriented

5. I will stop seeing first-run movies and rent videos instead.
    ☐ Positive ☐ Measurable ☐ Realistic ☐ Action/Solution Oriented

6. I will treat myself to a movie out this weekend if I eat and drink only food I bought from the grocery store.
    ☐ Positive ☐ Measurable ☐ Realistic ☐ Action/Solution Oriented

GOALS ANALYSIS PRACTICE EXERCISE ANSWERS

How did you do? Compare your answers to those below.

1. I want to get out of debt.
    [X] Positive   [ ] Measurable   [ ] Realistic   [ ] Action/Solution Oriented

    Comment: About the only thing we can say about this goal is that it's positive—getting out of debt is a positive step. However, there is no action or time frame attached to this goal. When will you get out of debt? *How?* This goal needs to be broken down into smaller steps.

2. I will wait forty-eight hours before buying an item costing over $20 to make sure I really need it.
    [X] Positive   [X] Measurable   [X] Realistic   [X] Action/Solution Oriented

    Comment: Parameters are clearly set: forty-eight hours and $20. The action: "wait." The goal is positive because it doesn't use words like "won't" or "not." It states "I will."

3. I want to pay off all of my debt in two years by disconnecting my cable television service, retiring my cell phone, and putting the money I save on these items toward debt.
    [X] Positive   [X] Measurable   [X] Realistic   [X] Action/Solution Oriented

    Comment: This goal has it all: a time frame, two distinctive actions, and a positive slant.

4. I want to save money by packing my lunch until my debt is paid off.
    [X] Positive   [X] Measurable   [X] Realistic   [X] Action/Solution Oriented

    Comment: A nice, small goal that is easily accomplished. The measure is not a distinct time frame but is defined: "until debt is paid off."

5. I will stop seeing first-run movies and rent videos instead.
    [ ] Positive   [ ] Measurable   [X] Realistic   [X] Action/Solution Oriented

    Comment: To put a more positive spin on this, try "I will rent videos instead of seeing first-run movies." Also, this goal has no time frame. Is it "forever" or "this month"?

6. I will treat myself to a movie out this weekend if I eat and drink only food I bought from the grocery store.
    [X] Positive   [X] Measurable   [X] Realistic   [X] Action/Solution Oriented

    Comment: Another small but well-defined goal with a short time frame—a week—and specific actions.

DETERMINING AN AVERAGE MONTH FOR VARIABLE INCOME

The key to determining a budget in the case of a variable income (due, for example, to your client receiving sales commissions or being self-employed) is to make a *conservative estimate* of net income for the coming year. Where possible, this would be done on the basis of the past several years' income. "Conservative" would be defined as not allowing one really good year to unduly influence the estimate for the coming year.

For example, if the past three years' net income were $37,000, $40,000, and $54,000—a really good year!—a conservative estimate for the coming year would be in the range of $44,000, not $56,000. Make the assumption that the client may not have the exceptionally good year they had last year.

In this example, the client's monthly budget would be $44,000 divided by 12, or $3,667. In the months they make more than that, the excess would be put into a short-term savings account, to be drawn on in months in which income is less than $3,667.

A wise approach to variable income also includes predetermining the best use of any additional funds, in the event God blesses and the client exceeds their estimated income for the year. Thoughtful consideration before the fact will prevent an impulsive decision if and when the money becomes available, avoiding regrets afterward that it had not been spent in some other, better way.

WHAT HAPPENS TO RAISES?

Most of the time, the extra money the client receives in raises "gets used up." Several months later, they're not quite sure where it went. Yet, even a modest raise on a modest salary can add up to a significant amount of additional income in just a few years.

A 4 percent Annual Raise on a $30,000 Salary

	Year 1	Year 2	Year 3
4% raise	$31,200	$32,448	$33,745
Base salary	$30,000	$30,000	$30,000
Additional $ income	$ 1,200	$ 2,448	$ 3,745
Total additional income in three years = $7,393			

Let's take the example of a $30,000 salary and a 4 percent raise and look at the additional income it produces over a three-year period:

- The first year there is a $1,200 increase (4 percent of $30,000).

- The second year the salary would increase to $32,448, an additional margin of $2,448 from the original salary of $30,000.

- The third year the salary would increase to $33,745, producing an increase from the original $30,000 of $3,745.

The total additional income in that three-year period adds up to almost $7,400, nearly one-fourth of the original salary! And that's just looking at a three-year period. Taxes obviously impact the amount the client doesn't give to charitable causes, but even the after-tax amount accumulates to a significant figure. Helping your client decide ahead of time how they will use the raises can be a key part of the strategy for reaching financial goals.

THE ENVELOPE RECORD-KEEPING SYSTEM

A form of the envelope system was used by many of our great-grandparents. They had a variety of containers—a coffee tin here and a sugar bowl there—in which money was placed. One container held money for groceries, one for clothes, and another for a rainy day. When a purchase was considered, they looked into the appropriate container and determined what could or could not be spent based on how much money was in it.

The envelope system is based on the same principle. It tangibly designates money for various expenses. Here is how it works.

ENVELOPE SYSTEM

All Income

Master Checking Account

Cash

Envelopes
(Variable Expenses)

The client deposits all their income into a master checking account. Each pay period they withdraw and distribute the cash among labeled envelopes.

In its purest form this system would have an envelope for each of the different expense categories like giving, savings, mortgage, utilities, giving, car payment, groceries, clothes, gifts, and household items. The monthly amount from the Spending Plan worksheet is written on each envelope, and that amount of cash is placed in each one. When it is time to make a purchase, the client looks in the appropriate envelope, checks how much money is available, and then uses the cash to make their purchase.

Obviously, it would not be practical or wise to have an envelope for every category on the Spending Plan worksheet—for example, having a mortgage envelope of $800. Your client probably doesn't want that kind of cash sitting around, and probably wouldn't find it very convenient to pay the mortgage with cash. Therefore, they write a check for those kind of expenses.

The diagram below includes these types of payments.

ENVELOPE SYSTEM

All Income

Master Checking Account

Checks
(Fixed Expenses)

Cash

Envelopes
(Variable Expenses)

Your client still deposits all income into a master checking account. But now, they don't have envelopes for those categories they write monthly checks for. This would include items like mortgage, giving, utilities, car payment, etc. Note that these expenses are often fixed monthly amounts, or usually paid just once a month, and controlling them is not a problem. The clients don't overspend on their rent payments! For the other variable categories, which are more difficult to control—food, clothes, entertainment, and household—they have envelopes.

This is all you need to know to help your client get started with the envelope system. An advantage of this system is that it is not necessary to keep written records. Another huge advantage is that each time they go to an envelope to get cash, it is a tangible reminder of how much they have to spend. That consistent feedback provides a powerful check-and-balance on their spending. The envelopes and their checkbook become their record-keeping system. Each pay period they put the budgeted amount of cash into each envelope. What's left at the end of the month tells them how much they spent.

KEEPING MONTH-TO-DATE AND YEAR-TO-DATE TOTALS ON THE SPENDING RECORD

Often it can be helpful for your client to know how they are doing in various categories, not just for the current month but since the beginning of the Spending Plan year. Lines 4 and 5 on the Spending Record provide that information.

Line 4 carries forward the amount each category was over or under the Spending Record from the month before. If this is done each month, and that figure is added to the over or under figure for the current month; the resulting figure represents the status of that category up to this point in the current budget year. This can be very helpful information in the case of variable expenses, as illustrated by the example on page 299 where the client has been tracking groceries, clothes, and going out.

This month the client was $34 under Spending Plan for groceries. In previous months, they spent a total of $118 less (line 4) than what had been allocated. That amount, added to the $34 under for this month, gives a Year-to-Date (YTD) total of $152 under the budget (line 5).

In the clothing category, the client spent $35 over budget for this month and was $142 over for the year at the end of the previous month. As a result, they are now $177 over for the year to date.

In the going out category, the client is $13 under the allotment for this month but was $96 over the allotment prior to this month. That leaves them $83 over the budget for the year.

This cumulative data can be very helpful as the year progresses. In this situation, as the holiday season approaches, we can see that because they have money in the grocery category, they can have guests over for nice holiday meals and still stay within the food budget for the year.

On the other hand, since they are behind in the clothing category, maybe they should pass the hint to others that it would be nice to get clothing gifts for Christmas! And moderation in the "going out" category is in order for the next several months.

Spending Record Example

Month __October__

Daily Variable Expenses

	Transportation		Household						Professional Services	Entertainment		
	Gas, etc.	Maint/ Repair	Groceries	Clothes	Gifts	Household Items	Personal	Other		Going Out	Travel	Other
(1) Spending Plan	80	40	320	60	80	75	50	—	—	100	70	40
	14	21	9	89	17	14	16	25		22	70	22 (sitter)
	17		87	46	55	22	18			46		
	9		43			9				19		
	19		106			31						
	11		21									
			7									
			13									
(2) Total	70	21	286	95	72	76	34	25	—	87	70	22
(3) (Over)/Under	10	19	34	(35)	8	(1)	16	(25)	—	13	—	18
(4) Last Month YTD			118	(142)						(96)		
(5) Total Year to Date			152	(177)						(83)		

~~1~~ ~~2~~ ~~3~~ ~~4~~ ~~5~~ ~~6~~ ~~7~~ ~~8~~ ~~9~~ ~~10~~ ~~11~~ ~~12~~ ~~13~~ ~~14~~ ~~15~~ ~~16~~ ~~17~~ ~~18~~ ~~19~~ ~~20~~ ~~21~~ ~~22~~ ~~23~~ ~~24~~ ~~25~~ ~~26~~ ~~27~~ ~~28~~ ~~29~~ ~~30~~ ~~31~~

- Use this page to record expenses that tend to be daily, variable expenses—often the hardest to control.
- Keep receipts throughout the day and record them at the end of the day.
- Total each category at the end of the month (line 2) and compare to the Spending Plan (line 1). Subtracting line 2 from line 1 gives you an (over) or under the budget figure for that month (line 3).
- To verify that you have made each day's entry, cross out the number at the bottom of the page that corresponds to that day's date.
- Optional: If you wish to monitor your progress as you go through the year, you can keep cumulative totals in lines 4 and 5.

MORE THAN ONE PAYCHECK PER MONTH

Item	Spending Plan ($)	1st Paycheck ($)	2nd Paycheck ($)
✓ Giving	250	125	125
✓ Saving	155		155
✓ Mortgage	970	970	
✓ Utilities	180		180
✓ Telephone	55		55
✓ Auto Payment	270		270
✓ Debt Repayment	110		110
Clothes	60		60
Gifts	80		80
Gas	80	40	40
Food	320	160	160
Household Misc.	75	30	45
Entertaiment	100	50	50
Misc. Small Exp.	45		45
Total	**2,750**	**1,375**	**1,375**

✓ = paid by check

Many clients are paid more than once per month and have difficulty with questions like "Which bill do I pay now?" and "Do I have enough for food and gas?" Helping your client make a one-time plan for how each paycheck will be allocated so they can refer to it each payday can be a wonderful way to ease their anxiety.

In the above example, the client receives net take-home pay of $2,750 per month and is paid twice a month ($1,375 per pay period.) The first column represents the Spending Plan for this family. They give $250 per month, save $155, have a mortgage payment of $970, etc.

Out of the first paycheck, checks are written for half of the monthly giving and for the mortgage. The rest of the check is used for cash for half of the allocation for gas, food, entertainment, and a portion of household/miscellaneous.

Out of the second paycheck, checks are written for the other half of giving, all short-term savings, utilities and telephone, auto payment, and debt repayment. The remainder of that check covers the other half of gas, food, household items, entertainment, and the total for the monthly miscellaneous cash expenditures category.

In developing such a plan, it may be necessary to adjust some payment dates to balance out payments from the two checks. Once the plan has been devised, a copy can be kept with your client's checkbook, and it will eliminate any question about how each paycheck is to be used.

MONEY BUILDING UP IN ACCOUNTS

With any kind of record-keeping system, there are certain expense categories that will tend to accumulate funds for a period of time. These include funds for an annual vacation, Christmas purchases, taxes, annual insurance premiums, etc. Rather than allowing these funds to accumulate in an envelope or checking account, it is wise for clients to put them in a short-term savings account until needed, preferably by direct deposit.

Once your client begins placing money for certain categories that tend to build up over time into a short-term savings account, the question may arise, "I have this savings account, and it has an amount of money in it, but how do I tell how much is for what category?"

The ledger sheet on page 304 shows an example to help answer this question. It is a ledger for a money market fund that contains short-term savings that have accumulated for several budgeted categories.

At the top, there is a description of the four funds into which money is being deposited each payday. In this case, the money is for emergencies, vacations, gifts, and auto repair. Lines 1 through 6 on the form are explained below.

Line 1 is the balance brought forward ($3,500) from the previous year. Based on the activity of that year, $2,100 of that $3,500 belongs to the emergency account, $500 belongs to the vacation account, $300 belongs to the gift account, and $600 belongs to the auto repair account.

Lines 2 through 6 show the activity in the fund for the most recent month. On January 8, Dan bought Wendy a birthday gift. He entered $40 in the total balance column with a parenthesis around it indicating it is an amount they need to subtract from the balance because they just spent $40. The $40 was also shown as being spent from the gift fund.

On January 15, Dan got paid. He deposited $235 to the fund, so $235 is shown under the total balance column. Of that $235, $100 was for the emergency fund, $70 was for the vacation fund, $30 was for the gift fund, and $35 was for the auto repair fund. They show those four figures under each of those funds. Since this was money being added to the funds, the figures do not have parentheses around them.

On January 17, Joe's Transmission Shop hit them hard with a $500 transmission job. They paid that out of their auto repair fund.

On January 25, they bought Sam and Mary a wedding present and recorded a $50 deduction from the total column, and a $50 deduction from the gift column.

On January 30, another paycheck was again distributed among the four categories.

The last line shows end-of-the-month totals based on adding and subtracting the transactions. The fund now has a total of $3,380, distributed as shown.

On page 305 is a blank form on which you can set up your own or your client's ledger to track savings.

Month __January__

Wendy and Dan's Money Market Fund for Short-Term Savings

	Date	Description	Total Fund Balance	Fund #1 Emergency	Fund #2 Vacation	Fund #3 Gift	Fund #4 Auto Repair	Fund #5
1	12/31	previous year balance forward	3500	2100	500	300	600	
2	1/8	Wendy's birthday gift	(40)			(40)		
3	1/15	paycheck	235	100	70	30	35	
4	1/17	Joe's transmission	(500)				(500)	
5	1/25	Sam and Mary's wedding	(50)			(50)		
6	1/30	paycheck	235	100	70	30	35	
		End of month total	3380	2300	640	270	170	

Form for Tracking Short-Term Savings

Month _____

Date	Description	Total Fund Balance	Fund #1	Fund #2	Fund #3	Fund #4	Fund #5

FINANCIAL AND LEGAL ISSUES

Important!

All tax and legal information contained in this section is current at the time of publication. Use this information only as a starting point. In the event such tax and legal information becomes critical to a case, it is always in the client's best interest to consult a tax or legal professional for current information.

COUNSELING LIABILITY GUIDELINES

As you build a counseling relationship with a client, you, may find them seeking your opinion on various financial decisions. In some cases this is because your past advice on budget issues or other matters has proven trustworthy. In other circumstances, you may be consulted because of your professional expertise.

If you provide guidance for situations not related to budget counseling or general financial direction, you may expose yourself and your church to the risk of legal liability for the advice you give.

In these situations you can best serve the client if you help them work through the issue factually. Aid their thinking process to be sure it is objective. Work through the numbers, computations, and budget questions the decision raises. Ask the questions they need to ask themselves. Slow them down if they need that. Keep them honest with themselves.

Avoid telling them specifically what to do. Direct them to professional assistance where appropriate. Do not relate what you would do if it were up to you. If you must give a recommendation, take off your counselor's hat with a disclaimer such as, "I'll give you my ideas on this, but remember this is not the opinion of [your church name]."

In other situations, you may be asked for legal advice. A client facing a legal dilemma will ask you what they can and cannot do. Armed with your Good $ense counselor training and resources, you may feel confident telling them what their rights are. The difficulty is that your information may be wrong. Either facts unique to their situation will permit actions of which you are unaware, or the law may have changed since you were educated on the matter. At the extreme, being too involved in giving legal advice could place you in jeopardy for practicing law without a license.

An appropriate balance is to share what you are reasonably certain is factual information, explaining you are not a lawyer and then encouraging them to seek legal advice to verify and go more deeply into the matter. If you make a specific referral to a lawyer, it is important that it be a competent person with appropriate expertise in the area of needed advice.

If you happen to have the professional expertise needed in the situation, it is important for you to maintain your counselor's role in that circumstance. Not only could your exercise of professional expertise create conflicts of interest, but also your objectivity as a counselor will be compromised. It is best to give them your time in the form of the budget counsel the Good $ense Ministry has promised to provide them. Remember, a Good $ense counselor may not benefit financially in any way through someone with whom they've come in contact as a Good $ense counselor.

Limiting your role in these ways will help you serve clients well, while avoiding risks you and your church do not wish to take.

NEGOTIATING WITH CREDITORS

Sometimes clients become seriously behind in their debt repayment and creditors have contacted them demanding repayment. In such cases, the client should immediately contact the creditors, explain the situation to them (including the fact that they are working with a counselor), and request additional time (several weeks—no more than four) to draw up and submit a repayment plan.

Making the Commitment

In the majority of cases, it is best that this contact be made by the client, not the counselor. Once a repayment plan is set up and is agreeable to the client, creditors should be notified *immediately* of the details of the plan. Whenever contact is made with creditors, it is important for clients to remember three things:

1. Be committed to repay the debt in full.

2. Be honest.

3. Be reliable . . . follow through with the commitment.

Emphasize to your client the need to initiate contact. Hiding from creditors only makes things worse. In order of preference, there are three methods which have proven most effective in dealing with creditors:

1. Personal meeting, face-to-face presentation.

2. Phone call followed by a letter summarizing the agreement.

3. Letter stating intent to pay and outlining the repayment plan.

Instruct your clients to be prepared when they contact creditors. They should be ready to explain the problem, the plan, and when the creditor will be paid. It is important that the creditor develop faith and trust in the debtor in order to accept the plan. If the client is sincere, the creditor's response is usually favorable. Most creditors react favorably to people who sincerely desire to make things right. Often the client will have to ask to deal with the supervisor rather than an employee who has no power to approve a new payment plan. Once that person is found, the client should try to deal exclusively with him or her. All future correspondence should be addressed to that person. Instruct the client to keep a copy of all letters exchanged and a log of all telephone discussions and meetings in case disputes or legal actions arise later.

If situations change, requiring a different monthly payment, the client should contact the creditor quickly and honestly explain the circumstances. If the debt is a bank loan, have the client set up an appointment with the office of the credit manager or collections department. If the debt is with a department store, have them contact the customer accounts department.

In such cases as these, Consumer Credit Counseling with its interest and abatement ability can be very helpful. (See Consumer Credit Counseling Service on page 311.)

Creditor's Legal Action

In the United States, before the creditor can legally attach a debtor's salary or property, the creditor must file a suit in the appropriate court. The court then issues a summons to the debtor informing the debtor of the step taken by the creditor. Once the summons is given to the debtor, the debtor normally has fourteen to thirty days to respond. If the debtor does not respond to the summons within the time granted by the summons, the court can make an assignment to the creditor.

If the creditor and debtor can agree to a repayment plan before the time limit on the summons expires, the suit can be dropped. Therefore, having the client or counselor contact the debtor immediately to work out a repayment plan is advisable. A lawyer may be contacted to attempt a compromise if the client and counselor fail to reach an accord. If a compromise can't be reached prior to court, the client, accompanied by the counselor or lawyer, should go to court with a repayment plan drawn up. For more on this topic, see "When Negotiations with Creditors Fail" on page 316.

Debt Moratoriums or Restructured Loans

Often a moratorium or temporary cessation of payments can be granted the client. Usually interest charges will still be required, but principle payback may be suspended briefly. If the creditor sees the problem as temporary in nature, the creditor may be willing to grant this. The creditor may also be willing to restructure the debt to allow for a longer loan with smaller payments than originally agreed upon. Negotiating these alternatives may be to the benefit of the client by reducing immediate monthly expenses. But, unless the client has fully repented from past debt mistakes or become aware of the dangers of borrowing, this step may reinforce an attitude that it is okay to push the problem into the future by paying more later to pay less now.

Bill consolidation is seldom a good idea. Certainly, total monthly payments can be reduced, but only by extending the duration of the loan. Commercial agencies offering bill consolidation services often charge exorbitantly high interest rates which, combined with the longer payback period, is obviously counterproductive.

Consumer Credit Counseling Service

CCCS is a non-profit national network of offices in the United States that, while offering similar services, are each independently operated. Thus, their fees, while nominal, do vary. For the nominal fee, they develop a debt repayment plan under which the client writes them one check and CCCS pays the various creditors. A significant advantage is that they have established relationships with most of the major credit card companies and are often able to arrange for the waiver of interest and in, some cases, an actual reduction in the principal amount owed. They have offices in most major U.S. cities.

A Christian-based organization that operates similarly to CCCS is Community Credit Counselors, which can be reached at the toll-free number (877) 603-0292.

SAMPLE LETTER FROM CLIENT TO CREDITOR*

Date

ABC Creditor
Street
City, State, Zip code

Dear [Creditor Name],

I am experiencing financial difficulties for the following reasons. [Provide a concise, honest summary]. I have explored every alternative and with the help of a budget counselor provided by my church, have developed a budget and repayment plan for all of my creditors. I can assure you it is doable and I am committed to following through on it.

In order to provide for my family's needs and to make planned payments to my creditors, I am asking creditors to accept a reduced payment until I am once again on sound financial ground. During the repayment period I am committed to incurring no additional debt.

In place of my regular payment of $XX, I request you accept payment of $YY each payment period until the balance is paid in full. I am enclosing the first of these payments [or indicate when the first payment will be made].

Thank you for your consideration. Should you need to contact me, I can be reached at [phone]. The best time to reach me is [time].

Sincerely,

Name
Street
City, State, Zip code

---

* Note: Keep a copy of all correspondence and a written record of any subsequent phone conversations.

SAMPLE LETTER FROM COUNSELOR TO CREDITOR*

Date

XYZ Creditor
Street
City, State, Zip code

Dear [Creditor Name]:

I am a member of the financial counseling ministry at [name of church]. I am currently working with [client name], one of your customers, regarding [his/her/their] overall financial and debt situation.

I understand [client name] has been in touch with you concerning the pay off plan they have developed. They indicated that you were not open to their proposal. I am writing to confirm that I am working with them on a regular basis and that I helped to develop the plan. It represents their ability to meet their obligations in the best way possible at this time. I will continue to work with them, encourage and hold them accountable and will notify all creditors if the conditions agreed upon are not being met.

The success of this plan depends upon all creditors concurring with it. Without this concurrence the only alternative appears to be a court-administered plan. Obviously, it is to everyone's advantage if this does not become necessary.

Please reconsider your initial response and agree to the submitted plan. Should you care to do so, you may contact me at [phone] between the hours of [time]. Your prompt response to this request will be appreciated.

Sincerely,

Name
Street
City, State, Zip code

* Note: Keep a copy of all correspondence and a written record of any subsequent phone conversations.

ADDITIONAL THOUGHTS ON NEGOTIATING WITH LAWYERS AND CREDITORS

Some clients may have been sued for a debt obligation. In those circumstances there are several avenues they may take to gain additional time, or to obtain a compromise of the debt due. Some of those situations are described here.

Contesting the Defensible Suit

In those few situations in which debtors have a well-grounded basis for disputing the existence or amount of the debt, they may wish to defend. In such a situation they must respond within the time permitted by filing an Answer to the Complaint with which they have been served. They need not hire a lawyer to do this; they can file their own papers. If the Complaint is verified or sworn to, the Answer must also be verified, using the verification language found on the Complaint.

Several rules must be observed in doing this, though. First, they must have been sued in the county of their residence or the place where the contract originated. If the suit is in another county, they should call a lawyer. Second, the original of any document including the debtor's Answer must be filed with the Clerk of the Court. There will be a filing fee for doing so. A copy of the Answer must be mailed to the lawyer who sued them.

Third, the Answer must contain a short statement denying the claim and stating the basis for the denial. It must be dated and signed by them, and they must certify that it was mailed to the lawyer who sued them. The lawyer may file additional papers to which they must respond.

A notice for trial will be given, at which they must appear. They will be permitted to tell their story and inspect any evidence and question witnesses the creditor presents. The judge will then decide the case. In a case where there is mandatory arbitration—usually for debts exceeding $2,500, but less than $50,000—a panel of arbitrators will decide the case.

The creditor's lawyer may attempt to negotiate settlement on the case at some point. In that event, the following information will help.

Compromising Debt Principle

Everyone is familiar with the axiom that a bird in the hand is worth two in the bush. Creditors know that phrase, too, and use it with some of their bad credit. In some circumstances, a client may have a source of funds that would permit them to liquidate some or all of the debt they will otherwise have to pay over time. The client must make a cash offer, usually beginning with 50 percent of the debt. Typically, creditor's attorneys will not bid against themselves.

Sometimes a creditor will accept half or less than half of a bad debt if they know they can get it today, rather than waiting for payments over time. While debtors should attempt to honor all commitments, in selective cases compromise could be explored as a means to reduce indebtedness.

Interest Reduction

In some cases, interest will have accumulated on a debt, but the interest is something the creditor may negotiate as well. In fact, the creditor may have already written off the debt and would be delighted to get their principle debt repaid. If they get favorable repayment terms, the creditor may forgive accrued interest to get an agreement. This may be true especially if the debtor is willing to sign a "Confession of Judgment," a legal document that permits a creditor to get judgment plus interest and attorneys' fees right away if the debtor defaults on the payments they agree to make.

Interest Waiver

Similarly, a creditor may waive future interest payments. This can be of great assistance to the debtor because interest can keep them from getting much benefit from the repayments they do make. An alternative for a client able to negotiate skillfully is to ask for an "interest waiver bonus," which would have the creditor waive interest payments at the end if the debtor makes all promised principle payments.

A client must remember in all negotiations to be specific in their offers; a creditor will respond best when there are firm terms presented. A creditor has nothing to lose if there is nothing specific on the table, and the creditor won't compromise voluntarily until offers are made. In any event, the worst a creditor can do is say no, but they will often say yes to good faith offers of compromise.

When Negotiations with Creditors Fail

When the initial attempt by the client fails to secure complete agreement to the repayment plan by the creditors, several steps are available. If one or two creditors are rejecting the plan, perhaps contacting them yourself can help persuade them. Reassure them that your client is genuine in their desire to repay the debt; the fact that you are involved may convince the creditor to accept the plan. A phone call is preferable, but a letter can also be sent (see the standard letter form on page 313). If the Spending Plan is reviewed and found void of any further areas to reduce spending and increase debt payments, consider one of the following options: Consider putting the original repayment plan into action anyway; request verification of the debt pursuant to the U.S. Fair Debt Collection Practices Act (FDCPA); go to court; consider Chapter 13 reorganization.

Consider Putting the Original Repayment Plan into Action Anyway

Many creditors may refuse to agree to the client's repayment amount, but may take no action as long as the money is paid. If the client can at least cover the interest or finance charges; make payments on schedule; and maintain contact with the creditor about their situation, the original repayment plan can succeed. The creditor is under no obligation to accept such a unilateral agreement, but many do so for a very good reason: it is simpler and less costly to do so than to use a collection agency or than taking the client to court.

Request Verification of the Debt Pursuant to the U.S. Fair Debt Collection Practices Act (FDCPA)

Attorneys as well as debt collectors are subject to the FDCPA and must stop all collection efforts until the request for verification is satisfied. A summary of the FDCPA is on page 327. The FDCPA is very specific about the types of communications that are permitted between creditors and debtors and is aimed at restraining and/or punishing abusive creditors. The FDCPA requires that persons who are deemed "collectors" must provide debtors with verification of the debt and must provide a thirty-day window of opportunity to negotiate the case or dispute the debt prior to filing suit. If the FDCPA is violated by a creditor, the penalties can be severe. Knowledge of the FDCPA can give the client leverage in dealing with an unfair or abusive creditor.

Going to Court

If the creditor fails to accept the repayment plan, the creditor can go to court against the client. The client will receive a summons to appear in court. When the client receives the summons, he or she must respond within thirty days by contacting the office of the court clerk or by going to court on the date specified on the summons. The client then should request a hearing and file an appearance by paying the appropriate fee. The purpose of a hearing is to give both sides a chance to speak. Legal consultation is recommended, but may not be necessary. When the client goes to court the client should:

- Prepare well in advance.

- Document income and assets.

- Document monthly expenses, using the Spending Plan to demonstrate where the money is going.

- Document the entire debt.

- Bring the repayment plan.

- Bring the log detailing the correspondence with creditors.

- Acknowledge the debt.

- Acknowledge the commitment to totally repay the debt.

- Acknowledge the commitment to incur no additional debt.

- Inform the court of the budget counseling help.

Deciding what the repayment amount should be is in the hands of the court or arbitration panel. If your client's plan is prudent and well supported by a realistic budget, the creditor will often have to accept the proposed amount. The judge has the option to allow the garnishment of the client's salary or demand a higher payment if he or she deems it appropriate. If this occurs, a Chapter 13 bankruptcy filing is a possible alternative.

The client has no guarantee of winning; nevertheless, if the client has been honest and fair, the chances for a favorable result are high.

Consider Chapter 13 Reorganization

A lawyer needs to be brought into the picture at this point to fully advise the client of the law. In a nutshell, Chapter 13, a section of the U.S. Federal Bankruptcy Act, allows an individual to work out an arrangement with the court and the creditors to pay back the debt. Thus, it protects the individual from unreasonable demands by a given creditor(s) that would be impossible for the individual to meet, but still obligates the repayment.

See page 337 for a more complete discussion of bankruptcy.

THE UNITED STATES INTERNAL REVENUE SERVICE

Occasionally Good $ense counselors may come across clients who owe money to the Internal Revenue Service. The IRS is similar to other creditors in that it desires to be paid back in full any money owed to it. The difference in dealing with the IRS is that it has, by law, more power and enforcement potential at its disposal than other creditor. Because of this fact, several things must be considered when there is a debt owed the IRS.

Here is a quick review of the collection process. On discovery of a person's income tax deficiency, the IRS sends a notice to the delinquent taxpayer, allowing ten days for a response. If no payment is received within the ten-day period, the IRS may attempt to contact the individual by telephone. If no response is forthcoming, the collection process moves to a more serious level. A member of the IRS will be assigned to investigate the delinquent taxpayer's background. The agent will seek to discover:

- the identity of the individual's employer

- what bank accounts are registered in the individual's name

- if there are any assets, such as automobiles, which the debtor owns that could be converted to cash.

If the IRS still has not heard anything from the delinquent taxpayer, then the following actions will typically be taken:

- Bank accounts will be frozen and levies made against them for available funds.

- Wages will be garnished. The IRS rules allow for all wages but $75 per week plus $15 per dependent.

- Tax liens will be put on assets.

To avoid this, if it hasn't already taken place, instruct the client to follow the same procedure that was suggested for dealing with any past-due creditor. Don't hide, but go to the IRS office. Honestly explain the relevant circumstances and offer a repayment plan. The IRS has on occasion reduced the balance owed in favor of a lump sum or payment plan. Remember, the IRS will be paid, and can enforce payment in full, yet negotiation as to the amount, rate of payment, and use of assets is possible. The client must be prepared to document the new budget plan and their spending needs, as well as the complete debt picture. The major difference in negotiating with the IRS is that they have more leverage in determining what a fair repayment plan will be. Bankruptcy threats don't scare them because their debts will not be reduced. Other creditors may be open to receiving your payment plan because a Chapter 13 reorganization ruling may cause them to receive less than full payment. But the IRS bill will eventually be paid totally unless an agreement for a reduction in the balance is made. In determining what payment rate is reasonable, the client will fill out a Collection Information Statement—documenting income and expenses (proof of heating bills, minimum payments to be made to other creditors, etc.).

Typically, the IRS will allow for reasonable expenses but will claim all surplus funds over and above those expenses. If equity in a home is available, the IRS will probably induce the taxpayer to sell it or borrow against it. As a general principal, the IRS is not going to loan a client money when equity is available. If it is affordable, and especially when the tax bill is large, seeking competent legal counsel is recommended. Yet because of the complex collection process involved, and with over 200 types of penalties, plus interest charges to deal with, few attorneys and CPAs may be qualified to negotiate effectively. Perhaps ex-IRS officers can best do the job.

In dealing with a client who will not be able to pay the upcoming tax bill, several bits of advice can be offered:

- File the return regardless. This avoids a failure-to-file penalty of 5 percent of the unpaid tax per month, up to a 25 percent maximum.

- Send in a partial payment. This reduces another penalty called the failure-to-pay penalty, which is half of 1 percent of the unpaid balance computed monthly (maximum is 25 percent of the unpaid balance). In addition, it verifies that the return was sent in.

- Negotiate with the IRS first before establishing a repayment plan with other creditors. This avoids having to adjust a repayment plan with creditors when the IRS enters the picture and wants its piece of the pie.

Don't feel pressured to know all about the IRS code. That is not the counselor's function. If IRS debts arise, just remember to counsel clients to deal with the agency swiftly and openly, recognizing that the power of the IRS to collect is different from that of any other creditor.

CREDIT SCORES

Jeff Gelles

Credit scores are an attempt to distill an individual's behavior patterns into an index number designed to predict how likely that person is to repay a loan or make timely credit payments. Scores are generated by computer models based on how well credit has been handled in the past by people with similar behavior patterns.

Credit scores are based on the following factors:

What is your payment history?

This consists of approximately 35 percent of your score.

Have you paid your bills on time? Your score reflects payment information on credit cards, retail accounts, and installment loans such as car loans, finance company accounts, and mortgage loans.

Generally, a payment that is thirty days late is not as bad as a payment that is ninety days late. But a thirty-day late payment made a month ago will count against you more than a ninety-day late payment from five years ago. How frequently you are late also counts.

Do you owe too much?

This makes up 30 percent of your score.

Owing money on various credit accounts doesn't automatically lead to a low score, but some borrowing patterns can hurt. One model weighs what is owed against the initial balances on installment loans and the lending limits on credit cards and other revolving accounts. The weight given to any factor may vary depending on other aspects of your credit profile. Also, although scores are based only on the information in your credit report, lenders may look at other factors when making a credit decision, such as your income and the kind of credit you are applying for.

How established is your credit?

This is 15 percent of your score.

In general, a longer credit history will increase your score. However, even people with short credit histories may get high scores depending on how the rest of the credit report looks.

Do you have a healthy mix of credit?

This is 10 percent of your score.

The score considers your mix of credit cards, retail accounts, installment loans, finance company accounts, and mortgage loans. It is not necessary to have one of each, and it is not advisable to open credit accounts you don't intend to use.

Are you taking on more debt?

This is 10 percent of your score.

Research shows that opening several credit card accounts in a short period of time does represent greater risk.

Your score may also be affected by repeated applications for credit, though the model treats multiple inquiries in a short period of time as a single inquiry to avoid penalizing consumers for shopping for the best rate.

Consumer advocates say credit scoring itself has contributed to the rise in delinquencies and defaults by fueling the growth of subprime lending: loans to people with less-than-perfect credit who can be charged higher interest rates because they pose greater risks.

Reprinted from the *Chicago Tribune*, (February 27, 2001), page 8.

EVICTION

Eviction proceedings are maintained by the legal action known as "forcible entry and detainer" or "ejectment." We'll just call it eviction.

Action by a landlord is typically triggered by the failure to pay rent. To evict in the U.S., the landlord must give the tenant at least five days to respond to a "demand for rent." A legal document bearing this name will be served on the tenant, unless they have waived their rights or have additional rights given to them in a lease. Generally, if the tenant brings rent current and there are no other defaults, they will be able to stay put, but that is not universally true.

If they continue in default, the landlord will follow the demand for rent with a Summons for the tenant to appear in court. This appearance will be required within seven to forty days from the date the Summons is issued. The tenant need not do anything if they intend to go to the court hearing, but they must respond in writing to the landlord and court if they will not appear.

Unless the tenant has good reason for nonpayment, which is rare, they will be evicted. The court may allow them some additional minimal time to vacate. If they do not remove themselves, the sheriff will remove them, by order of the court. In all events, the tenant is still liable for back rent owed.

In summary, the tenant in default usually has approximately three weeks, possibly more, from the date they are served the eviction notice to make other arrangements. Any rent due must be paid.

If the client has questions about the legality of the notices given or about the eviction process, he or she can sometimes obtain legal advice over the phone at no cost from free legal agencies such as Bar Association Volunteer Lawyer programs or the Legal Aid Society. A call to the county Bar Association can provide the numbers of these agencies in the client's area.

MORTGAGE FORECLOSURE

When a person finances the purchase of a residence, he or she gives the lender a mortgage securing repayment of the debt. If the purchaser defaults on payments, the creditor has the right to "foreclose" the mortgage, obtaining the property to satisfy the debt.

In the U.S., a foreclosure suit is started the same as other suits: by service of a Summons and Complaint. The debtor has thirty days after service to respond. If they do not respond, judgment will be taken against them.

How long can the debtor stay in the house after foreclosure starts? State laws vary on this issue and so it is good to contact a lawyer for accurate information in your state.

What options does the debtor have once they are sued for foreclosure? First, once every five years the debtor may reinstate the mortgage after suit is started by paying all defaults and the expenses the lender has incurred. Reinstatement must happen within ninety days after suit starts. Second, they may "redeem" the property by paying the amount specified in the foreclosure judgment, usually the amount due to the lender—plus interest and approved court costs—within seven months after suit starts, or three months after the foreclosure judgment is entered, whichever is later.

The debtor can be liable for any debt still owing after the proceeds of sale are applied to the debt and the expenses of foreclosure and sale. There are two ways to avoid this "deficiency" debt. One way is to give the creditor a "deed in lieu of foreclosure." This deed transfers the debtor's interest to the creditor and results in the creditor waiving any rights to claim a deficiency is due. The second way to avoid a deficiency situation is through a "consent foreclosure." This may be offered by the lender in the context of the foreclosure suit, and the debtor may respond by consenting to such a judgment being entered. In such a case the creditor waives all rights to a deficiency judgment.

In summary, when a debtor is foreclosed upon, they have thirty to ninety days to respond to the situation by moving or paying the amount they are in default, plus the creditor's expenses. They also have at least seven months to redeem the property by paying the judgment amount. If they do not retain the property, they should try to avoid a deficiency claim by using a deed in lieu of foreclosure or a consent foreclosure.

A QUICK SUMMARY OF THE U.S. FAIR DEBT COLLECTION PRACTICES ACT

Elizabeth V. Maring

Under the act, who is a debtor?

If you owe on credit cards, household items, personal loans, or other personal, family, or household matters, you are a debtor. If you fall behind on any of your debts, you may be contacted by a debt collector.

Under the act, who is a debt collector?

Anyone who regularly engages in the collection of a debt for others is a debt collector. This includes attorneys and collection agencies.

Do you have any rights as a debtor?

The Fair Debt Collection Practices Act is a law that protects debtors from unfair or unconscionable means by debt collectors to collect or attempt to collect a debt.

Can a debt collector contact you about your debt?

A debt collector may contact you at home or at work by mail, in person, or by fax, telephone, or telegram. However, the collector must not contact you at unreasonable times or places, which usually means that the collector must contact you after 8:00 A.M. or before 9:00 P.M. unless you agree otherwise. In addition, the collector must not contact you if he or she knows you are represented by an attorney, and cannot contact you at work if the collector knows that your employer disapproves or if you disapprove.

The debt collector must tell you the following information within five days after the initial communication with you or in the initial communication with you:

- The amount of the debt

- The name of the creditor to whom the debt is owed

- A statement that unless you, the debtor, contact the collector in writing and dispute the validity of the debt, the debt will be assumed to be valid by the debt collector

- A statement that if you notify the collector within the thirty day period that the debt, or any portion thereof, is disputed, that the debt collector will obtain verification of the debt and a copy will be mailed to the debtor, and

- A statement that upon written request within the thirty days that the collector will provide the name and address of the original creditor, if different from the current creditor.

What if you think you do not owe the money?

If you are contacted by a collector about a debt you do not think you owe, or if you dispute the balance the collector indicates you owe, you have a right to contact the collector in writing—*within thirty days of the first contact*—and contest the debt. The collector must send you proof of the debt before resuming collection activities.

Can you stop communication by a collector?

If you do not want to be contacted by a debt collector, you can contact the collector in writing and tell them to stop contacting you. Upon receipt of the letter, the collection agency or collector must not contact you except to let you know that they will cease communications with you or merely to notify you if the creditor intends to take specific action, such as file a lawsuit against you.

Can a debt collector contact anyone but you about your debt?

If you are represented by an attorney, a debt collector cannot contact any third parties and can contact only your attorney. If you are not represented by an attorney, a debt collector may contact third parties, but only to obtain location or job information about you. When contacting third parties, a collector must identify himself or herself but cannot discuss the debt. Collectors are usually prohibited from contacting third parties more than once and cannot tell anyone that you owe money.

What types of collection practices are prohibited?

1. False Statements

   A debt collector cannot:

   - falsely imply that they are an attorney or a government representative

   - falsely imply that you have committed a crime

   - falsely imply or represent that they work for a credit bureau

   - misrepresent the amount of the debt

   - misrepresent that an attorney is involved with the collection of the debt

   - indicate that documents sent to you are legal forms if in fact they are not, or indicate that the forms are not legal forms when in fact they are.

2. Harassment

   Debt collectors may not harass, oppress, or abuse anyone. For example, a debt collector cannot:

   - advertise your debt

   - telephone people and not identify themselves

   - use obscene or profane language

   - repeatedly telephone to annoy and harass someone

   - use threats of violence or harm against the person, property, or reputation of someone.

3. Unfair Practices

Debt collectors may not engage in unfair practices to collect the debt such as:

- collect more money than you owe on the debt unless allowed by law
- deposit a post-dated check prematurely
- contact you by postcard
- take or threaten to take your property unless it can be done legally
- make the debtor pay for telegrams or pay for collect calls.

4. Other

Debt collectors may not:

- use a false name
- send you anything that looks like it is from a court or government agency when it is not
- give false information about you to anyone
- state that you will be arrested if you do not pay your debt
- threaten that they will seize, garnish, attach, or sell your property or wages *unless* it is legal to do so and the collection agency or the creditor *intends to do so.*

Payment of multiple debts

If you owe more than one debt with a creditor, any payment you make must be applied to the debt that you indicate. A debt collector may not apply a payment to any debt that you dispute.

What you can do if you think a debt collector has violated the law

You have the right to sue a debt collector in state or federal court within one year from the date you believe the law was violated. If you have trouble with a debt collector and you believe the debt collector has violated the law, you can contact your state Attorney General and/or the Federal Trade Commission.

A poor credit history may be of concern to the client, but it's not the end of the world. Remember, the client should probably not be using credit cards or debt to sustain his or her lifestyle anyway. In addition, even homes and cars can be obtained with loans, even with poor credit histories. However, it usually requires more shopping around and paying a higher rate.

Credit records do change. After seven to ten years, such items as canceled accounts or Chapter 13 experiences are deleted from credit histories.

Preserving a good credit record should not be the ultimate goal of the client, at the expense of other financial considerations.

HOW TO OBTAIN A CREDIT REPORT

Copies of an individual's credit report may be obtained by contacting one of the following agencies. The report is available for a nominal fee.

Equifax
P.O. Box 740241
Atlanta, GA 30374-0241
(800) 685-1111
www.equifax.com

Experian (formerly TRW)
P.O. Box 949
Allen, TX 75013-0949
(888) 397-3742
www.experian.com

Trans-Union Consumer Disclosure Center
P.O. Box 390
Springfield, PA 19064-0390
(800) 916-8800
www.tuc.com

DRAWING ON ASSETS

Life Insurance

One way to reduce debt and lower monthly cash outlay for some clients is to review their life insurance portfolios. Many people who are paying for life insurance own some form of cash value insurance (whole life, universal life, variable life, endowment, etc.).

Remember, cash value insurance is simply death protection (term insurance) plus some form of forced savings. The premium consists of a charge for insurance and an additional charge for the savings. Since these savings programs traditionally pay low interest rates and/or have assorted fees and costs associated with them, clients may better utilize the savings charge of the premium to reduce debt and later to establish their emergency, replacement, and long-term savings accounts.

The following plans can be considered for two different situations:

1. If the insureds are in good health, they may consider securing a new policy of renewable term life insurance (pure death protection) to cover their needs. They can combine all of their family's policies into one. Having a husband and wife together on one policy, saves the cost of policy fees. Also, a rider to cover an adequate amount of death benefit for the children can be added to the family policy for very little cost, if applicable. Once the new lower cost term insurance policy has been issued, the cash value policies can be surrendered. Monthly cash outlay for insurance has been lowered and the clients still have the same protection. Any cash value that the previous policy had can be used to reduce debt. Be sure that new insurance is in effect before the old policy is cancelled.

2. If the insured cannot qualify for new insurance due to ill health, they can write a letter to each insurance company involved to get necessary information needed to reduce the monthly cost and/or borrow or obtain any cash that might be available. The letter should be addressed to the home office of the insurance company and should include the policy number. The following information should be included in their request:

- What is the current face amount and cash surrender value of this policy?

- Is the cash value available for a loan, or can the money be obtained by other means without lapsing the policy?

- What interest rate or fees are involved in the above?

- If all cash available is removed, what would the minimum monthly premium be to keep this policy in force? (Please use dividends, if available, to reduce premiums.)

- In addition, ask the company to send a printout, illustrating the above requests.

The company's reply to the above request will help to determine a correct decision regarding meeting the client's insurance needs.

Retirement Funds

Taxable distributions and borrowing are two ways of taking money out of qualified employee plans.

Taxable Distributions

Under current U.S. regulations, this is permitted if a person:

- Has reached age fifty-nine and a half

- Has been separated from military service

- Has died or become disabled

- Is involved in a plan which has been terminated

- Has certain medical expenses or qualified hardship caused by immediate and heavy financial needs that cannot be reasonably satisfied from other resources

- Is a nonparticipant under a divorce court order.

In each of the above situations, the recipient will have to pay tax on the amount of the distribution. In the event the recipient is separated from military service and is under age fifty-five, they will be subject to a 10 percent premature distribution penalty in addition to the tax. If the plan is terminated and the person is under fifty-nine-and-a-half, they are also subject to the regular tax plus the 10 percent premature distribution tax. The tax and the premature distribution tax can be avoided if funds are rolled over into another tax sheltered account (such as an IRA) within a sixty-day period after distribution. "Certain medical expenses" and "qualified hardships" are not clearly defined, so the 10 percent penalty may or may not apply.

Borrowing against a Qualified Plan

- An employee may borrow the greater of $10,000 or half the present value of their nonforfeitable accrued benefit up to an aggregate loan amount of $50,000. Any amounts greater than this will be considered a taxable distribution.

- A loan to an employee from deductible employee contributions is treated as a distribution regardless of the amount or term of the loan.

- There is a five-year repayment requirement. A loan to a participant that is not required to be repaid within five years is automatically treated as a taxable distribution. The time period should be determined at the time the loan is made. If repayments are not all made under a plan of five years or less, the amount still owed at the end of five years is then considered a taxable distribution. A loan that is treated as a distribution because of a greater than five-year repayment period will still be treated as taxable even though it is paid within five years. Determining the time frame at the beginning is vital.

- There is one exception to the five-year repayment rule. If the loan is used to acquire (not construct or reconstruct) a principal residence of the participant (not a member of his or her family), the five-year repayment is not applicable.

- A retirement plan loan must be amortized in equal payments, not less than quarterly over the life of the loan.

- There is a short-term period of sixty days in which IRA funds can be used during a rollover period. You are limited to one rollover per investment, per twelve-month period.

The client should thoroughly review all the preceding points with their retirement plan coordinator. A given plan may vary, but it should be within this framework. If you are unsure of what to do, and since tax laws frequently change, it is wise to consult a tax professional if this option is relevant for your client.

BANKRUPTCY LAWS*

The two provisions of the U.S. Bankruptcy Code that are most often considered are Chapter 13 and Chapter 7.

Chapter 13 is a personal financial reorganization. Under this provision the court determines the repayment plan between creditors and debtors. Chapter 13 is often seen as a refuge from creditors whose repayment demands may be seen as excessive under current circumstances. It is also frequently used to protect certain assets from being turned over to lenders. It is not specifically designed to eliminate debts, but to pay back the debts the court deems repayable and at a rate the court rules is feasible. Some debts may be reduced or eliminated, however, and interest charges and penalty costs may be waived. The court trustee who works with the debtor and creditors to establish a repayment plan must see a flow of income coming in that will enable the debts to be retired within three years. In some cases four- or five-year repayment plans will be acceptable. The steps leading a person to file for Chapter 13 often follow this pattern.

Step 1 The creditor is owed $5,000, with a minimum monthly installment of $100 per month needed to retire the debt. The debtor hasn't paid anything in the past six months, so the creditor seeks legal remedy and files a suit with the court to collect.

Step 2 The debtor receives a summons informing him or her of legal action and typically has fourteen to thirty days to respond.

Step 3 The debtor cannot work out a reduced installment plan with the creditor and, to prevent the debtor from seizing assets or garnishing wages, the debtor files for Chapter 13 protection.

Step 4 The debtor, with help of an attorney or other counselor, drafts a repayment plan to be reviewed by a court-appointed trustee. If the plan is judged as fair to creditors, the plan is accepted and approved by a judge. If judged unfair, the trustee will make adjustments and seek court acceptance.

* Important note: At time of publication, U.S. federal legislation was pending on significant changes to the bankruptcy laws. Consult an attorney for current information.

Step 5 The plan goes into operation until debts are retired.

It should be noted that some debts such as IRS obligations and governmentally approved educational loans will not be reduced through Chapter 13 proceedings. Debts occasioned by fraudulent conduct will not be removed through bankruptcy. Similarly, Chapter 7 protection does not exempt the debtor from paying these debts.

Chapter 7 of the U.S. Bankruptcy Code is a more severe step for the debtor to take, in that all debt is cleared up by matching assets against liabilities. Under this provision, the judge exempts certain amounts of money from creditors' claims and then arranges the liquidation of all other assets to be turned over pro-rata to the creditors. Common exemptions include:

- Necessary clothing

- Bibles

- School books

- Family photos

- Equity interest in other property up to the amount of $2,000

- Equity interest in a motor vehicle up to $1,200

- Equity interest in any professional books or tools up to the amount of $750

- Professionally prescribed health aids for the person or a dependent

- All proceeds payable because of the death of the insured and the aggregate net cash value of any or all life insurance and endowment policies and annuity contracts payable to a wife or husband of the person or to a child, parent, or other person dependent upon the person

- A person's right to receive Social Security benefits, unemployment compensation, worker's compensation benefits, public assistance benefits, veteran's benefits, disability, illness or unemployment benefit, alimony support, or separate maintenance to the extent reasonably necessary for the support of the person and any dependent of the person

- A homestead exemption of up to $7,500 ($15,000 for married couple filing jointly) in property owned by the person that is used as a residence

- Retirement plan, if it qualifies as a retirement plan under the Internal Revenue Code or the person's state pension code.

These are some of the general guidelines to how much can be kept by the debtor. Chapter 7 legally clears away all debts (except IRS, school loans, and fraudulently incurred obligations) and seeks to provide the family with a new start.

Important: Remember to tell each client that you are not legally trained and do not purport to know all the facts surrounding Chapter 13 and Chapter 7. The information provided here is not comprehensive and may not be current or fully accurate. Your counsel is not a substitute for that of a lawyer.

For a biblical perspective on bankruptcy, see page 284.

MISCELLANEOUS ARTICLES

THE CUMULATIVE EFFECT OF LITTLE THINGS OVER AN EXTENDED PERIOD

A faucet dripping once a second can release fifty gallons in one week. In the same way, a slow trickle of money can gradually fill financial reservoirs to overflowing or drain them dry. Since everything we have ultimately belongs to God, every financial splash we make can have eternal significance and consequence. To have the financial freedom God intends, we need to learn how to use—rather than be victimized by—the cumulative effect of little things over an extended period.

To get a clearer picture of this important principle—what the Bible has to say about it and how small financial decisions really do add up—consider the Scriptures and examples below.

What the Bible Says

Scripture is clear in its support of the cumulative effect of a little effort over an extended period.

- "Go to the ant, you sluggard; consider its ways and be wise! . . . it stores its provisions in summer and gathers its food at harvest" (Proverbs 6:6–8).

- "If you have not been trustworthy in handling worldly wealth, who will trust you with true riches?" (Luke 16:11).

- "Everyone who competes in the games goes into strict training. They do it to get a crown that will not last; but we do it to get a crown that will last forever" (1 Corinthians 9:25).

Just a Dollar a Day

The cumulative effect of a little money, just one dollar a day, can be tremendous over a forty-five-year career depending on whether it is saved or added to debt. The chart below compares saving the dollar in a piggy bank, or a tax-sheltered mutual fund with a 10 percent return, versus charging the dollar to a credit card and incurring a 20 percent interest charge.

Years	Piggy bank	Invested in a mutual fund with a 10 percent rate of return	Charged to a credit card with a 20 percent interest rate
5	$1,825	$2,329	−$2,957
10	$3,650	$6,080	−$10,316
15	$5,475	$12,121	−$28,626
20	$7,300	$21,849	−$74,190
25	$9,125	$37,518	−$187,566
30	$10,950	$62,752	−$469,681
35	$12,775	$103,391	−$1,171,674
40	$14,600	$168,842	−$2,918,457
45	$16,425	$274,250	−$7,265,012

Major Purchases

The cumulative effect has a great impact on every major purchase. A $20,000 item can cost as little as $17,700 or as much as $25,500 depending on whether we allow the cumulative effect to work for us by saving for it in advance, or against us by incurring debt to purchase now. Consider this example:

To accumulate $20,000 in five years at 5 percent interest monthly payments to ourselves will have to be $295 and the total of the sixty payments will be $17,700.	To borrow $20,000 for five years at 10 percent interest monthly payments to the finance company will have to be $425 and the total of the sixty payments will be $25,500.

Start Young

Although students and young adults may not feel they have much in the way of assets, the greatest asset they have is *time.*

Saving $100 a month during the first fifteen years of a career, and then saving nothing more for the next twenty-five years with a 10 percent return, results in savings of $431,702.	Saving nothing during the first fifteen years of a career, and then saving $100 a month for the next twenty-five years with a 10 percent return, results in savings of $123,332.

It's Never Too Late

It's never too late to start making a little extra effort. For example, a $100,000 home loan for thirty years at 7 percent interest would have a monthly payment of $665, and the final cost of the loan would be double what was borrowed. However, paying just a little extra every month could dramatically reduce the total cost of the loan.

Extra Payment	Out of Debt	Total Interest
$0/month	30 years	$139,511
$25/month	<27 years	$121,296
$50/month	<24 years	$107,856
$100/month	<21 years	$ 89,003

A BIG DIFFERENCE IN A SHORT TIME

Question: My client is determined to be a better steward of God's resources. It would be an encouragement if they could do something that would make a big difference in a short time. Do you have a suggestion?

Answer: Except for housing (an expense that is pretty hard to change), cars are the biggest drain on most budgets. The average price of a new car in the United States is $19,000. Although cars remain reliable for an average of ten years and 120,000 miles, Americans tend to keep cars an average of only four-and-a-half years and 41,000 miles. Hanging on to their present car—or buying a good used car instead of a new one—may be the "one big thing" the client could do to free up a significant amount of money for higher purposes.

Here are some facts you might share with your client as they decide whether having an older car would be appropriate:

- A car loses most of its trade-in value in the first four years. If they trade in a new car after four years or less, they're paying a tremendous price for less than half the useful life of the car. On the other hand, if they buy a good used vehicle, they can get more than half the useful life of the car at a relatively thrifty price.

- We usually assume that new cars are more reliable than used cars. However, according to *Consumer Reports,* cars less than one year old make as many trips to the repair shop as cars that are four or five years old. The most reliable years of a car's life are the second and third years.

- When they select a new car, they have to base their decision on the manufacturer's claims, but used cars have a track record that they can check. Most libraries have the *Consumer Reports Annual Buying Guide,* which has a chapter called "Ratings of Cars as Used Cars" and a huge chart giving "Six-Year Repair Records" for most models. Also, the National Highway Traffic Safety Administration has a toll-free hotline they can use to see if a used car has ever been recalled: (800) 424-9393.

- As a car gets older, the costs for maintenance increase, but the costs for collision and theft insurance decrease.

- New car dealers typically save the best trade-in cars to sell on their own used car lots. These cars are often thoroughly checked and backed by a used-car warranty. In some cases, used car buyers may even inherit the remainder of the manufacturer's new car warranty.

- Recently, leasing has become a popular option and is pushed heavily by many auto dealers. No wonder—it's a good deal for them. The appeal to many unsuspecting folks is the lower monthly payment. Payments *should* be lower! At the end of the lease they don't own anything! The up side for used-car buyers is that an increasing number of leased cars are being turned in at the end of the lease and then turn up on used car lots.

Bottom line:

- A recent comparison of the cost differential of keeping a four-year-old car for another four years and spending more on gas, oil, tires and maintenance versus buying a new car showed the savings in keeping the four-year-old car to be over $5,000 . . . assuming the new car would be paid for in cash. Add a couple thousand more dollars if it would be financed.

- A comparison of buying a two-year-old used car and keeping it for eight years versus leasing a new car every three years over a "driving life time" of forty-eight years revealed a staggering (almost unbelievable) differential of over $400,000.

You might quibble over some of the assumed costs, and the equation might change by some thousands of dollars, but the point is clear—huge savings are possible in the area of automobiles.

When Jesus spoke about avoiding "treasures on earth, where moth and rust destroy, and where thieves break in and steal," he could have been speaking of cars. Probably his advice to Christian families today would be, "Keep the heap," and "Store up for yourselves treasures in heaven, where moth and rust do not destroy, and where thieves do not break in and steal. For where your treasure is, there your heart will be also" (Matthew 6:19–21).

Information on costs and savings taken from "A Big Difference in a Short Time" by Jon Kopke, *College Hill Presbyterian Church Belltower News* (November 1996).

NOTHING DOWN, NOTHING A MONTH

Dave Ramsey

One way products and services are sold is by offering consumers unbelievable financing. Have you ever heard of "ninety days same as cash" or "no finance charges until January" or "no-interest financing"? Did it ever occur to you that in a world driven by money markets, a company offering zero interest with no ulterior motive would soon go broke?

Here is how it really works. First, the product is priced higher to cover the expense of the zero-interest financing. So there is actually no savings to begin with. But the story just starts there. Most dealers then sell the financing contract to a finance company to buy. And why would a finance company buy a contract at zero interest? Because the dealer (a furniture store, department store, electronics store, etc.)—who marked the item up in the first place—sells the financing contract to the finance company at a discount. Everyone but the purchaser wins. The dealer got what they wanted—an immediate sale at a regular profit (after the discount to the finance company). And when the buyer pays off the finance company, the finance company makes a profit because they got the buyer's contract at a discount from the dealer.

Second, and more importantly, over 70 percent of the time *the buyer does not pay off the dealer within the stated period.* Then the finance company gladly begins to charge interest and initiates a longer payment plan. When this occurs, the buyer often pays over 24 percent interest (if that state allows it) and the contract is on prepaid interest or "rule of 78's," which means there is a huge prepayment penalty. Plus, the company will add interest for the original ninety days, which is only "free" if paid off within the ninety days. They also typically will sell overpriced life and disability insurance to pay off their overpriced loan should something happen to your overpriced self. I once met a man who had life insurance on a loan against a rototiller!

This brilliant zero-interest plan now has turned into one of the worst financial decisions ever made because of the total cost of that item. A $1,000 couch at 25 percent for three years with credit life and disability insurance can end up costing at least $1,900.

Adapted from *Financial Peace,* Dave Ramsey (Viking Press, New York, 1992, 1997), pages 39-40.

WHAT THE BIG PRINT GIVETH, THE SMALL PRINT TAKETH AWAY

Mary Hunt

The other day I got a note from J.K. expressing disgust with her credit card company. It seems that in response to her monthly statement, J.K.—wishing to respond responsibly—sent two checks along with clear instructions:

- The check for $150 was to pay in full the portion of her balance that was being charged 15.7 percent interest.

- The second check was the required $134 payment on the big balance—the amount she transferred to this card in the first place so she could take full advantage of that dubious 3.9 percent interest rate.

The company completely ignored her instructions and applied both amounts to the low-interest portion of her balance, leaving that $150 intact, growing like crazy at 15.7 percent per year.

Her question: Don't we, as consumers, have any say over this or are we at the mercy of whoever is processing the checks that day?

My answer: No, you silly woman! You have no say. You have no rights. You kissed them good-bye the day you signed that highly deceptive credit card application. You agreed to let the company decide how your payments will be allocated. And they will always do that to their advantage, not yours.

I just happen to have that fine print and a high-powered magnifying glass right here in front of me. Take a look:

Payment Allocation: Your payment will be allocated in the manner the company deems appropriate including applying your payment to transfer balances before purchases and cash advance balances. Did you get that? The manner the company deems appropriate. Gotcha!

While I have this application handy, let's take a look at the rest of the fine print. Now, I know this material is probably a great cure for insomnia, but remember this is the stuff that's getting many of you into financial trouble because you assume naively that transferring balances to these slick new "low-interest" cards is some kind of noble financial move.

So buck up! Pay attention. Don't even think about turning this page, yet!

Annual Percentage Rate: This particular application, starting with the envelope and cute letter from Anne Geddes (would somebody please tell me what in the world cute babies in pea pods have to do with credit cards?), shouts "3.9 fixed rate!" But read the fine print: 3.9 percent on balance transfers and purchases until April 1, 1999; after that a 9.99 percent rate on purchases and balance transfers, and 19.99 percent APR on cash advances. Does that look like "3.9 fixed rate" to you? Gotcha!

Note Buried at the Bottom: If payment is late once during the introductory period, the rate goes to 9.99 percent. If payment is received late twice in any six-month period, 19.99 percent takes effect. If you do not make payments for two consecutive months, 22.99 percent takes effect on all balances on your account. Did you get that? If you are late—and believe me, that means even five minutes and for any reason—you lose. Do it twice and you're toast. To make matters even worse, those new punitive rates apply to the entire statement balance, not just future purchases and balance transfers. Gotcha!

Transaction Fee: For ATM and bank cash advances, 2 percent of the advance, but not less than $10. That means if you take a $20 cash advance you will immediately pay 19.99 percent interest on $30, not just the $20 you withdrew. Gotcha!

Grace Period: Twenty to twenty-five days from the date of the periodic statement (provided you paid your previous balance in full by the due date). If you carry a balance, no grace. Period. Gotcha!

Billing method. Two-Cycle Average Daily Balance Method (including new purchases). Watch out for this one. Hardly anyone knows what it means so it's easy to ignore it. Two-cycle billing has become quite standard with the new "low fixed-rate cards." This is one of the ways the company can recapture the interest they give up on the front end. If you don't pay in full each month, two-cycle billing can kill you interest-wise. Two-cycle calculations require you pay in full two months in a row or they reach back to eliminate the grace period between cycles. If the bill is not paid in full at the first billing, interest becomes retroactive—back to the purchase date. One-cycle cards look at each billing period on its own.

Example: If you paid your $600 January bill in full, but only $300 of your $800 bill in February, a two-cycle method will go back and charge you two months' worth of interest in March, wiping out your grace period from February. Gotcha!

Late Payment Fee: $29 every time you are late! Keep in mind that's in addition to the punitive interest rate increases for being late. Double Gotcha!

Over-the-Credit-Limit-Fee: $25 each month your balance is over limit. Even if you are only $1 over limit, you'll get nailed with a $25 fee that immediately accrues interest. That should keep you over limit next month, too. And next . . . gotcha!

The final blow: Every credit card agreement carries a just-in-case-we-missed-anything provision like this: I understand that the terms of my account are subject to change at any time and for any reason. Gotcha! Gotcha! Gotcha!

The new low fixed-rate interest rates—even as low 2.9 percent—lose their glamour once you consider and fully understand the serious ramifications of the small print. Read it and weep.

Reprinted from "Cheapskate Monthly," Vol. 8, Number 3 (March 1999), page 1. Copyright 1999 Mary Hunt.

UNPLUGGING FROM THE CONSUMPTIVE SOCIETY

*"There are two ways of getting enough; one is to continue to accumulate more of it, the other is to desire less."**

Here are ten tips on simplifying life and being a good steward that you may wish to share with your clients.

1. **Know where your money goes—develop a budget.**
   If we make no more than $25,000 per year for forty-five working years, we will have been the stewards of $1,125,000! How dare we consider handling that amount of money without keeping records and knowing where it went! Also, treat the giving portion of your budget differently than your operating budget. The goal of the operating budget is to hold down expenditures, but the goal of giving is to increase expenditures.

2. **Actively reject the advertising industry's persuasive and pervasive attempt to squeeze you into its mold.**
   Greet with sarcastic laughter all the patently false claims of phony TV commercials. Have your family shout in unison, "Who do you think you're kidding?" The goal of advertising is to create a desire for products. This is often done by creating dissatisfaction with what you now have, even though it may be quite satisfactory. Avoid settings that subject you to these overt efforts to create a mindset that is antithetical to Christ's teachings. Don't watch ads on TV. Don't read mail-order catalogs. Don't window shop in malls. Look at advertisements only after you have carefully determined your need for a particular product, and then only to seek the best quality at the lowest price.

3. **When you do decide it is right to purchase an item, see if God will provide it without you having to buy it.**
   Pray about it for a week, then consider if you still need it. If God hasn't provided it and you do still need the item, go ahead and purchase it. This practice integrates our needs with the concept of God's provision and has the additional benefit of avoiding impulse buying.

---

* Source of quote unknown.

4. **Stress the quality of life above quantity of life.**
Refuse to be seduced into defining life in terms of having, rather than being. Learn the wonderful lesson that to increase the quality of life means to decrease material desire—not vice versa.

5. **Make recreation healthy, happy, and gadget free.**
Consider noncompetitive games—why must there always be a winner? Avoid "spectatoritis." Modern spectator sports programs are obscene in their waste of human and material resources. It is a joy to watch some games, but addiction to doing so is another thing altogether. Develop the habit of homemade celebrations. Read together, play games, tell stories, have skits, invite other families in (and don't kill yourself preparing for them).

6. **Learn to eat sensibly and sensitively.**
Eliminate prepackaged dinners. Plan menus ahead, and buy only to meet the menu. Eliminate nonnutritious snack foods. Be conscious of the bio food chain. Grain-fed animals that require ten pounds of grain to produce one pound of meat are a luxury that the bio food chain cannot sustain for the masses of humanity. Get in on the joy of gardening. Dwarf fruit trees can supply large quantities of fresh fruit. Explore food cooperatives. Eat out less and make it a celebration when you do. Go without food one day a month and give the money you save to the poor. Buy less food rather than diet pills!

7. **Learn the difference between significant travel versus self-indulgent travel.**
Give your travel purpose. Travel inexpensively. Become acquainted with people as well as places.

8. **Buy things for their usefulness, not their status.**
Clothes can be quite presentable but inexpensive. Furniture can be used, refinished. Significant amounts of money can be saved buying good used cars and less expensive models. Are you alone after having raised your family? Consider inviting extended family, a college student, or single young person to live with you.

9. **Learn to enjoy things without owning them.**
Possession is an obsession in our culture. If we own it, we feel we can control it, and if we control it, we feel it will give us more pleasure. This is an illusion. Enjoy the beauty of the beach without the compulsion to buy a piece of it. Many things can be shared among neighbors and friends. Give some things away just for the freedom it brings.

10. **Teach your children by word and deed about the varied uses of money. Provide clear guidelines about what you consider reasonable and unreasonable expenditures.**
Culture trains children to desire everything in sight when they enter a store. You do them no favor when you give in to their incessant demands. Get them what they need, not what they want; and in time, they will come to want what they need. Provide children with the experience of a growing self-governance. At a young age, offer them an allowance to give them the experience of saving and giving away, and decide with them how to spend the rest. In time, as their allowances and earning abilities grow, go one-half with them on necessities. Eventually, let them pay for everything themselves. Consider the goal of handling all income and expenses except for food and housing by age sixteen and financial independence, except for college expenses, by age eighteen. Consider approaching the cost of college as the young adult's responsibility, with parents acting as a safety net, as opposed to the cost of college being the parents' responsibility, with the young adult chipping in what they can—a very significant difference in philosophy.

---

* Adapted from *Celebration of Discipline,* Richard J. Foster, (HarperCollins, San Francisco, 1978, 1988, 1998), pages 78-83.

RECOMMENDED RESOURCES

BOOKS

Randy Alcorn, *Money, Possessions and Eternity.* **Tyndale House Publishers, 1989.**

Excellent integration of biblical truths and practical ways to live them out. Very challenging. Highly recommended for all counselors.

Ron Blue, *Master Your Money.* **Thomas Nelson, 1997.**

Nuts and bolts information and forms presented in a biblical context.

Larry Burkett, *The Word on Finances.* **Moody Press, 1994.**

Burkett has organized relevant Scriptures into this reference guide with more than seventy topics included under eight major headings. Each topic is preceded by a brief commentary. A helpful reference.

Larry Crabb, *Connecting.* **W Publishing, 1997.**

Crabb casts a vision that communities of ordinary Christians might better accomplish most of the good we now depend on mental health professionals to provide. While Good $ense counselors cannot replace mental health professionals, "connecting" with clients and helping them with their personal finances can accomplish much more than we often imagine. This is an excellent book from which to gain a deeper understanding of the potential impact of a counselor's role.

David Henderson, *Culture Shift.* **Baker Books, 1998.**

In part two entitled, "Who We Are: Consumers," Henderson gives a well-documented history and analysis of how our culture has "manufactured the consumer." Interesting and sobering reading.

Mary Hunt, *Mary Hunt's Debt-Proof Your Kids*. Broadman and Holman Publishers, 1998.

An excellent, hard-hitting book with lots of straight talk and good ideas for debt-proofing kids. Hunt also publishes the *Cheapskate Monthly* newsletter, which can be ordered by calling 800-550-3502.

Rollo May, *Art of Counseling*, Revised Edition. Amereon Press, 1989.

Good book on counseling techniques.

John Ortberg, Laurie Pederson, Judson Poling, *Giving: Unlocking the Heart of Good Stewardship*. Zondervan, 2000.

The questions at the end of each chapter of this small group study guide make it good material for group study and discussion.

Austin Pryor, *Sound Mind Investing*, Revised Edition. Victor Books, 2000.

Pryor does an excellent job of presenting thoroughly researched material on a complex topic in layperson's terms . . . and does it all from a clear Christian perspective. He also publishes a monthly newsletter and has a website that's well worth checking into: www.soundmindinvesting.com

David Ramsey, *Financial Peace*. Viking Press, 1992, 1997.

Practical advice on avoiding "stuffitis" and on learning how sacrifices now can produce long-term peace.

Juliet B. Schor, *The Overspent American*. HarperCollins, 1998.

Schor is a senior lecturer at Harvard and a professor at Tilburg University who has analyzed the crisis of the American consumer in a culture where "spending has become the ultimate social act." Not written from a Christian perspective but full of thought-provoking information.

Thomas J. Stanley, William D. Danko, *The Millionaire Next Door*. Longstreet Press, 1996.

This book reveals seven common factors characteristic of those who have accumulated wealth. These factors, as well as the identity of the millionaires, may surprise you.

AUDIO TAPES

The following audio tapes may be obtained by calling (800) 570-9812 or by logging on to www.willowcreek.com.

M0014	Bill Hybels	*Living Excellent Lives Financially*
M0003	Bill Hybels	*Tools for the New Millenium: The Palm Pilot*
M0004	Bill Hybels	*The Calculator and Managing Your Finances*
M0042	John Ortberg	*It All Goes Back in the Box*
C9516	John Ortberg	*What Jesus Really Taught about Greed*
M9402	Bill Hybels	*The Truth about Earthly Treasures*
C9122	Bill Hybels	*The Gift of Giving*
M9903	Bill Hybels	*The Financial Ten Commandments*
M9816 M9817 M9818	Bill Hybels	*What Money Can't Buy* (three-tape series)
M9949	Bill Hybels	*Truths that Transform, Part 9: Learn to be Content in All Circumstances*
DF9906	Bill Hybels/ Dick Towner	*Establishing Financial Good $ense*

WEB SITES

www.GoodSenseMinistry.com
The Good $ense web site is intended to foster an online community to support leaders of Good $ense ministries in the local church. It casts a vision for and encourages biblically-based stewardship ministries, supports the implementation and maintenance of Good $ense ministries through coaching and equipping, acts as an exchange for stewardship ideas and information, and creates mutual support networks among churches.

www.debtfree.org
This site, sponsored by Consolidated Credit Counseling Services, Inc., features a debt calculator that will help you figure out the amount of time needed to pay off any debt by inputting the principal amount, the interest rate, and any monthly payment.

www.cfcministry.org
The Crown Financial Concepts web site features debt calculators, budgeting tools, articles, software, and more.

www.bankrate.com and www.cardtrak.com
These two sites enable you to search for credit cards by lowest interest rate, lowest yearly fee, etc. They also provide information on highest C.D. rates and other financial information.

www.debtorsanonymous.org
The official site of the Debtor's Anonymous organization.

www.nfcc.org
The National Foundation for Credit Counseling site features credit facts, legislative updates on consumer credit issues, budget calculators, budgeting forms, and many useful fact sheets.

www.ssa.gov/retire
This site provides retirement income calculations and similar tools. You can also check the websites of major brokerage firms.

www.pueblo.gsa.gov
This U.S. federal government site features consumer education publications, including useful books and pamphlets.

CREDIT REPORT WEB SITES

Visit the following sites for information on obtaining credit reports.

www.experian.com

www.transunion.com

www.equifax.com

ORGANIZATIONS

Consumer Credit Counseling Service

Provides low-cost debt counseling. Call (800) 388-2227 for the nearest location. They can sometimes arrange for interest rate abatement.

Community Credit Counselors

A Christian-based organization that operates similarly to Consumer Credit Counseling Service. Their toll free number is (877) 603-0292.

Debtor's Anonymous

Support program for people with compulsive spending habits. Local chapters meet regularly and are typically listed in telephone directories. The official web site is www.debtorsanonymous.org.

LOCAL RESOURCE LIST

Check with your ministry administrator. He or she may have a list of resources and organizations in your community.

PRE-READING FOR THE GOOD $ENSE COUNSELOR TRAINING WORKSHOP

IMPORTANT NOTE

In order for the workshop to be as valuable and productive as possible, it is important to complete the pre-reading on the following pages prior to attending the workshop.

Thank you!

WELCOME!

This pre-reading section of the Participant's Guide and Manual is intended to give you a brief orientation to some of the topics that will be covered during the *Good $ense Counselor Training Workshop.* Everything in the pre-reading will be expanded on in the workshop itself.

As you review these materials, you will note that more attention is given to relationship building and to Biblical Financial Principles than is given to purely financial matters. Your selection as a counselor candidate indicates you already have enough financial expertise to be of help to a Good $ense client. However, the most astute biblically-based financial counsel will neither be received nor acted on unless the client hears it from someone they trust and feel genuinely cares for them. It is also important that the counsel you offer is in the context of biblical truth and a Christian worldview. Therefore, your training in the workshop will focus on these two areas—interpersonal skills and Biblical Financial Principles.

When you complete the pre-reading, feel free to review the rest of the Participant's Guide and Manual, especially the Appendix. Note any questions you have. If your questions are not addressed in the workshop, feel free to bring them to the attention of your instructor. You may also wish to log on to the Good $ense web site for information, www.GoodSenseMinistry.com.

Let's begin the journey!

MISSION AND PURPOSE OF A GOOD $ENSE MINISTRY

The mission of a Good $ense Ministry is to educate people about the Biblical Financial Principles of money management so they can move out of financial bondage into financial freedom.

To fulfill this mission, Good $ense has two primary strategies. The first is to teach and encourage people in the practical application of Biblical Financial Principles. This teaching is contained in the *Good $ense Budget Course.* The *Good $ense Budget Course* addresses:

- What the culture says about money. We call this the "Pull of the Culture."
- What the Bible says about money. We call this the "Mind and Heart of God," and explore how it contrasts with the Pull of the Culture.
- The tools, insight, and information by which people can implement Biblical Financial Principles in their own lives.
- The motivation and encouragement to do so!

The second strategy is to train and equip a select group of Good $ense counselors to provide free, biblically-based, confidential counsel to assist individuals and families in addressing financial difficulties or, better yet, to help them avoid encountering financial difficulties to begin with.

THE BIBLICAL FINANCIAL PRINCIPLES: FOUNDATIONS OF THE GOOD $ENSE MINISTRY

The Good $ense Ministry is founded on a set of Biblical Financial Principles that express the ministry's beliefs about how the Bible tells us to manage money.

The overarching and most important of the principles is the cultivation of a steward's mindset. By that, we mean the mindset of one who is managing resources rather than owning them. A modern analogy to that of being a steward would be being a trustee. If you were incapacitated and someone was made the trustee of your estate, that person would have no rights to the assets that belonged to you, simply the responsibility to manage them in the way that was in your best interest.

In a similar fashion, the Bible makes it clear that, in the eternal perspective, we own nothing; God has simply entrusted us with resources that ultimately belong to him. Consequently, we are to use them in ways that honor and please God.

The concept of stewardship/trusteeship versus ownership is at the heart of everything the Bible has to say about money and our proper relationship to it.

The remaining Biblical Financial Principles center around the five financial areas of our lives: earning, giving, saving, debt, and spending. These areas represent the usual way in which we get money (earning) and the four things we can do with it once we have it—we can give it away, save it, pay debt with it, or spend it. The Bible is clear and has much to say on each of these topics. We are to be diligent earners, generous givers, wise savers, cautious debtors, and prudent spenders. The biblical basis for this statement appears below in summary form. Before attending the workshop, take some time to study and reflect on these scriptures.

Steward's Mindset

God created everything and retained ownership of all he created. Therefore, whatever we possess is entrusted to us by God. We are not owners but trustees.

> God created everything. (Genesis 1:1)
> God owns everything. (Psalms 24:1; 50:10, 12b)
> We are trustees. (1 Corinthians 4:1-2)

Earning

In the Garden of Eden God shared the ongoing work of creation with Adam and Eve; this gave dignity to all work. Work is not a curse but a blessing, and we are to work as unto the Lord, with gratitude for our ability to do so.

Be diligent. (Colossians 3:23)
Be purposeful. (Colossians 3:23, I Timothy 5:8)
Be grateful. (Deuteronomy 8:18)

Giving

Since we are made in the image of a loving and generous God, we are made to give. Giving has multiple purposes, one of which is to break the hold money can otherwise have on us. We are to give:

As a response to God's goodness. (James 1:17)
To focus on God as our source of security. (Mathew 6:19-20a, 23b-33)
To achieve economic justice.
To bless others. (Genesis 12:2-3)
To break the hold of money.

Saving

It is wise to save for the unexpected but we must answer the question, when is enough, enough?

It is wise to save. (Proverbs 6:8, 21:20)
It is sinful to hoard. (Luke 12:16-21)

Debt

If we are in debt it is our obligation to repay it. Better yet, we are cautioned to avoid debt.

Repay debt. (Psalm 37:21)
Avoid debt. (Proverbs 22:7)

Spending

Our spending should be disciplined and marked by contentment. Materialism is a competing theology and leads to envy and greed.

Beware of idols. (Deuteronomy 5:8; Romans 1:25)
Guard against greed. (Luke 12:15)
Be content. (Philippians 4:12)

THE COUNSELING PROCESS

The counseling process is a key part of the Good $ense mission: educating people about the Biblical Financial Principles of money management, and training them in the practical application of those principles to personal finances. The counselor provides both teaching and training and, importantly, the support and encouragement the client needs to change lifetime financial habits. To accomplish this, the counselor needs to have both financial skills and listening skills. Both are vital ingredients for building a relationship characterized by trust and understanding.

The following steps are the usual process by which clients enter the ministry and are assigned to a counselor.

Step 1: Profile Received

The client receives a Client Profile and an instruction sheet on how to fill it out. The profile asks for basic personal and financial information and what the client's hopes are for the counseling process. A copy of the Client Profile and instruction sheet is on pages 203–207 of the Appendix. The client completes the Client Profile and submits it to the Good $ense administrator.

Step 2: Profile Screened

The Client Profile is reviewed by the administrator in preparation for assignment to a counselor.

Step 3: Counselor Assigned

In assigning counselors, factors such as age, gender, marital status, profession, severity of the financial condition, and previous counseling history (if any) are taken into consideration.

While every effort is made to carefully match the client with the counselor, in certain circumstances, a counselor may be asked to handle a case outside his or her preference. For instance, a counselor preferring less severe financial cases may be asked to meet with a severe case if other counselors are not available.

A typical case load is two clients. The second case is assigned after the first case is well underway and its time commitment has lessened.

And then—

Upon receiving the profile, the counselor uses the following process:

COUNSELING PROCESS

1. Analyze the Client Profile.

2. Call the client.

3. Conduct the first meeting.

4. Provide ongoing counseling.

5. Close the case.

1. **Analyze the Client Profile.** Reviewing the profile provides considerable initial information about your client that will help you prepare for the first meeting.

2. **Call the client.** Call the client to arrange for the first meeting and to affirm their decision to contact the ministry.

3. **Conduct the first meeting.** The first meeting is crucial. This is when you begin to establish the rapport and trust necessary for a productive client-counselor relationship.

4. **Provide ongoing counseling.** Ongoing counseling is provided for approximately four to six months. During ongoing counseling you work with the client to create and monitor a Spending Plan and Debt Reduction Plan.

5. **Close the case.** At the appropriate time, the case is closed. Ideally, the client will have achieved the goals established for counseling when the case is closed.

This process will be discussed in detail during the workshop.

PRE-COUNSELING PREPARATION AND THE FIRST MEETING

Being prepared for your first meeting is critically important for the success of your relationship with a client. But before walking into your first meeting, it is important to do two things: pray and analyze the Client Profile.

Pray

Prayer lays the foundation for your relationship. As a counselor, you have been entrusted with an individual or family who needs not just counsel but godly counsel. Good $ense is not primarily in the budget business. Rather, we are in the business of building God's kingdom.

For many in severe financial difficulty, only divine intervention can help. In Good $ense we often refer to the concept of "God's math." On paper the situation may appear hopeless, if not impossible. But when Biblical Financial Principles are applied and appropriate actions are taken, God honors those actions and amazing things often happen. Psalm 50:14-15 should be a theme for both the counselor and client: "Sacrifice thank offerings to God, fulfill your vows to the Most High, and call upon me in the day of trouble; I will deliver you, and you will honor me." The client needs to claim this promise, as does the counselor.

Pray both for yourself and for your client. Ask God to give you wisdom, discernment, compassion, and patience. Ask God to give the client courage to be completely honest and broken about his or her situation, as well as strength to take the necessary next steps.

Analyze the Client Profile

The second action a counselor takes prior to the first meeting is analyzing the Client Profile. The Client Profile can give you a good overview of the client's situation but will be far from a complete picture. The workshop will teach you how to effectively analyze the Client Profile.

Now you're prepared to walk into your first meeting.

The First Meeting

The focus of your first meeting with the client is to gather information and build the relationship. If there is a creditor crisis or other urgent problem, it may be appropriate to offer an immediate action step. However, it is not necessary to map out solutions at the first meeting. In fact, given the potential lack of reliable data you have at the first meeting, mapping out solutions may even be unwise.

Meeting Duration and Counseling Timeframe

The length of your meetings with a client will vary. However, meetings will rarely be less than an hour. Initial meetings in which you are taking time to get to know the client, establish trust, and collect information, typically take an hour-and-a-half to two hours. As you and your client continue to meet and finalize a Spending Plan and Debt Reduction Plan, the meeting focus will shift to checking in and accountability which take less time.

It is important to keep the meeting focused. Clients often find it difficult or embarrassing to talk about finances and so may be easily sidetracked onto other issues or topics. They may dwell on the ongoing impact of their poor financial choices, such as marital stress or self-esteem issues. Listen attentively and sensitively but always look for the first opportunity to redirect the conversation to budget counseling. If you sense they have a need for professional counseling in other areas, refer them to ministries that provide such help.

The typical timeframe for working with a client is four to six months. The majority of financial counseling is precipitated by a crisis, and most crises do not occur all at once—they evolve. The need for counseling is often the end result of a series of poor decisions that took place over an extended period of time. Since the client did not get into difficulty in one day, the client is unlikely to get out of it quickly as well.

Meeting Location

The best location for meetings is the church. It is neutral territory. In rare situations, it may be appropriate to meet either in your home or the client's home. Meeting in the client's home may provide additional insight into lifestyle choices the client has made, which could be helpful in the counseling process. However, the disadvantages of interruptions and a non-professional setting most often outweigh this advantage.

Similarly, meeting in your home may pose challenges, such as interruptions from family members or the telephone. The client may also make comparisons between your circumstances and theirs, which may not be helpful for the counseling relationship. Counseling in your home could even cause a client to see you in a less professional context and lower the value and credibility of your advice.

Specific steps for conducting the first and subsequent client meetings will be covered in the workshop.

COUNSELING DYNAMICS

by Steve Sherbondy*

Helping people change their financial behavior is a difficult task. That task can become nearly impossible unless you are able to establish a caring and understanding relationship. As a counselor candidate, your Good $ense Ministry believes you already have the financial expertise to help clients. The key issue to address now is whether you will be able to establish a relationship of trust that will make it easy for clients to receive your counsel and act on it.

In initial meetings, your client will be asking—consciously or unconsciously—the following questions:

- Are you interested in me?
- Do you understand me?
- Do you like me?
- Can I trust you?

To better understand how important these questions are, think for a moment of someone who has had a significantly positive influence on your life. Picture them in your mind. If you were to ask this person these questions, almost certainly the answer to all of them would be a resounding yes. You knew they were interested in you, that they understood and liked you, that you could trust them. That person had influence in your life because you were certain they cared about you. As a counselor, your clients need to feel this way about you—they need to be certain you care about them.

Your major focus, especially in early meetings, should be on the relationship, not on the task. A good phrase to remember is, "Relationship must precede resolution." In Luke 10, Jesus gently rebuked Martha for being distracted from a relationship with him by all the work that needed to be done. Christ also rebuked the Pharisees in much stronger terms for rigidly adhering to the law, but neglecting the weightier, relationship-oriented matters that the spirit of the law was designed to protect and honor.

One of the key ways in which you can build a caring relationship with a client is to be a good listener.

* Steve Sherbondy is a licensed clinical professional counselor and author of *Changing Your Child's Heart*. A member of Willow Creek Community Church since 1976, Steve has been a volunteer trainer of Good $ense counselors for thirteen years.

Listening Skills

The Bible is clear on the importance of listening: "Everyone should be quick to listen, slow to speak. . ." (James 1:19). Nevertheless, we often err on the side of saying too much rather than listening too much. In fact, it has been said that a picture is worth a thousand words—but some people still prefer the thousand words.

Good listening involves much more than just hearing and being able to repeat the words that were spoken. It is the act of focusing on the other person and what they have to say.

Good listening also involves discerning the feelings behind the words. If a person believes you understand how they feel, it lessens their anxiety and creates an environment in which they feel safe, understood, and cared for. Learn to listen intently not only to a person's words, but to their heart as well. Sometimes people don't mean what they say and sometimes they mean more than they say. Discerning feelings often requires reading between the lines; it always requires paying attention to more than just the words spoken. Body language and other non-verbal behaviors are important communications to pay attention to. Non-verbals—a person's tone of voice, how they move, sit, look—are an even more important part of how they communicate than the words they use.

In Matthew 13:14, Jesus described those who listened to him teach as "ever hearing but never understanding." This should never be said of a Good $ense counselor! But there is even more to good listening than understanding. The goal of listening is not merely to understand; it is to make the other person *feel* understood. A listener can be very good at understanding what someone is saying, but it won't matter unless the person feels that the listener understands.

The only sure way to determine whether or not your client feels understood is to give them feedback about what you sense they are feeling. Typically, the client will be quick to either verify or correct your perceptions. The process of showing the client you have not only heard the words but also grasped his or her feelings will significantly enhance your relationship.

It is also possible that your perception and articulation of their feelings will help the client to gain insights of his or her own. The story is told of radio personality and author Studs Terkel who was interviewing people in an impoverished area. After taping a conversation with a poor woman who had never had her voice recorded, her excited children begged Terkel to play back the tape. Although the children giggled with delight at what they heard, the woman listened with sober intensity. After Terkel stopped the tape, he could tell the woman had been deeply moved in some way and so he asked what she was thinking. "I never knew I felt like that," she responded. Sensitively discerning and mirroring back your perceptions of a client's feelings can have the same impact. It can help the client better understand thoughts and feelings they aren't even aware they have.

In addition to listening for feelings, listen for strengths, joys, and things the client is proud of. Listen for struggles, sorrows, and things to work on. Perhaps most importantly, listen for opportunities. Opportunities to:

- cheer the client's efforts
- affirm and encourage
- challenge the client's assumptions and misconceptions
- teach and reflect on Biblical Financial Principles

Avoid dwelling on failures. Ask about how the client has already tried to fix the situation. Look for ways to be an encouragement—clients need lots of it!

As a counselor, you are in a position of authority and influence. Careful listening gives the client a place of dignity and respect in the counseling relationship. It is important to remember that good listening earns you the right to influence the client. Remember the person you thought of earlier who had a significantly positive influence on you? Did they not earn that right before the influence actually occurred? You only have as much influence as the client grants you and good listening can help you earn their trust.

Good listening is also an important counselor discipline—it trains you to focus on the client as a person and not just on the advice you want to give them. When you really listen to someone, you give them rare gifts; the gifts of value, insight, and understanding.

Boundaries

In addition to establishing a relationship of trust, you also need to set appropriate boundaries with your client. The fact that you have been chosen to become a counselor indicates you have a genuine desire to help people. That's a good thing! However, helping too much can be detrimental not only to you, but also to the client.

Setting appropriate boundaries includes things like clarifying roles and responsibilities and making sure you don't end up working harder than the client. Clients need to own the responsibility for doing the work to remedy their situation; they may be prohibited from doing so if their counselor takes on too much responsibility.

Common boundary problems include a client who wants the counselor to:

- do their work for them
- make decisions for them
- lend them money
- provide a "magic" answer to their problems that requires no effort or sacrifice on their part
- provide help or advice with problems other than financial problems

The best model we have for helping people while maintaining appropriate boundaries is Jesus. Based on Christ's ministry and example, there are five basic principles Good $ense counselors can follow to establish and maintain appropriate boundaries with clients:

- Know who you are and are not.
- Know your energy level and feelings.
- Know your mission.
- Know what your client expects.
- Test the resolve of your client.

Know Who You Are and Are Not

John 6:15 says, "Jesus, knowing that they intended to come and make him king by force, withdrew again to a mountain by himself." Jesus knew he was not to be a political king; his kingdom was not of this world. Some clients may want to make you their financial savior. You are not. You are their financial counselor/coach/adviser. It is important to be very clear on what you are committing yourself to do, what your responsibilities are, and what role you play.

Roles you are *not* to play include drill sergeant, prison guard, IRS agent, detective, friend, or sibling. Appropriate roles include coach, leader, cheerleader, teacher, and, at times, even a parent. If your past financial circumstances were difficult, you may also wish to share your story as "wounded healer." Your testimony can be an effective relationship builder if presented in a way that builds hope and assurance in God's ability to help solve their financial difficulties.

In navigating what role to play with your client, keep these general guidelines in mind:

- Be friendly, but not a friend.
- Have a servant attitude, but don't be the client's slave.
- Be a leader, but not a dictator.

Know Your Energy Level and Feelings

In Luke 8:45 a woman who had been bleeding for many years touched Jesus' robe and was healed. Though he hadn't seen the woman, Jesus was instantly aware that something unusual had happened. Someone had not merely bumped against him in the crowd but had touched him intentionally with expectation. Something had been asked of him and healing energy was released from him. Christ had feelings about this; he needed to find out who had touched him and why.

As you relate to your client, pay attention to your energy level and feelings. God gave us feelings because they help us understand what is going on. Are you tired and worn out? Do you feel frustrated, irritated, or burdened? Do you find yourself trying to avoid the client? Do you feel guilty if you say no to one of their requests? Such feelings often signal that something is wrong, that a boundary problem may exist.

It is natural for you to feel frustrated by the situations in which many clients find themselves. However, if God is at work in your relationship there should be a sense of freedom and hope about your ministry. Second Corinthians 3:17 states, "where the Spirit of the Lord is, there is freedom."

Know Your Mission

Early in Christ's ministry he had what appeared to be a great ministry opportunity. The day after he taught and performed miracles, the whole town of Capernaum came out to hear him speak. His disciples were excited but Christ said, "Let us go somewhere else—to the nearby villages—so I can preach there also. That is why I have come." Christ knew who he was and "why he had come."

The purpose of your relationship with the client is to offer financial counsel, to teach biblical stewardship, and to lead them to financial freedom by helping them assume responsibility for their finances. Beware of being pulled into other tasks that at first glance may seem like good things to do, but are not part of your expressed mission.

Know What Your Client Expects

Matthew 20:30-34 tells the story of blind men who called out to Jesus for mercy. In response, Jesus asked them a question to which the answer seemed obvious, "What do you want me to do for you?" Their answer was what one would expect—the men wanted Jesus to restore their sight. By asking them the question, Christ forced the men to do two things: to state their need and to acknowledge their inability to meet it. It humbled them and put them in a teachable mindset. It also prepared them to truly rejoice when their need was met.

To understand what your client expects, ask these three questions in your first meeting:

- What do you want to accomplish?
- How are you hoping I can help you?
- How are you going to contribute to those goals?

These questions require the client to clarify their expectations and communicate them to you. This gives you the opportunity to articulate an appropriate counseling relationship as well as roles and responsibilities for both of you.

Test the Resolve of Your Client

Jesus frequently tested the resolve of those who asked him for help. He invited the rich young ruler to come and follow him, but only if the ruler would give away his riches. The ruler went away sad; he could not give up his riches. It could be said that Jesus "failed" to save him. In Matthew 15 and Mark 7, a Canaanite woman with a demon possessed daughter persistently asked Jesus to heal her child. To add strength to her request, she used a clever analogy—even dogs get to eat crumbs from a master's table. After testing her resolve, Jesus praised her persistence and wisdom and healed the woman's daughter.

You should consistently test the resolve of your client. Maintain high expectations that they will follow through on homework assignments. In the event they come to a meeting and have not completed their assignments, you could approach the situation in a couple different ways.

If you feel a gentle approach would be best, you might ask:

- Do you need more time?
- Am I expecting too much?
- May we finish your assignment right now?

A more direct approach would be to ask:

- Do you really want to do this? Why?
- What is it going to take for us to accomplish this?
- What are the obstacles?
- What were you expecting to do in our meeting since you don't have your assignment?
- Would you like to call and reschedule once you've completed the assignment?

Testing the client's resolve and holding them accountable may feel difficult or uncomfortable, but is always in their best interest. Often, even in the midst of their resistance, your resolve will be interpreted as an indication that you really care. Your own modeling is also important. Being on time, being prepared, and following through on your commitments is key. Actions are internalized more than words.

Setting appropriate boundaries is a loving act. Boundaries communicate respect. They say, "You are capable and therefore responsible for yourself. You may not feel or behave that way, but you are!" The old adage about the value of giving a person a fish versus teaching them to fish has application here. Metaphorically speaking, your goal is not to give your client a fish to merely feed them now; but to teach them to fish so they can feed themselves for a lifetime. In other words, healthy boundaries will not only help your client to do the work, but also to develop the skills they need to maintain solid financial practices for a lifetime of good stewardship.

YOUR PRE-READING IS COMPLETE!

This concludes your pre-reading. As previously mentioned, feel free to read through the Appendix and to consult other resources for additional insights. If you can only read one other resource, Randy Alcorn's *Money, Possessions and Eternity* is an especially good one.

Thanks once again for your willingness to become a very important part of the Good $ense Ministry. May God bless you as you train and begin actively serving in the ministry.

FORMS

This section contains the following forms and documents to assist you in your role as a Good $ense counselor:

- Biblical Financial Principles (expanded)
- Client Profile
- Tips for Filling Out Your Client Profile
- Good $ense Budget Counseling Covenant
- Spending Record
- Client Progress Report
- Spending Plan
- Debt Reduction Plan
- Case Completion Report
- Client Profile: Mark and Carol Olsen
- Client Profile: Joe and Sharlene Moore
- Client Profile: Barb Leonard
- Client Profile Analysis Chart

These forms are perforated so they can be removed and photocopied. Your Good $ense administrator may also have copies of these forms available for your use. Electronic copies of these forms are included on the *Good $ense Counselor Training Workshop* PowerPoint CD-ROM.

BIBLICAL FINANCIAL PRINCIPLES

FOUNDATION OF THE GOOD $ENSE MINISTRY
Cultivate a steward's mindset.

GOD CREATED EVERYTHING
In the beginning there was nothing, and God created (Genesis 1:1).

GOD OWNS EVERYTHING
"'The silver is mine and the gold is mine,' declares the LORD Almighty" (Haggai 2:8). "Every animal of the forest is mine, and the cattle on a thousand hills" (Psalm 50:10). "The earth and the fullness thereof belong to the Lord and all those who live within" (Psalm 37:21 KJV).

Flowing out of the fact that God created and owns everything is the logical conclusion that whatever we possess is not really ours, but belongs to God; we are simply entrusted with our possessions. Therefore, we are trustees, not owners. Although 1 Corinthians 4 (quoted below) does not directly refer to material possessions, its counsel is applicable to this aspect of life as well.

WE ARE TRUSTEES
"A person who is put in charge as a manager must be faithful" (1 Corinthians 4:1-2 NLT).

WE CAN'T SERVE TWO MASTERS
"No one can serve two masters. For you will hate one and love the other, or be devoted to one and despise the other. You cannot serve both God and money" (Matthew 6:24 NLT).

USE RESOURCES WISELY
"His master replied, 'Well done, good and faithful servant! You have been faithful with a few things; I will put you in charge of many things. Come and share your master's happiness!'" (Matthew 25:21-28).

PURSUE BIBLICAL, FINANCIAL KNOWLEDGE
"Buy the truth and do not sell it; get wisdom, discipline and understanding" (Proverbs 23:23). "Plans fail for lack of counsel, but with many advisers they succeed" (Proverbs 15:22).

MEASURABLE GOALS AND REALISTIC PLANS
"Commit to the LORD whatever you do, and your plans will succeed" (Proverbs 16:3).

TRUSTWORTHINESS MATTERS
"Whoever can be trusted with very little can also be trusted with much, and whoever is dishonest with very little will also be dishonest with much. So if you have not been trustworthy in handling worldly wealth, who will trust you with true riches? And if you have not been trustworthy with someone else's property, who will give you property of your own?" (Luke 16:10-12).

EARNING
The Diligent Earner—One who produces with diligence and purpose and is content and grateful for what he or she has.

God established work while Adam and Eve were yet in the Garden of Eden. God invited them to join him in the ongoing act of caring for creation. Work before the fall of Adam and Eve is a blessing, not a curse. All work has dignity. Our work should be characterized by the following principles.

BE DILIGENT; SERVE GOD
"Whatever you do, work at it with all your heart, as working for the Lord" (Colossians 3:23).

PROVIDE FOR OURSELVES AND THOSE DEPENDENT ON US
"Those who won't care for their own relatives, especially those living in the same household, have denied what we believe. Such people are worse than unbelievers" (1 Timothy 5:8 NLT).

BE GRATEFUL; REMEMBER FROM WHOM INCOME REALLY COMES
"Remember the LORD your God, for it is he who gives you the ability to produce wealth" (Deuteronomy 8:18).

ENJOY YOUR WORK; BE CONTENT IN IT
"It is good for people to eat well, drink a good glass of wine, and enjoy their work—whatever they do under the sun—for however long God lets them live. And it is a good thing to receive wealth from God and the good health to enjoy it. To enjoy your work and accept your lot in life—that is indeed a gift from God" (Ecclesiastes 5:18-19 NLT).

BE TRANSFORMED WORKERS
"Slaves, obey your earthly masters with respect and fear, and with sincerity of heart, just as you would obey Christ. Obey them not only to win their favor when their eye is on you, but like slaves of Christ, doing the will of God from your heart" (Ephesians 6:5-6).

EARN POTENTIAL, SHARE EXCESS
"If you are a thief, stop stealing. Begin using your hands for honest work, and then give generously to others in need" (Ephesians 4:28 NLT).

GIVING
The Generous Giver—One who gives with an obedient will, a joyful attitude, and a compassionate heart.

WE ARE MADE TO GIVE
We are made in the image of God (Genesis 1:26-27). God is gracious and generous. We will lead a more satisfied and fulfilled life when we give to others.

GIVE AS A RESPONSE TO GOD'S GOODNESS
"Every good and perfect gift is from above" (James 1:17). Therefore, we give out of gratefulness for what we have received.

GIVE TO FOCUS ON GOD AS OUR SOURCE AND SECURITY
"But seek first his kingdom and his righteousness and all these things will be given to you as well" (Matthew 6:33).

GIVE TO HELP ACHIEVE ECONOMIC JUSTICE
"Our desire . . . is that there might be equality. At the present time your plenty will supply what they need" (2 Corinthians 8:13-14). Throughout Scripture, God expresses his concern for the poor and calls us to share with those less fortunate.

GIVE TO BLESS OTHERS
"I will make you into a great nation and I will bless you; I will make your name great, and you will be a blessing. And I will bless you, and make your name great; and so you shall be a blessing" (Genesis 12:2-3). If we are blessed with resources beyond our needs, it is not for the purpose of living more lavishly but to bless others. We are blessed to be a blessing.

BE WILLING TO SHARE
"Command them [the rich] to do good, to be rich in good deeds, and to be generous and willing to share" (1 Timothy 6:18).

GIVE TO BREAK THE HOLD OF MONEY
Another reason to give is that doing so breaks the hold that money might otherwise have on us. While the Bible doesn't specifically say so, it is evident that persons who give freely and generously are not controlled by money but have freedom.

GIVE JOYFULLY, GENEROUSLY, IN A TIMELY MANNER
"Out of the most severe trial, their overflowing joy and their extreme poverty welled up in rich generosity. For I testify that they gave as much as they were able, and even beyond their ability. Entirely on their own, they urgently pleaded with us for the privilege of sharing in this service to the saints" (2 Corinthians 8:1-5).

GIVE WISELY
"We want to avoid any criticism of the way we administer this liberal gift" (2 Corinthians 8:20).

GIVE EXPECTANTLY AND CHEERFULLY
"The one who plants generously will get a generous crop. You must each make up your own mind as to how much you should give. Don't give reluctantly or in response to pressure. For God loves the person who gives cheerfully" (2 Corinthians 9:6-7 NLT; see also verses 10-14).

MOTIVES FOR GIVING ARE IMPORTANT

Unless our motives are right, we can give all we have—even our bodies as sacrifices—and it will be for naught (I Corinthians13). We can be scrupulous with tithing and still not have the right motives. Jesus rebuked the religious leaders of his day for this very thing: "You hypocrites! You give a tenth of your spices—mint, dill and cummin. But you have neglected the more important matters of the law—justice, mercy and faithfulness" (Matthew 23:23).

SAVING

The Wise Saver—One who builds, preserves, and invests with discernment.

IT IS WISE TO SAVE

"In the house of the wise are stores of choice food and oil, but [the] foolish ... devour all [they have]" (Proverbs 21:20). "Go to the ant, you sluggard; consider its ways and be wise! It has no commander, no overseer or ruler, yet it stores its provisions in summer and gathers it food at harvest" (Proverbs 6:8).

IT IS SINFUL TO HOARD

And he gave them an illustration: "A rich man had a fertile farm that produced fine crops. In fact, his barns were full to overflowing. So he said, 'I know! I'll tear down my barns and build bigger ones. Then I'll have room enough to store everything. And I'll sit back and say to myself, My friend, you have enough stored away for years to come. Now take it easy! Eat, drink, and be merry!' But God said to him, 'You fool! You will die this very night. Then who will get it all?' Yes, a person is a fool to store up earthly wealth but not have a rich relationship with God" (Luke 12:16-21 NLT).

CALCULATE COST; PRIORITIZE

"But don't begin until you count the cost. For who would begin construction of a building without first getting estimates and then checking to see if there is enough money to pay the bills? Otherwise, you might complete only the foundation before running out of funds. And then how everyone would laugh at you! They would say, 'There's the person who started that building and ran out of money before it was finished!'" (Luke 14:28-30 NLT).

AVOID GET-RICH-QUICK SCHEMES

"The trustworthy will get a rich reward. But the person who wants to get rich quick will only get into trouble" (Proverbs 28:20 NLT).

SEEK WISE COUNSELORS

"Let the wise listen and add to their learning, and let the discerning get guidance" (Proverbs 1:5).

ESTABLISH A JOB BEFORE BUYING HOME

"Finish your outdoor work and get your fields ready; after that, build your house" (Proverbs 24:27).

DIVERSIFY YOUR HOLDINGS

"Give portions to seven, yes to eight, for you do not know what disaster will come upon the land" (Ecclesiastes 11:2).

DEBT

The Cautious Debtor—One who avoids entering into debt, is careful and strategic when incurring debt, and always repays debt.

REPAY DEBT AND DO SO PROMPTLY

"The wicked borrow and do not repay, but the righteous give generously" (Psalm 37:21). "Do not say to your neighbor, 'Come back later; I'll give it tomorrow'—when you now have it with you" (Proverbs 3:28).

AVOID THE BONDAGE OF DEBT

"The rich rule over the poor, and the borrower is servant to the lender" (Proverbs 22:7).

DEBT PRESUMES ON THE FUTURE

"Now listen, you who say, 'Today or tomorrow we will go to this or that city, spend a year there, carry on business and make money.' Why, you do not even know what will happen tomorrow. What is your life? You are a mist that appears for a little while and then vanishes" (James 4:13-14).

DEBT CAN DENY GOD THE OPPORTUNITY TO WORK IN OUR LIVES AND TEACH US VALUABLE LESSONS

God may wish to show us his love by providing us with something we desire but for which we have no resources. If we go into debt to get it anyway, we deny him that opportunity (see Luke 12:22-32). In the same way that parents refrain from giving a child everything the child wants because parents know it isn't in the child's best interest, incurring debt can rob God of the opportunity to teach us through denial. Ecclesiastes 7:14 reminds us: "When times are good, be happy; but when times are bad, consider: God has made the one as well as the other."

DEBT CAN FOSTER ENVY AND GREED

"Beware! Don't be greedy for what you don't have. Real life is not measured by how much we own" (Luke 12:15).

GIVE AND PAY WHAT YOU OWE

"Give everyone what you owe them: Pay your taxes and import duties, and give respect and honor to all to whom it is due" (Romans 13:7 NLT).

DON'T CO-SIGN

"Do not co-sign another person's note or put up a guarantee for someone else's loan. If you can't pay it, even your bed will be snatched from under you" (Proverbs 22:26-27 NLT).

DEBT CAN DISRUPT SPIRITUAL GROWTH

"The fruit of the Spirit is love, joy, peace, patience, kindness, goodness, faithfulness, gentleness and self-control. Against such things there is no law" (Galatians 5:22-23).

SPENDING

The Prudent Consumer—One who enjoys the fruits of their labor yet guards against materialism.

BEWARE OF IDOLS

"You shall not make yourself an idol in the form of anything in heaven above or on the earth beneath or in the waters below" (Deuteronomy 5:8). Materialism—which so saturates our culture—is nothing less than a competing theology in which matter (things) is of ultimate significance; that is, things become gods or idols. "They ... worshipped and served created things rather than the Creator" (Romans 1:25).

GUARD AGAINST GREED; THINGS DO NOT BRING HAPPINESS

"Beware! Don't be greedy for what you don't have. Real life is not measured by how much we own" (Luke 12:15).

SEEK MODERATION

"Give me neither poverty nor riches, but give me only my daily bread. Otherwise, I may have too much and disown you and say, 'Who is the LORD?' Or I may become poor and steal, and so dishonor the name of my God" (Proverbs 30:8-9).

BE CONTENT

"I know what it is to be in need, and I know what it is to have plenty. I have learned the secret of being content in any and every situation, whether well fed or hungry, whether living in plenty or in want. I can do everything through him who gives me strength" (Philippians 4:12-13).

"Godliness with contentment is great gain. For we brought nothing into the world, and we can take nothing out of it. But if we have food and clothing, we will be content with that" (1 Timothy 6:6-8).

DON'T WASTE GOD'S RESOURCES

"When they had all had enough to eat, he said to his disciples, 'Gather the pieces that are left over. Let nothing be wasted'" (John 6:12).

ENJOY A PORTION OF GOD'S PROVISION

"Command those who are rich in this present world not to be arrogant nor to put their hope in wealth, which is so uncertain, but to put their hope in God, who richly provides us with everything for our enjoyment. Command them to do good, to be rich in good deeds, and to be generous and willing to share. In this way they will lay up treasure for themselves as a firm foundation for the coming age, so that they may take hold of the life that is truly life" (1 Timothy 6:17-19).

WATCH YOUR FINANCES (BUDGET)

"Be sure you know the condition of your flocks, give careful attention to your herds; for riches do not endure forever, and a crown is not secure for all generations" (Proverbs 27:23-24).

Client Profile

Number _____

Date Mailed _____

Date Received _____

Date Counselor Assigned _____

Name of Counselor _____

Counseling Completed _____

NAME_____ AGE _____

MARITAL STATUS _____

SPOUSE'S NAME _____

ADDRESS _____

CITY_____ ZIP _____

HOME PHONE ( ) _____

WORK PHONE ( ) _____

NATURE OF EMPLOYMENT:

    SELF_____

    SPOUSE _____

NAME(S)/AGE(S) OF CHILDREN _____

_____

_____

_____

WHAT I OWN

Checking Accounts   _____

Savings Account   _____

Other Savings   _____

Insurance (cash value)   _____

Retirement Funds   _____

Home (market value)   _____

Auto (age_____ make_____)   _____

Auto (age_____ make_____)   _____

Other Possessions (estimate)   _____

Money Owed to Me   _____

Other   _____

Other   _____

WHAT I OWE

	Total Owed	Min. Mo. Payment	Interest	Other	Total Owed	Min. Mo. Payment	Interest
Mortgage (current bal.)	$_____	_____	____%	_____	$_____	_____	____%
Home Equity Loan	_____	_____	____%	_____	_____	_____	____%
Credit Cards:	_____	_____	____%	_____	_____	_____	____%
_____	_____	_____	____%	_____	_____	_____	____%
_____	_____	_____	____%	_____	_____	_____	____%
_____	_____	_____	____%	_____	_____	_____	____%
_____	_____	_____	____%	_____	_____	_____	____%
Car Loans	_____	_____	____%	_____	_____	_____	____%
Education Loans	_____	_____	____%	_____	_____	_____	____%
Family/Friends	_____	_____	____%	_____	_____	_____	____%

WHAT I MAKE

Use take-home pay figures (the amount of the check):   My spouse gets a check for:

Job #1 $_____ ☐ weekly ☐ every other week   Job #1 $_____ ☐ weekly ☐ every other week

☐ monthly ☐ twice a month   ☐ monthly ☐ twice a month

Job #2 $_____ ☐ weekly ☐ every other week   Job #2 $_____ ☐ weekly ☐ every other week

☐ monthly ☐ twice a month   ☐ monthly ☐ twice a month

Other Income (explain)_____

Total Monthly Income_____

WHAT I SPEND

EARNINGS/INCOME PER MONTH
Salary #1 (net take-home) _____
Salary #2 (net take-home) _____
Other (less taxes) _____
TOTAL MONTHLY INCOME: [_____]

GIVING
Church _____
Other Contrib. _____
TOTAL GIVING [_____]

SAVINGS _____
TOTAL SAVINGS [_____]

DEBT
CREDIT CARDS
Visa _____
Master Card _____
Discover _____
Am. Express _____
Gas Cards _____
Dept. Stores _____
EDUCATION LOANS _____
OTHER LOANS:
Bank Loans _____
Credit Union _____
Family/Friends _____
Other _____
TOTAL DEBT [_____]

HOUSING
MORTGAGE/TAXES/RENT _____
MAINTENANCE/REPAIRS _____
UTILITIES:
Electric _____
Gas _____
Water _____
Trash _____
Telephone/Internet _____
Cable TV _____
OTHER _____
TOTAL HOUSING [_____]

AUTO/TRANSPORTATION
CAR PAYMTS./LICENSE _____
GAS/BUS/TRAIN/PKING. _____
OIL/LUBE/MAINT. _____
TOTAL AUTO [_____]

INSURANCE (paid by you)
AUTO _____
HOMEOWNERS _____
LIFE _____
MEDICAL/DENTAL _____
OTHER: _____
TOTAL INSURANCE [_____]

HOUSEHOLD/PERSONAL
GROCERIES _____
CLOTHES/DRYCLEANING _____
GIFTS _____
HOUSEHOLD ITEMS _____
PERSONAL
Liquor/Tobacco _____
Cosmetics _____
Barber/Beauty _____
OTHER
Books/Magazines _____
Allowances _____
Music Lessons _____
Personal Technology _____
Education _____
Miscellaneous _____
TOTAL HOUSEHOLD [_____]

ENTERTAINMENT
GOING OUT:
Meals _____
Movies/Events _____
Babysitting _____
TRAVEL (VAC./TRIPS) _____
OTHER:
Fitness/Sports _____
Hobbies _____
Media Rental _____
Other _____
TOTAL ENTERTAINMENT [_____]

PROFESSIONAL SERVICES
CHILD CARE _____
MED./DENTAL/PRESCRIP. _____
OTHER:
Legal _____
Counseling _____
Union/Prof. Dues _____
Other _____
TOTAL PROFESSIONAL [_____]

MISC. SMALL CASH EXPENSES [_____]

TOTAL EXPENSES =======

TOTAL MONTHLY INCOME	$_____
LESS TOTAL EXPENSES	$_____
INCOME OVER/(UNDER) EXPENSES	$_____

REQUEST

How can the Good $ense Ministry help you? _____

_____

_____

_____

What steps are you taking to improve your present situation?_____

_____

_____

_____

_____

_____

_____

_____

Have you ever seen a financial planner/advisor?   ❏ Yes   ❏ No   If yes, who? _____

How were you helped? _____

_____

_____

_____

AGREEMENT

MY (OUR) AGREEMENT WITH _____

I (we) hereby make the commitment to actively participate with the Good $ense Ministry in seeking a resolution to the issues that brought me (us) to this place.

I (we) understand that Good $ense will attempt to assist me (us) in developing a plan, and that the consultant or volunteer agents do not make any representations or warranties with respect to the results of its services or its ability to help me (us) with my (our) credit/financial management.

I (we) understand that Good $ense is being offered to me (us) without charge or obligation, and that the people in Good $ense are volunteers who are donating their time to people requesting their assistance. Good $ense personnel have pledged to not benefit monetarily in any way as a result of their involvement in the ministry and are thereby prohibited from selling any services or products to persons who seek their counsel.

I (we) further agree to indemnify and hold harmless all volunteers of the Good $ense Ministry, the sponsor church and its employees, agents, counselors, officers, and directors from any claim, suit, action, demand or liability of any kind and any nature arising out of, or in any manner connected with, my (our) participation in Good $ense.

X _____   Date_____

X _____   Date_____

(If married, both spouses should sign.)

TIPS FOR FILLING OUT YOUR CLIENT PROFILE

The information on your Client Profile is confidential. Please fill it out as completely and accurately as possible. The information will be used by you and your counselor to develop a budget and debt retirement plan.

Please return the Client Profile as soon as possible.

WHAT I OWN

Fill in the blanks as requested. For "Other Possessions," simply estimate the market value of your major assets. If you had to sell everything, what would you be able to get?

WHAT I OWE

What liabilities do you have? To whom do you owe money and how much? What interest rate are you paying on each debt? Include the minimum monthly payment on each debt.

WHAT I MAKE

The income figures should be those which you *take home* after taxes and other deductions. Make a note of any deductions other than taxes (such as medical insurance, retirement, etc.). Where those items occur under expenses, enter an asterisk with the footnote "payroll deduction." If your income varies from month to month, use a conservative monthly average based on the last two or three years' earnings. Referring back to your income tax records could be helpful in that determination. Remember, you want to note after-tax, take-home income.

WHAT I SPEND

Gather as much information as you can to determine a *monthly average* for expenses in each category. Going through your check book register for the past year will probably be helpful. Be sure to include such items as auto insurance, property taxes, etc., that may not be paid on a monthly basis. If you've not kept records in the past, some of the categories may be difficult to estimate. Give it your best shot, recognizing that if you don't have records showing how much you're spending in a particular area, it's probably more than you think!

If what you are spending adds up to more than your take-home income, changes will need to be made. Your counselor will help clarify your options. Some changes may not be easy to make, but when done with a willing spirit, God will be pleased and will help! We look forward to working with you.

The Good $ense Ministry

GOOD $ENSE
BUDGET COUNSELING COVENANT

As a Good $ense client, you are asked to commit to the following:

1. A *significant effort* to develop better financial habits.

2. Regular *prayer* for learning and adopting new financial practices.

3. *Honesty* and openness—no financial surprises two months down the road.

4. An *honest effort* to act upon the counselor's guidance.

5. A consistent commitment of *time,* more at first but then tapering off gradually.

6. A willingness on your part to *be accountable* to the budget you and your counselor design for you.

As a counselor, I commit to you:

1. *Encouragement.*

2. Regular thoughts and *prayers* for you and your situation.

3. Respect for your *privacy.* All information you convey to me is kept *confidential.*

4. *Time* to meet with you.

5. *Training* seminars to sharpen my skills and knowledge.

6. My *skills* and expertise in budget counseling and the application of the Biblical Financial Principles to my own life.

7. *Ideas* to challenge you in your spiritual growth in the financial area of your life.

_____   _____
Client Signature   Counselor Signature

_____
Spouse Signature

_____   _____
Date   Date

BIBLICAL FINANCIAL PRINCIPLES

Steward's Mindset

God created everything. (Genesis 1:1)
God owns everything. (Psalms 24:1; 50:10, 12b)
We are trustees. (1 Corinthians 4:1-2)

Earning

Be diligent. (Colossians 3:23)
Be purposeful. (Colossians 3:23; 1 Timothy 5:8)
Be grateful. (Deuteronomy 8:18)

Giving

Giving is a key to a satisfied and fulfilled life. We are to give:

As a response to God's goodness. (James 1:17)
To focus on God as our source of security. (Matthew 6:19-20a; 23b-33)
To achieve economic justice.
To bless others. (Genesis 12:2-3)
To break the hold of money.

Saving

It is wise to save. (Proverbs 6:8; 21:20)
It is sinful to hoard. (Luke 12:16-21)

Debt

Repay debt. (Psalm 37:21)
Avoid debt. (Proverbs 22:7)

Spending

Beware of idols. (Deuteronomy 5:8; Romans 1:25)
Guard against greed. (Luke 12:15)
Be content. (Philippians 4:12)

Spending Record

Month _____

Daily Variable Expenses

	Transportation		Household						Professional Services	Entertainment		
	Gas, etc.	Maint/ Repair	Groceries	Clothes	Gifts	Household Items	Personal	Other		Going Out	Travel	Other
(1) Spending Plan												
1												
2												
3												
4												
5												
6												
7												
8												
9												
10												
11												
12												
13												
14												
15												
16												
17												
18												
19												
20												
21												
22												
23												
24												
25												
26												
27												
28												
29												
30												
31												
(2) Total												
(3) (Over)/Under												
(4) Last Month YTD												
(5) Total Year-to-Date												

- Use this page to record expenses that tend to be daily, variable expenses—often the hardest to control.
- Keep receipts throughout the day and record them at the end of the day.
- Total each category at the end of the month (line 2) and compare to the Spending Plan (line 1). Subtracting line 2 from line 1 gives you an (over) or under the budget figure for that month (line 3).
- To verify that you have made each day's entry, cross out the number at the bottom of the page that corresponds to that day's date.
- Optional: If you wish to monitor your progress as you go through the year, you can keep cumulative totals in lines 4 and 5.

Spending Record

Month _____

Monthly Regular Expenses
(generally paid by check once a month)

	Giving		Savings	Debt			Housing				Auto	Insurance		Misc. Cash Exp.
	Church	Other		Credit Cards	Educ.	Other	Mort./Rent	Maint.	Util.	Other	Pmts.	Auto/Home	Life/Med.	
(1) Spending Plan														
(2) Total														
(3) (Over)/Under														
(4) Last Mo. YTD														
(5) This Mo. YTD														

- This page allows you to record major monthly expenses for which you typically write just one or two checks per month.
- Entries can be recorded as the checks are written (preferably) or by referring back to the check ledger at a convenient time.
- Total each category at the end of the month (line 2) and compare to the Spending Plan (line 1). Subtracting line 2 from line 1 gives you an (over) or under the budget figure for that month (line 3).
- Use the "Monthly Assessment" section to reflect on the future actions that will be helpful in staying on course.

Monthly Assessment

Area	(Over)/Under	Reason	Future Action

Areas of Victory _____

Areas to Watch _____

Client Progress Report
Good $ense Ministry

Counselor_____   **Case No.** _____

Client _____

Instructions: This report serves as a summarized record of meetings with your client. Include the results of previous action items, observations about your client's behavior and attitudes, thoughts on your client's progress, and action items assigned for the next meeting. At the completion of this case, all progress reports should be forwarded to the ministry office.

Meeting Date:_____   Next Meeting Date:_____

      Time:_____   Time:_____

Results of previous action items:

_____
_____
_____

Observations about the client's behavior and attitudes:

_____
_____
_____
_____
_____

Thoughts on the client's progress:

_____
_____
_____
_____
_____
_____

Action items assigned for the next meeting:

_____
_____
_____
_____
_____
_____

Observations about the client's spiritual condition:

_____
_____
_____
_____

SPENDING PLAN

EARNINGS/INCOME PER MONTH	TOTALS
Salary #1 (net take-home)	_____
Salary #2 (net take-home)	_____
Other (less taxes)	_____
TOTAL MONTHLY INCOME	$_____

% GUIDE

1. GIVING $_____

Church _____
OTHER CONTRIBUTIONS _____

2. SAVING   5–10% $_____

EMERGENCY _____
REPLACEMENT _____
LONG TERM _____

3. DEBT   0–10% $_____

CREDIT CARDS:
  VISA _____
  Master Card _____
  Discover _____
  American Express _____
  Gas Cards _____
  Department Stores _____
EDUCATION LOANS _____
OTHER LOANS:
  Bank Loans _____
  Credit Union _____
  Family/Friends _____
  OTHER _____

4. HOUSING   25–38% $_____

MORTGAGE/TAXES/RENT _____
MAINTENANCE/REPAIRS _____
UTILITIES:
  Electric _____
  Gas _____
  Water _____
  Trash _____
  Telephone/Internet _____
  Cable TV _____
  OTHER _____

5. AUTO/TRANSP.   12–15% $_____

CAR PAYMENTS/LICENSE _____
GAS & BUS/TRAIN/PARKING _____
OIL/LUBE/MAINTENANCE _____

* This is a % of total monthly income. These are guidelines only and may be different for individual situations. However, there should be good rationale for a significant variance.

6. INSURANCE
(Paid by you)   5% $_____

AUTO _____
HOMEOWNERS _____
LIFE _____
MEDICAL/DENTAL _____
Other _____

7. HOUSEHOLD/PERSONAL   15–25% $_____

GROCERIES _____
CLOTHES/DRY CLEANING _____
GIFTS _____
HOUSEHOLD ITEMS _____
PERSONAL:
  Liquor/Tobacco _____
  Cosmetics _____
  Barber/Beauty _____
OTHER:
  Books/Magazines _____
  Allowances _____
  Music Lessons _____
  Personal Technology _____
  Education _____
  Miscellaneous _____

8. ENTERTAINMENT   5–10% $_____

GOING OUT:
  Meals _____
  Movies/Events _____
  Baby-sitting _____
TRAVEL (VACATION/TRIPS) _____
OTHER:
  Fitness/Sports _____
  Hobbies _____
  Media Rental _____
  OTHER _____

9. PROF. SERVICES   5–15% $_____

CHILD CARE _____
MEDICAL/DENTAL/PRESC. _____
OTHER
  Legal _____
  Counseling _____
  Professional Dues _____

10. MISC. SMALL CASH EXPENDITURES   2–3% $_____

TOTAL EXPENSES $_____

TOTAL MONTHLY INCOME	$_____
LESS TOTAL EXPENSES	$_____
INCOME OVER/(UNDER) EXPENSES	$_____

Debt Reduction Plan

Item	Amount Owed	Interest	Minimum Monthly Payment	Additional Payment $_____	Payment Plan and Pay-off Dates				
Total									

- The first and second columns list to whom the debt is owed and the amount owed. Debts are listed in the order of lowest to highest amount.
- The third and fourth columns list the interest rate and the minimum monthly payment for each debt.
- The fifth column indicates the amount of additional payment above the minimum that can be made and adds that amount to the minimum payment for the first (smallest) debt listed.
- The remaining columns show how, as each debt is paid, the payment for it is rolled down to the next debt. Pay-off dates can be calculated in advance or simply recorded as they are achieved.

CASE COMPLETION REPORT
Good $ense Ministry

Instructions: At the completion of a case, this form should be forwarded with the Client Progress Reports to the Good $ense administrator.

Date _____   **Client Name** _____

Last date of contact _____   **Counselor** _____

How terminated: ❏ In person   ❏ By telephone   ❏ No contact

Who decided: ❏ Mutual   ❏ Counselor   ❏ Client

In view of counselor:
Original problem that brought about referral :_____
_____

Is this problem now: ❏ Resolved   ❏ Improved   ❏ Unchanged   ❏ Worse

Additional problems worked on: Is each problem:
_____   ❏ Resolved   ❏ Improved   ❏ Unchanged   ❏ Worse
_____   ❏ Resolved   ❏ Improved   ❏ Unchanged   ❏ Worse

NOTE: Upon completion of a case, successful or unsuccessful, a goal is to have the client connected somewhere within the church—a ministry that can further help them or a small group that can help them grow, etc. Please indicate the results of your efforts in that regard: Client ❏ Is ❏ Is NOT connected elsewhere. Explain:
_____
_____

Counseling Results:
Success is judged by the following criteria: 1) the client is embracing the Biblical Financial Principles and making decisions based upon these principles; 2) the client has a Spending Plan in place and has been following it for at least three months; 3) the client has a Debt Reduction Plan in place and has been following it for at least three months; 4) the client has met his/her goals.

❏ Successful   ❏ Partial   ❏ Unsuccessful
 (met all criteria)   (met some criteria)   (met no criteria)

Comments:
_____
_____
_____
_____

Is there something about this case that could help and/or encourage other counselors or clients? If so, what?
_____
_____
_____
_____
_____

Client Profile

Number _____ *178* _____

Date Mailed _____ *2/14* _____

Date Received _____ *3/1* _____

Date Counselor Assigned _*3/19*_____

Name of Counselor _*Roger Liston*_____

Counseling Completed _*5/1*_____

NAME_____ *Mark Olsen* _____ AGE ___*32*____

MARITAL STATUS ___*Married*_____

SPOUSE'S NAME ___*Carol*_____

ADDRESS ___*7708 Geneva Street*_____

CITY_____ *Westport* _____ ZIP ___*01623*___

HOME PHONE (*921*) _*555-6623*_____

WORK PHONE (*921*) _*555-5412*_____

NATURE OF EMPLOYMENT:

SELF___ *Data Processing* _____

SPOUSE _____

NAME(S)/AGE(S) OF CHILDREN _____ *Ben, 4*_____

WHAT I OWN

Checking Accounts	30
Savings Account	100
Other Savings	–
Insurance (cash value)	–
Retirement Funds	20,000 (401k)
Home (market value)	174,000
Auto (age _7_ make _Suburban_)	13,475 (11,425) Retail (Wholesale)
Auto (age _10_ make _Sunbird_)	?
Other Possessions (estimate)	–
Money Owed to Me	–
Other	–
Other	–

WHAT I OWE

	Total Owed	Min. Mo. Payment	Interest	Other	Total Owed	Min. Mo. Payment	Interest
Mortgage (current bal.)	$125,000	1236	8.25 %	Bank Loan	$ 7954	182	13 * %
Home Equity Loan			%	Child. Hosp.	1000	20	0 %
Credit Cards:			%				%
Master Card	4417	137	17.65 %				%
Discover	265	18	19.8 %				%
			%				%
			%				%
Car Loans			%				%
Education Loans			%				%
Family/Friends	3400	–	0 %				%

Tax deductible – Travel trailer

WHAT I MAKE

(Use take-home pay figures (the amount of the check):

Job #1 $ 2074   ☐ weekly   ☒ every other week
                 ☐ monthly ☐ twice a month

Job #2 $_____ ☐ weekly   ☐ every other week
                 ☐ monthly ☐ twice a month

Other Income (explain) _None_

Total Monthly Income $ 4494

My spouse gets a check for:

Job #1 $_____ ☐ weekly   ☐ every other week
                 ☐ monthly ☐ twice a month

Job #2 $_____ ☐ weekly   ☐ every other week
                 ☐ monthly ☐ twice a month

EARNINGS/INCOME PER MONTH

Salary #1 (net take-home)   _4494_
Salary #2 (net take-home)   _____
Other (less taxes)   _____
TOTAL MONTHLY INCOME: | 4494 |

GIVING

Church   _—_
Other Contrib.   _—_
TOTAL GIVING | 0 |

SAVINGS

_—_
TOTAL SAVINGS | 0 |

DEBT

CREDIT CARDS:
  Visa   _____
  Master Card   _137_
  Discover   _18_
  Am. Express   _____
  Gas Cards   _____
  Dept. Stores   _____
EDUCATION LOANS   _____
OTHER LOANS:
  Bank Loans   _182_   _trailer payments_
  Credit Union   _____
  Family/Friends   _____
  Other   _20_   _(Children's Hospital)_
TOTAL DEBT | 357 |

HOUSING

MORTGAGE/TAXES/RENT   _1236_
MAINTENANCE/REPAIRS   _____
UTILITIES:
  Electric   _79_
  Gas   _52_
  Water   _14_
  Trash   _13_
  Telephone/Internet   _77_
  Cable TV   _25_
OTHER   _____
TOTAL HOUSING | 1496 |

AUTO/TRANSPORTATION

CAR PAYMTS./LICENSE   _8_   _(license)_
GAS/BUS/TRAIN/PKING.   _90_
OIL/LUBE/MAINT.   _10_
TOTAL AUTO | 108 |

INSURANCE (paid by you)

AUTO   _62_
HOMEOWNERS   _—_
LIFE   _42_
MEDICAL/DENTAL   _108_
OTHER: _—_
TOTAL INSURANCE | 212 |

HOUSEHOLD/PERSONAL

GROCERIES   _650_
CLOTHES/DRYCLEANING   _____
GIFTS   _____
HOUSEHOLD ITEMS   _____
PERSONAL
  Liquor/Tobacco   _____
  Cosmetics   _____
  Barber/Beauty   _____
OTHER
  Books/Magazines   _7_
  Allowances   _____
  Music Lessons   _____
  Personal Technology   _____
  Education   _____
  Miscellaneous   _____
TOTAL HOUSEHOLD | 657 |

ENTERTAINMENT

GOING OUT:
  Meals ⎫
  Movies/Events ⎬ _As $ avail. (not very often)_
  Babysitting ⎭
TRAVEL (VAC./TRIPS)   _____
OTHER:
  Fitness/Sports   _____
  Hobbies   _5_
  Media Rental   _____
  Other   _____
TOTAL ENTERTAINMENT | 5 |

PROFESSIONAL SERVICES

CHILD CARE   _____
MED./DENTAL/PRESCRIP.   _316_
OTHER:
  Legal   _____
  Counseling   _____
  Union/Prof. Dues   _____
  Other   _____
TOTAL PROFESSIONAL | 316 |

MISC. SMALL CASH EXPENSES

| |

TOTAL EXPENSES   _3151_

TOTAL MONTHLY INCOME	$ _4494_
LESS TOTAL EXPENSES	$ _3151_
INCOME OVER/(UNDER) EXPENSES	$ _1343_

REQUEST

How can the Good $ense Ministry help you? _Help me establish a budget to start a cash reserve for future needs. Provide an evening (or day or hour) of child care (fluent in sign language) so we can get some time alone. Most important, help us get out of debt._

What steps are you taking to improve your present situation?

- started going to work in car pool

- opened second checking account to transfer funds for bills, hoping to avoid dipping into funds needed for known bills

- Hoping to find work we can do from home to bring in additional income

Have you ever seen a financial planner/advisor? ☒ Yes ☐ No   If yes, who? _____

How were you helped? _Was shown how to cash in life insurance policies to pay off previous debts. The planner did not help evaluate how funds were budgeted to see if I had money set aside or if I had a reserve._

AGREEMENT

MY (OUR) AGREEMENT WITH _____

I (we) hereby make the commitment to actively participate with the Good $ense Ministry in seeking a resolution to the issues that brought me (us) to this place.

I (we) understand that Good $ense will attempt to assist me (us) in developing a plan, and that the consultant or volunteer agents do not make any representations or warranties with respect to the results of its services or its ability to help me (us) with my (our) credit/financial management.

I (we) understand that Good $ense is being offered to me (us) without charge or obligation, and that the people in Good $ense are volunteers who are donating their time to people requesting their assistance. Good $ense personnel have pledged to not benefit monetarily in any way as a result of their involvement in the ministry and are thereby prohibited from selling any services or products to persons who seek their counsel.

I (we) further agree to indemnify and hold harmless all volunteers of the Good $ense Ministry, the sponsor church and its employees, agents, counselors, officers, and directors from any claim, suit, action, demand or liability of any kind and any nature arising out of, or in any manner connected with, my (our) participation in Good $ense.

X _Mark Olsen_ Date _3/17_

X _Carol Olsen_ Date _3/17_

(If married, both spouses should sign.)

Client Profile

Good $ense Ministry

Number _____ *183* _____

Date Mailed _____ *3/1* _____

Date Received _____ *3/7* _____

Date Counselor Assigned _____ *3/19* _____

Name of Counselor _____ *Jose Garcia* _____

Counseling Completed _____ *8/11* _____

NAME _____ *Sharlene Moore* _____ AGE *45* _____

MARITAL STATUS _____ *Married* _____

SPOUSE'S NAME _____ *Joe* _____

ADDRESS _____ *113 Cascade* _____

CITY _____ *Meadowview* _____ ZIP *84312* _____

HOME PHONE (*413*) *555-6305* _____

WORK PHONE (*413*) *555-0712* _____

NATURE OF EMPLOYMENT:

   SELF _____ *Self Employed* _____

   SPOUSE _____ *Retail (Part-time student)* _____

NAME(S)/AGE(S) OF CHILDREN _____ *—* _____

_____

_____

_____

WHAT I OWN

Checking Accounts	0
Savings Account	0
Other Savings	0
Insurance (cash value)	0
Retirement Funds	0
Home (market value)	115,000
Auto (age _10_ make _Chev Blazer_)	0
Auto (age ____ make _____)	–
Other Possessions (estimate)	–
Money Owed to Me	–
Other	–
Other	–

WHAT I OWE

	Total Owed	Min. Mo. Payment	Interest	Other	Total Owed	Min. Mo. Payment	Interest
Mortgage (current bal.)	$ 851		8 %	Dept. Store	$ 203	10	12 %
Home Equity Loan	–		%	Dept. Store	859	17	8 %
Credit Cards:			%				%
Visa Preferred	5558	111	12 %				%
Visa Gold	4907	98	15.6 %				%
Master Card Monogram	500	10	17 %				%
			%				%
Car Loans	3482	322	9.75 %				%
Education Loans	12,000	240	7 %				%
Family/Friends			%				%

WHAT I MAKE

(Use take-home pay figures (the amount of the check):

Job #1 $ 760   ☒ weekly ☐ every other week
                ☐ monthly ☐ twice a month

Job #2 $_____   ☐ weekly ☐ every other week
                      ☐ monthly ☐ twice a month

My spouse gets a check for:

Job #1 $ 120   ☒ weekly ☐ every other week
                ☐ monthly ☐ twice a month

Job #2 $_____   ☐ weekly ☐ every other week
                      ☐ monthly ☐ twice a month

Other Income (explain) _____

Total Monthly Income $ 3813

EARNINGS/INCOME PER MONTH

Salary #1 (net take-home)   *3293*
Salary #2 (net take-home)   *520*
Other (less taxes)   _____
TOTAL MONTHLY INCOME: *3813*

GIVING

Church   *20*
Other Contrib.   _____
TOTAL GIVING   *20*

SAVINGS

TOTAL SAVINGS   —

DEBT

CREDIT CARDS:
Visa *Preferred*   *150*
Master Card   *50*
~~Discover~~ *Visa Gold*   *300*
Am. Express   —
Gas Cards   —
Dept. Stores   *50*
EDUCATION LOANS   *500*
OTHER LOANS:
Bank Loans   —
Credit Union   _____
Family/Friends   _____
Other   _____
TOTAL DEBT   *1050*

HOUSING

MORTGAGE/TAXES/RENT   *851*
MAINTENANCE/REPAIRS   _____
UTILITIES:
Electric   *82*
Gas   *133*
Water   *33*
Trash   *10*
Telephone/Internet   *150*
Cable TV   _____
OTHER   _____
TOTAL HOUSING   *1259*

AUTO/TRANSPORTATION

CAR PAYMTS./LICENSE   *322*
GAS/BUS/TRAIN/PKING.   *80*
OIL/LUBE/MAINT.   *25*
TOTAL AUTO   *427*

INSURANCE (paid by you)

AUTO   *30*
HOMEOWNERS   _____
LIFE   _____
MEDICAL/DENTAL   _____
OTHER: _____
TOTAL INSURANCE   *30*

HOUSEHOLD/PERSONAL

GROCERIES   *500*
CLOTHES/DRYCLEANING   *50*
GIFTS   *50*
HOUSEHOLD ITEMS   _____
PERSONAL
Liquor/Tobacco   *140*
Cosmetics   _____
Barber/Beauty   *50*
OTHER
Books/Magazines   *30*
Allowances   _____
Music Lessons   _____
Personal Technology   _____
Education   *100*
Miscellaneous   _____
TOTAL HOUSEHOLD   *920*

ENTERTAINMENT

GOING OUT:
Meals   *180*
Movies/Events   *300*
Babysitting   _____
TRAVEL (VAC./TRIPS)   _____
OTHER:
Fitness/Sports   *50*
Hobbies   _____
Media Rental   _____
Other   _____
TOTAL ENTERTAINMENT   *530*

PROFESSIONAL SERVICES

CHILD CARE   _____
MED./DENTAL/PRESCRIP.   _____
OTHER:
Legal   _____
Counseling   *225*
Union/Prof. Dues   _____
Other   _____
TOTAL PROFESSIONAL   *225*

MISC. SMALL CASH EXPENSES

TOTAL EXPENSES   *4461*

TOTAL MONTHLY INCOME	$ *3813*
LESS TOTAL EXPENSES	$ *4461*
INCOME OVER/(UNDER) EXPENSES	$ *(648)*

REQUEST

How can the Good $ense Ministry help you? _____

We need to receive help in managing budgeting areas.

What steps are you taking to improve your present situation?_____

#1—Setting up an appointment with Good Sense.

#2—Giving back what we can to God at church and a lot of praying.

Have you ever seen a financial planner/advisor? ☐ Yes ☒ No   If yes, who? _____

How were you helped? _____

AGREEMENT

MY (OUR) AGREEMENT WITH _____

I (we) hereby make the commitment to actively participate with the Good $ense Ministry in seeking a resolution to the issues that brought me (us) to this place.

I (we) understand that Good $ense will attempt to assist me (us) in developing a plan, and that the consultant or volunteer agents do not make any representations or warranties with respect to the results of its services or its ability to help me (us) with my (our) credit/financial management.

I (we) understand that Good $ense is being offered to me (us) without charge or obligation, and that the people in Good $ense are volunteers who are donating their time to people requesting their assistance. Good $ense personnel have pledged to not benefit monetarily in any way as a result of their involvement in the ministry and are thereby prohibited from selling any services or products to persons who seek their counsel.

I (we) further agree to indemnify and hold harmless all volunteers of the Good $ense Ministry, the sponsor church and its employees, agents, counselors, officers, and directors from any claim, suit, action, demand or liability of any kind and any nature arising out of, or in any manner connected with, my (our) participation in Good $ense.

X _*Sharlene Moore*_____   Date_*3/19*_____

X _*Joe Moore*_____   Date_*3/19*_____

(If married, both spouses should sign.)

Client Profile

Good $ense Ministry

Number _____ 444 _____

Date Mailed _____ 12/4 _____

Date Received _____ 12/6 _____

Date Counselor Assigned _____ 12/11 _____

Name of Counselor _____ Susan Dean _____

Counseling Completed _____ 5/1 _____

NAME _____ Barb Leonard _____ AGE _____ 26 _____

MARITAL STATUS _____ Divorced _____

SPOUSE'S NAME _____

ADDRESS _____ 1900 Talbot Drive _____

CITY _____ Prospect _____ ZIP _____ 44201 _____

HOME PHONE (662) _____ 555-4900 _____

WORK PHONE (662) _____ 555-4812 _____

NATURE OF EMPLOYMENT:

   SELF _____ Sales Rep _____

   SPOUSE _____

NAME(S)/AGE(S) OF CHILDREN _____ Cindy / 4 yrs. old _____

_____

_____

_____

WHAT I OWN

Checking Accounts	0
Savings Account	0
Other Savings	0
Insurance (cash value)	0
Retirement Funds	0
Home (market value)	0
Auto (age _10_ make _Volvo_)	1000
Auto (age____ make_____)	0
Other Possessions (estimate)	0
Money Owed to Me	0
Other	0
Other	

WHAT I OWE

	Total Owed	Min. Mo. Payment	Interest	Other	Total Owed	Min. Mo. Payment	Interest
Mortgage (current bal.)	$ —		__%	Bank Loan	$ 1400	28	0 %
Home Equity Loan	—		__%	IRS Debt	400		__%
Credit Cards:	—		__%				__%
			__%				__%
			__%				__%
			__%				__%
			__%				__%
Car Loans			__%				__%
Education Loans			__%				__%
Family/Friends	7500		0 %				__%

WHAT I MAKE

(Use take-home pay figures (the amount of the check):

Job #1 $ _847_ ☐ weekly ☒ every other week ☐ monthly ☐ twice a month

Job #2 $_____ ☐ weekly ☐ every other week ☐ monthly ☐ twice a month

My spouse gets a check for:

Job #1 $_____ ☐ weekly ☐ every other week ☐ monthly ☐ twice a month

Job #2 $_____ ☐ weekly ☐ every other week ☐ monthly ☐ twice a month

Other Income (explain) _Commission on 22nd every month $700_

Total Monthly Income _2535_

WHAT I SPEND

EARNINGS/INCOME PER MONTH
Salary #1 (net take-home) _____
Salary #2 (net take-home) _____
Other (less taxes) _____
TOTAL MONTHLY INCOME: | 2535 |

GIVING
Church _____20_____
Other Contrib. _____
TOTAL GIVING | 20 |

SAVINGS
_____—_____
TOTAL SAVINGS | 0 |

DEBT
CREDIT CARDS:
Visa _____—_____
Master Card _____—_____
Discover _____—_____
Am. Express _____—_____
Gas Cards _____—_____
Dept. Stores _____—_____
EDUCATION LOANS _____
OTHER LOANS:
Bank Loans _____—_____
Credit Union _____—_____
Family/Friends _____—_____
Other _____100_____
TOTAL DEBT | 100 |

HOUSING *(monthly)*
MORTGAGE/TAXES/RENT _____910 – rent
MAINTENANCE/REPAIRS _____
UTILITIES:
Electric _____
Gas _____
Water _____
Trash _____
Telephone/Internet _____100_____
Cable TV _____
OTHER _____
TOTAL HOUSING | 1010 |

AUTO/TRANSPORTATION
CAR PAYMTS.(LICENSE) _____70_____
GAS/BUS/TRAIN/PKING. _____50_____
OIL/LUBE/MAINT. _____60_____
TOTAL AUTO | 180 |

INSURANCE (paid by you)
AUTO _____
HOMEOWNERS _____
LIFE _____
MEDICAL/DENTAL _____
OTHER: _____
TOTAL INSURANCE | — |

HOUSEHOLD/PERSONAL
GROCERIES _____140_____
CLOTHES/DRYCLEANING _____
GIFTS _____
HOUSEHOLD ITEMS _____—_____
PERSONAL
Liquor/Tobacco _____
Cosmetics _____
Barber/Beauty _____40_____
OTHER
Books/Magazines _____40_____
Allowances _____
Music Lessons _____
Personal Technology _____
Education _____
Miscellaneous _____
TOTAL HOUSEHOLD | 220 |

ENTERTAINMENT
GOING OUT:
Meals _____
Movies/Events _____
Babysitting _____
TRAVEL (VAC./TRIPS) _____
OTHER:
Fitness/Sports _____90_____
Hobbies _____
Media Rental _____
Other _____
TOTAL ENTERTAINMENT | 90 |

PROFESSIONAL SERVICES
CHILD CARE _____750_____
MED./DENTAL/PRESCRIP. _____30_____
OTHER:
Legal _____
Counseling _____
Union/Prof. Dues _____
Other _____
TOTAL PROFESSIONAL | 780 |

MISC. SMALL CASH EXPENSES | |

TOTAL EXPENSES _____2400_____

TOTAL MONTHLY INCOME	$ 2535
LESS TOTAL EXPENSES	$ 2400
INCOME OVER/(UNDER) EXPENSES	$ 135

REQUEST

How can the Good $ense Ministry help you? _Shopping tips, budgeting._

What steps are you taking to improve your present situation? _Taking the Good $ense Budget Course was a big step._

Have you ever seen a financial planner/advisor? ☐ Yes ☒ No   If yes, who? _____

How were you helped? _____

AGREEMENT

MY (OUR) AGREEMENT WITH _____

I (we) hereby make the commitment to actively participate with the Good $ense Ministry in seeking a resolution to the issues that brought me (us) to this place.

I (we) understand that Good $ense will attempt to assist me (us) in developing a plan, and that the consultant or volunteer agents do not make any representations or warranties with respect to the results of its services or its ability to help me (us) with my (our) credit/financial management.

I (we) understand that Good $ense is being offered to me (us) without charge or obligation, and that the people in Good $ense are volunteers who are donating their time to people requesting their assistance. Good $ense personnel have pledged to not benefit monetarily in any way as a result of their involvement in the ministry and are thereby prohibited from selling any services or products to persons who seek their counsel.

I (we) further agree to indemnify and hold harmless all volunteers of the Good $ense Ministry, the sponsor church and its employees, agents, counselors, officers, and directors from any claim, suit, action, demand or liability of any kind and any nature arising out of, or in any manner connected with, my (our) participation in Good $ense.

X _Barb Leonard_   Date _12/5_

X _____   Date _____

(If married, both spouses should sign.)

Client: _____

Date: _____

Client Profile Analysis Chart

As you review the Client Profile, note positive things you can affirm and questions you want to ask. Place a check in the + or ? colums to indicate whether it is an affirmation or a question.

CHECKLIST	+	?	NOTES
FRONT COVER			
Is the client married? If so, the spouse should participate in the counseling meetings.			
How old is the client? This will give you an idea about future career income and of how adequate their savings are for college expenses and retirement, etc.			
What is the nature of the client's employment? If self-employed, there may be income stability issues and a question of whether they are current on their quarterly estimated tax payments.			
What are the names and ages of the client's children? This will help you understand the types and amount of their expenses as well as provide information that may be helpful in building rapport with your client.			
WHAT I OWN			
How much money is in the checking and savings accounts? This indicates whether your client has any buffer to work with.			
Are there any other savings listed for the client to draw on? The cash value of life insurance may be such a resource.			

CHECKLIST	+	?	NOTES
WHAT I OWN (continued)			
Has the client begun to save for retirement?			
What is the value of the home? How much money is owed on the home (from the "What I Owe" section)? This is a key part of their overall financial evaluation.			
Check the ages of the cars. If the cars are old, a savings plan for a new used car may be a top priority.			
What is the value of other possessions? If high, there may be an opportunity to sell some assets to jump-start debt repayment.			
WHAT I OWE			
Total all the consumer debts. Include all debts, *except* mortgage.			
WHAT I MAKE			
Verify the total monthly income figure. Note the frequency of paychecks. "Every other week" means that there are twenty-six paychecks per year. "Weekly" means fifty-two checks per year. Since we are interested in monthly income, you'll have to do the math to calculate the monthly income. Note also that these pay arrangements can create some cash flow complexities since paydays come on different dates each month.			

QUESTIONS	+	?	NOTES
WHAT I SPEND			
Is the client giving and saving anything?			
How do the consumer debt payments in this section compare to the minimum monthly payments listed in the "What I Owe" section?			
Based on the ages of the cars in the "What I Own" section, is a realistic amount listed for auto maintenance?			
Are there any missing items? Pay attention to the household/personal section. Clothes/dry cleaning, gifts, cosmetics, and barber/beauty are typically underestimated or left blank, yet just about everyone has these expenses.			
Total the monthly expenses and subtract from the monthly income to get an idea of cash flow.			
Check for any expenses in any of the categories that appear to be unusually high. Be prepared to learn why these expenses are high.			

QUESTIONS	+	?	NOTES
REQUEST			
Carefully read the answers to the open-ended questions. Look for clues about the client's attitude toward his/her situation and for action steps you can affirm.			
AGREEMENT			
If your clients are married, check whether they both signed the agreement. If not, ask about it at the first meeting.			

Needed for the first meeting:

NOTES

NOTES

NOTES

NOTES

NOTES

NOTES

NOTES

NOTES

WILLOW CREEK ASSOCIATION

Vision, Training, Resources

for Prevailing Churches

This resource was created to serve you and to help you in building a local church that prevails!

Since 1992, the Willow Creek Association (WCA) has been linking like-minded, action-oriented churches with each other and with strategic vision, training, and resources. Now a worldwide network of over 7,000 churches from more than ninety denominations, the WCA works to equip Member Churches and others with the tools needed to build prevailing churches. Our desire is to inspire, equip, and encourage Christian leaders to build biblically functioning "Acts 2" churches that reach increasing numbers of unchurched people, not just with innovations from Willow Creek Community Church in South Barrington, Illinois, but from any church in the world that has experienced God-given breakthroughs.

Willow Creek Conferences

Each year, thousands of local church leaders, staff and volunteers—from WCA Member Churches and others—attend one of our conferences or training events. Conferences offered on the Willow Creek campus in South Barrington, Illinois, include:

- Prevailing Church Conference—Offered twice a year, it is the foundational, overarching, training conference for staff and volunteers working to build a prevailing local church.
- Select ministry workshops—A wide variety of strategic, day-long workshops covering seven topic areas that represent key characteristics of a prevailing church; offered multiple times throughout the year.
- Promiseland Conference—Children's ministries; infant through fifth grade.
- Student Ministries Conference—Junior and senior high ministries.
- Arts Conference—Vision and training for Christian artists using their gifts in the ministries of local churches.
- Leadership Summit—Envisioning and equipping Christians with leadership gifts and responsibilities; broadcast live via satellite to scores of cities across North America.
- Contagious Evangelism Conference—Encouragement and training for churches and church leaders who want to be strategic in reaching lost people for Christ.
- Small Groups Conference—Exploring how developing a church of small groups can play a vital role in developing authentic Christian community that leads to spiritual transformation.

To find out more about WCA conferences, visit our website at www.willowcreek.com.

Regional Conferences and Training Events

Each year the WCA team leads a variety of topical conferences and training events in select cities across the United States. Ministry and topic topic areas include leadership, next-generation ministries, small groups, arts and worship, evangelism, spiritual gifts, financial stewardship, and spiritual formation. These events make quality training more accessible and affordable to larger groups of staff and volunteers.

To find out more about upcoming events in your area, visit our website at www.willowcreek.com.

Willow Creek Resources®

Churches can look to Willow Creek Resources® for a trusted channel of ministry tools in areas of leadership, evangelism, spiritual gifts, small groups, drama, contemporary music, financial stewardship, spiritual transformation, and more. For ordering information, call (800) 570-9812 or visit our website at www.willowcreek.com.

WCA Membership

Membership in the Willow Creek Association as well as attendance at WCA Conferences is for churches, ministries, and leaders who hold to an historic, orthodox understanding of biblical Christianity. The annual church membership fee of $249 provides substantial discounts for your entire team on all conferences and Willow Creek Resources, networking opportunities with other outreach-oriented churches, a bimonthly newsletter, a subscription to the Defining Moments monthly audio journal for leaders, and more.

To find out more about WCA membership, visit our website at www.willowcreek.com.

WillowNet www.willowcreek.com

This Internet resource service provides access to hundreds of Willow Creek messages, drama scripts, songs, videos, and multimedia ideas. The system allows you to sort through these elements and download them for a fee.

Our website also provides detailed information on the Willow Creek Association, Willow Creek Community Church, WCA membership, conferences, training events, resources, and more.

WillowCharts.com www.WillowCharts.com

Designed for local church worship leaders and musicians, WillowCharts.com provides online access to hundreds of music charts and chart components, including choir, orchestral, and horn sections, as well as rehearsal tracks and video streaming of Willow Creek Community Church performances.

The NET http://studentministry.willowcreek.com

The NET is an online training and resource center designed by and for student ministry leaders. It provides an inside look at the structure, vision, and mission of prevailing student ministries from around the world. The NET gives leaders access to complete programming elements, including message outlines, dramas, small group questions, and more. An indispensable resource and networking tool for prevailing student ministry leaders!

Contact the Willow Creek Association

If you have comments or questions, or would like to find out more about WCA events or resources, please contact us:

Willow Creek Association
P.O. Box 3188
Barrington, IL 60011-3188
Phone: (800) 570-9812 or (847) 765-0070
Fax (888) 922-0035 or (847) 765-5046
Web: www.willowcreek.com

Resources You've Been Waiting For . . .

To Build the Church You've Been Dreaming About

Willow Creek Resources

What do you dream about for your church?

At the Willow Creek Association we have a dream for the church . . . one that envisions the local church—your church—as the focal point for individual and community transformation.

We want to partner with you to make this happen. We believe when authentic, life-changing resources become an integral part of everyday life at your church—and when they become an extension of how your ministries function—transformation is inevitable.

It then becomes normal for people to:
- identify their personal style of evangelism and use it to bring their unchurched friends to Christ
- grow in their ability to experience God's presence with them in each moment of the day
- feel a deep sense of community with others
- discover their spiritual gifts and put them to use in ministry
- use their resources in ways that honor God and care for others

If this is the kind of church you're dreaming about, keep reading. The following pages highlight just a few of the many Willow Creek Resources available to help you. Together, we can build a local church that transforms lives and transfigures communities. We can build a church that *prevails.*

Good $ense

Transformational Stewardship for Today's Church

DICK TOWNER
with contributions from the Good $ense Ministry team of
Willow Creek Community Church

GRACE. JOY. FREEDOM.
Are these the first words that come to mind when you think of stewardship? They could be! Grace, joy, and freedom are words people most often use to describe Good $ense—a field-tested, proven resource for changing hearts and lives in the area of finances.

There is a tremendous need for churches to educate and assist people with managing their resources in God-honoring ways. Implementing a Good $ense Ministry in your church does that. It can relieve the crushing stress and anxiety caused by consumer debt, restore marriages torn by conflict over money, and heal the wounded self-esteem and shattered confidence resulting from poor financial decisions.

Most significantly, a Good $ense Ministry can be used by God to remove stumbling blocks to spiritual growth. This is *transformational stewardship.* The result is a congregation whose finances—and lives—are characterized by grace, joy, and freedom.

Complete Kit	0744137241
Casting a Vision for Good $ense video	0744137268
Implementation Guide	074413725X
Budget Course Leader's Guide	0744137276
Budget Course Participant's Guide	0744137284
Budget Course Video	0744137292
Budget Course PowerPoint CD-ROM	0744137306
Counselor Training Workshop Leader's Guide	0744137314
Counselor Training Workshop Participant's Guide	0744137322
Counselor Training Workshop Video	0744137330
Counselor Training Workshop PowerPoint CD-ROM	0744137349

cal Stewardship Ministry that Transforms Lives

Based on over sixteen years of ministry at Willow Creek Community Church, Good $ense includes resources designed to train and equip: church leaders, volunteer counselors, and everyone in your church.

Envision Church Leaders and Implement the Ministry

Good $ense Implementation Guide
Casting a Vision for Good $ense Video

FOR: Senior church leaders.

PURPOSE: To envision and equip leaders to launch and lead a year-round stewardship ministry.

CONTENTS: The Implementation Guide provides a roadmap for implementing a Good $ense Ministry as well as the practical tools to do so. The video provides an inspiring tool to help leaders cast vision for a Good $ense Ministry.

Equip Volunteer Counselors

Good $ense Counselor Training Workshop

FOR: Volunteer counselors.

PURPOSE: To train and equip laypersons to provide free, biblically-based, confidential counsel to assist families and individuals in addressing financial questions or difficulties.

CONTENTS: This one-day, five-session workshop offers training for volunteers to become Good $ense budget counselors.

Train Everyone in Your Church

Good $ense Budget Course

FOR: Everyone in your church—not just those in financial difficulty.

PURPOSE: To train every believer to integrate Biblical Financial Principles into their lives—financially and spiritually.

CONTENTS: Contrasts the Pull of the Culture with the Mind and Heart of God in five areas—earning, giving, saving, spending, debt. Six, fifty-minute sessions can be taught in a variety of formats.

Experience the Reality of God's Presence Every Day

An Ordinary Day with Jesus

JOHN ORTBERG AND RUTH HALEY BARTON

An Ordinary Day with Jesus uses aspects of an ordinary day and illustrates how we can connect with Jesus in those moments. Participants will learn how to:

- wake up and go to sleep in Jesus' name
- review their day with God
- silence competing voices in order to hear God's leadings
- experience time alone with God as an opportunity not an obligation
- use their own unique spiritual pathway to connect with God
- eliminate hurry and simplify their pace of life
- and much more!

	WCA ISBNs	Zondervan ISBNs
Leader's Guide	0744137217	0310245850
Participant's Guide	0744137225	0310245869
Drama Vignettes Video	0744136652	0310245575
PowerPoint CD-ROM	0744137195	0310245885
Complete Kit	0744136555	0310245877

Link People and Their Gifts with Ministries and Their Needs

Network

Bruce Bugbee, Don Cousins, Bill Hybels

This proven, easy-to-use curriculum helps participants to discover their unique spiritual gifts, areas of passion for service, and individual ministry style.

Network helps believers better understand who God made them to be, and mobilizes them into meaningful service in the local church.

Using *Network,* your whole church can share a vision for each member and understand the vital role each plays in building God's Kingdom.

Leader's Guide	0310412412
Participant's Guide	0310412315
Drama Vignettes Video	0310411890
Overhead Masters	0310485282
Consultant's Guide	0310412218
Vision/Consultant Training Video	0310244994
Implementation Guide	0310432618
Complete Kit	0310212790

Train Believers to Share Christ Naturally

Becoming a Contagious Christian

Mark Mittelberg, Lee Strobel, Bill Hybels

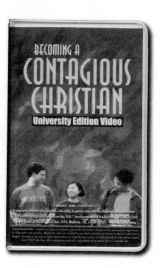

Over 500,000 believers have been trained to share their faith confidently and effectively with this proven curriculum. In eight, fifty-minute sessions, participants experience the joy of discovering their own unique evangelism style, learn how to transition conversations to spiritual topics, present gospel illustrations, and more.

Leader's Guide	0310500818
Participant's Guide	0310501016
Drama Vignettes Video	0310201691
Overhead Masters	0310500915
Complete Kit	0310501091

Also available—*Becoming a Contagious Christian* University Edition Video. Developed in partnership with InterVarsity Christian Fellowship, these drama vignettes feature college students building relationships with seekers. Designed to be used with the adult version of the curriculum.

Video	1558920412

Equip Students to Lead this Generation to Christ

Becoming a Contagious Christian Youth Edition

Mark Mittelberg, Lee Strobel, Bill Hybels

Revised and expanded for students by Bo Boshers

The award-winning *Becoming a Contagious Christian* curriculum has been revised and expanded to equip junior high and high school students to be contagious with their faith.

In eight, fifty-minute sessions, students learn how to:
- Develop relationships intentionally
- Transition an ordinary conversation to a spiritual conversation
- Tell their personal story of meeting Christ
- Share the gospel message using two different illustrations
- Answer ten common objections to Christianity
- Pray with a friend to receive Christ

Real stories of students who have led their friends to Christ make the material come alive as students see how God can work through them.

Leader's Guide	0310237718
Student's Guide	0310237734
Drama Vignettes Video	0310237742
Complete Kit	0310237696

Bestselling Books by John Ortberg

If You Want to Walk on Water, You've Got to Get Out of the Boat

With engaging illustrations, humor, and relevant applications, John Ortberg explains how discerning God's call, rising above fear, and taking next steps can strengthen your faith.

Hardcover   0310228638

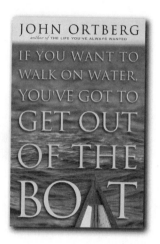

The Life You've Always Wanted

Gain a fresh perspective on the power of spiritual disciplines and how God can use them to deepen your relationship with him.

Hardcover   0310212146
Softcover   0310226996

Love Beyond Reason

Filled with poignant illustrations, real-life applications, and humor, *Love Beyond Reason* describes the numerous facets of God's reason-defying, passionate love.

Hardcover   0310212154
Softcover   0310234492

Life-changing Small Group Resources

Pursuing Spiritual Transformation Series

John Ortberg, Laurie Pederson, Judson Poling

Explore fresh, biblically-based ways to think about and experience life with God through Willow Creek's Five Gs: Grace, Growth, Groups, Gifts, and Good Stewardship (Giving). Each study challenges the popular notion that merely "trying harder" will lead to Christlikeness. Instead, this series helps you identify the practices, experiences, and relationships God can use to help you become the person he longs for you to be.

Fully Devoted	0310220734
Grace	0310220742
Growth	0310220750
Groups	0310220769
Gifts	0310220777
Giving	0310220785

New Community Series

Bill Hybels, John Ortberg

New Community studies provide in-depth Bible study, thought-provoking questions, and community building exercises so groups can grow in faith together.

1 John: Love Each Other	0310227682
1 Peter: Stand Strong	0310227739
Acts: Build Community	0310227704
Colossians: Discover the New You	0310227690
Exodus: Journey Toward God	0310227712
James: Live Wisely	0310227674
Philippians: Run the Race	0310233143
Romans: Find Freedom	0310227658
Parables: Imagine Life God's Way	0310228816
Revelation: Experience God's Power	0310228824
Sermon on the Mount, part 1: Connect with God	0310228832
Sermon on the Mount, part 2: Connect with Others	0310228840

Bible 101 Series

Bill Donahue, Kathy Dice, Judson Poling, Michael Redding, Gerry Mathisen

Bible 101 provides a solid, foundational understanding of God's Word in a format uniquely designed for a small group setting.

Cover to Cover	0830820639
Foundations	0830820612
Great Themes	0830820671
Interpretation	0830820655
Parables and Prophecy	0830820663
Personal Devotion	083082068X
Study Methods	0830820647
Times and Places	0830820620

InterActions Series

Bill Hybels

InterActions studies encourage participants to share interests, experiences, values, and lifestyles, and uses this common ground to foster honest communication, deeper relationships, and growing intimacy with God.

Authenticity	031020674X
Community	0310206774
Lessons in Love	0310206804
Marriage	0310206758
The Real You	0310206820
Commitment	0310206839
Essential Christianity	0310224438
Evangelism	0310206782
Freedom	0310217172
Getting a Grip	0310224446
Parenthood	0310206766
Serving Lessons	0310224462
Overcoming	0310224454
Character	0310217164
Fruits of the Spirit	0310213150
Jesus	0310213169
Prayer	0310217148
Psalms	0310213185
Transparency	0310217156
Transformation	0310213177

Walking with God Series

Don Cousins, Judson Poling

Practical, interactive, and biblically based, this dynamic series follows a two-track approach. Series 1 plugs new believers into the transforming power of discipleship to Christ. Series 2 guides mature believers into a closer look at the church.

Series 1

"Follow Me"	0310591635
Friendship with God	0310591430
The Incomparable Jesus	0310591538
Leader's Guide	0310592038

Series 2

Building Your Church	031059183X
Discovering Your Church	0310591732
Impacting Your World	0310591937
Leader's Guide	0310592135

Tough Questions Series

Garry Poole, Judson Poling

Created for seeker small groups, this series guides participants through an exploration of key questions about and objections to Christianity.

How Does Anyone Know God Exists?	0310222257
Is Jesus the Only Way?	0310222311
How Reliable Is the Bible?	0310222265
How Could God Allow Suffering/Evil?	0310222273
Don't All Religions Lead to God?	031022229X
Do Science and the Bible Conflict?	031022232X
Why Become a Christian?	0310222281
Leader's Guide	0310222249

Build a Church Where Nobody Stands Alone

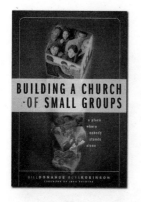

Building a Church of Small Groups

Bill Donahue, Russ Robinson

Experience the vision, values, and necessary initial steps to begin transitioning your church from a church *with* small groups to a church *of* small groups in this groundbreaking book.
Hardcover   0310240352

The Connecting Church

Randy Frazee

Pastor Randy Frazee explores the three essential elements of connecting churches: Common Purpose, Common Place, and Common Possessions. An excellent resource to help leaders create the kind of church where every member feels a deep sense of connection.
Hardcover   0310233089

Leading Life-Changing Small Groups

Bill Donahue

Leading Life-Changing Small Groups covers everything from starting, structuring, leading, and directing an effective small group, to developing effective leaders.
Softcover   0310205956

The Coaches Handbook

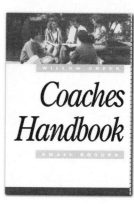

This comprehensive resource provides teaching and tools to those who coach small group leaders. An excellent resource for small group ministry leaders.
Softcover   0744106567